The Law&You

A guide to key employment rights (

The law and you: *A guide to key employment rights*
3rd edition
June 2005
Designed and produced by UNISON Communications.
Published by UNISON, 1 Mabledon Place, London WC1H 9AJ.
Printed by Communisis Print Management, London EC2.

ISBN: 0 904198 19 7

www.unison.org.uk

Communications/June 2005/14835/stock no. 1895.

Contents

Introduction

UNISON believes that many problems arising in members' work-places are capable of resolution by negotiation and agreement. However, there will always be situations where this is not possible and that is where knowledge of legal rights will be particularly helpful. It can of course also be used in the process of negotiation itself.

How can this book help?

This book is designed to assist those who represent members (be they regional or branch officers or branch stewards) in as practical a manner as possible. It will empower them in representing the interests of our most important asset – our members – and help them to persuade others who are not yet our members of the benefits of joining us.

Answering queries from individual members

Members' queries may appear simple, but the underlying legal position can be complex. A key skill for representatives is to know enough about the law:

→ To identify where a legal issue needs follow-up advice.

→ To avoid misleading over-simplified advice which leads members to make wrong decisions.

→ To ensure tribunal time-limits are not missed.

Representing members at disciplinaries and grievances.

These internal hearings are often a first stage of a situation which will end with dismissal or a tribunal case for dismissal or discrimination. It is important you know the general legal considerations which would apply so that you can handle the hearing appropriately. Obviously there will also be other non-legal factors.

Negotiating on policy

It is important to know where you have the backing of the law and where you do not. You also want to know where the law is inadequate, so that therefore negotiation is crucial to fill the gap.

This is not a complete legal text. It is not possible in one book to provide information on every legal issue which may come up, but we have tried to deal with the most common issues. Nor are we trying to make you into a lawyer, because that is a full-time occupation. While we cannot include every aspect of the areas we cover, the book sets out the legal principles which apply and draws attention to the relevant issues, myths and dangers. It also directs you to sources of follow-up information. Far greater detail on law and practice would be needed to take tribunal cases (see Bibliography on page 314 for materials).

The book is presented in a "problem-centred" way. You need to remember that the member may only ask your advice on one issue, but may have rights that s/he does not know about. For example, a redundant employee who asks you about redundancy pay, may also have rights to claim unfair dismissal or discrimination. The text and checklists try to cross-refer you to possible other claims, but of course they cannot cover everything and you need to be alert.

This book was commissioned and edited by Adam Creme, Head of Employment Rights at UNISON and written for UNISON by Tamara Lewis. Adam is a solicitor specialising in employment law who has run some of the leading UK employment cases. Tamara is a solicitor specialising in employment law at Central London Law Centre. She has conducted extensive legal training for UNISON and is author of "Employment Law: An Adviser's Handbook", which gives further guidance on the law and running tribunal cases.

This book is accurate on the law as known at 1st April 2005. You need to be aware of any major changes in the law since then. Please note that the author cannot be responsible for advice given on the basis of the contents of this book.

Legal overview and new employment rights

What employment rights do workers' have?

Members have two kinds of legal rights in their employment. A great many rights are given by acts of parliament. These are known as statutory rights and they are generally dealt with by employment tribunals. Such rights include protection against discrimination and unfair dismissal, and regulation of certain terms and conditions such as minimum pay, rest breaks and holidays.

Not every worker is eligible to claim under every statutory right. Each statutory right has its own eligibility requirements, eg a minimum length of service with the particular employers or status as an "employee" or "worker" as defined by the relevant statute.

In addition, members have particular rights in their contract of employment. These are rights which are agreed between the individual workers and employer and deal with issues such as pay, hours and workplace. In UNISON organised areas, eg local authorities and NHS trusts, there are nationally agreed terms and conditions, which become incorporated into individual contracts.

Although contractual rights form the basis of many statutory rights, their legal value is less straightforward. If the employers break any contract term, the legal position and consequences are complex to deal with. Contract terms are very important and good terms should be negotiated. However, not all contractual rights are easily enforceable and often it is statutory rights such as not to be unfairly dismissed, which are more relevant to the member's legal position. Too much emphasis on abstract contract terms can be rather academic when dealing with practical problems.

Employment law is one of the fastest developing areas of law. It is a huge subject with constant change and new laws. It is heavily influenced by political change in Britain and Europe. Many of the most recent legal developments have resulted from ever increasing European legislation in the form of Directives which member states must implement into national law. The most important influences from Europe have come in the area of anti-discrimination and laws promoting the work-life balance and family life.

Tribunal time-limits are extremely strict and tend to be short. It is essential you are familiar with these and that the member is informed at the first opportunity of any deadline.

Legal aid is not available for employment tribunal cases except in limited circumstances in Scotland. There are currently many plans for changing the tribunal system.

The Human Rights Act

The Human Rights Act incorporating the European Convention on Human Rights came into effect on 2nd October 2000. There are a number of rights which could be relevant to employment law, eg the right to a fair hearing (article 6), the right to respect for private life (article 8), freedom of religion (article 9), freedom of expression (article 10) and the right to peaceful assembly (article 11). There must also be no discrimination on any ground in the enjoyment of the Convention rights (article 14).

The courts and tribunals are supposed to take Convention rights into account when interpreting UK law. Public sector employees may also be able to enforce these rights directly. So far, the Human Rights Act has not made a great impact in the employment field, mainly because the various rights tend to be subject to balances and qualifications.

Why is the legal position so often uncertain?

Knowing what the law says is important, but it is more important to understand how it applies in practice and to individual situations. The book aims to give pointers on this. You will probably find it frustrating that the law never seems to give a clear-cut answer to problems. Members naturally want reliable and simple answers as to the legal position they are in, but unfortunately this is rarely possible. It is important to remember that in each individual situation, the law has to be applied to a particular and unique set of facts. This often makes the legal outcome hard to predict with any certainty. Many legal rights depend on unscientific concepts such as "reasonableness", eg

➔ In unfair dismissal cases, whether it was reasonable for the employers to dismiss the member.

➔ In some redundancy pay or maternity leave cases, whether an alternative job offer was suitable and whether the member unreasonably turned it down.

➔ In cases of indirect race or sex discrimination, whether the employers can justify discriminating.

➔ In disability discrimination cases, whether the employers should have made a reasonable adjustment.

It will be the tribunals and courts that ultimately decide these issues, and although a lawyer can usually judge whether a case has a chance of winning, s/he can rarely guarantee what the outcome will be. This book tries to indicate the sort of factors that affect the decision on reasonableness etc., but you must be cautious about advising in individual cases.

To take an illustrative example: a member can lose the right to statutory redundancy pay if s/he unreasonably refuses an offer of suitable alternative employment. A member who is made an offer may ask you if s/he will still get the redundancy pay if s/he rejects it. To answer this question, you need to know whether a tribunal would consider (1) that the offer was "suitable" and (2) that the member had "unreasonably" refused it.

To take another example: when a woman returns from additional maternity leave, her legal right is to return to the same job if it is reasonably practicable to do so, but if not, to return to a suitable and appropriate alternative. If the member turns down a suitable alternative offer in these circumstances, she may not win an unfair dismissal claim. The law sounds straightforward until you try to advise a woman who is offered a different job instead of her own, whether or not to accept it. This is because you may not be absolutely certain:

→ Whether a tribunal would think that it was or was not "reasonably practicable" for her to have been allowed to return to her original job.

→ What a tribunal would consider her original job actually was. Whether the alternative offer was "suitable" and "appropriate" for her to do.

→ Whether there were other suitable alternatives which should have been offered.

The answer to these questions will affect whether or not the member would win her case and therefore whether she can risk rejecting the alternative offer. When you get into areas like this it is best to consult with your regional organiser/officer.

In many chapters you will find clues as to what tribunals may consider "reasonable" "suitable" and "justifiable" etc., but you need to remember that within the general legal guidelines, tribunals have a lot of room for discretion.

Scotland and Northern Ireland

Although employment law provisions in Scotland and Northern Ireland are mostly the same as those in England and Wales, some legislation and regulations differ. In Scotland and Northern Ireland, stewards / branches should therefore check with your regional office.

Terminology: 'workers'

This book refers to "workers" or "members" throughout. As explained above, you do need to be precise on each legal right as to whether it is owed to all workers or purely to employees. The text indicates in respect of the major rights which workers are eligible.

Legal support from UNISON

Where a steward encounters a legally complex situation, it would normally be wise to consult colleagues working in the branch.

All of our branches have access to advice and assistance from regional staff who work as part of teams in the relevant regional office. They will normally be able to deal with most enquiries referred to them on employment issues.

In the event that regional staff need further advice, UNISON has entered into arrangements with solicitors to whom they can turn for advice on behalf of the branch.

Where it becomes necessary to start legal proceedings, in particular in tribunals, the decision will rest in the hands of the region and trained branch or regional officers will usually provide representation. Again, if there are any legal issues they need advice on in the run up to a hearing they can take advantage of the arrangements with solicitors mentioned above.

UNISON has a strategic in-house unit, the Employment Rights Unit, responsible for overseeing the employment advice and assistance scheme. It also deals with core areas of employment law which are key to our members' interests, such as equal pay or the monitoring of the use of new legislation.

We hope that, in conjunction with those services, you will find this book helps you in the important work you do every day.

Chapter 1:

The contract of employment

Contents

Introduction

Every employee has a contract of employment. The contract consists of the agreement between the worker and the employers about working arrangements, eg pay, hours, workplace and duties. Each of these agreements is known as a contract term.

A contract of employment may or may not be in writing. Often some contract terms are written down but others are not. For example, a contract may set out a worker's holiday entitlement, but may not say whether s/he can get paid for untaken holiday when s/he leaves.

It is often hard to work out what the contract says about a particular point, especially if it is not in writing. There are rules about how to work this out.

Section 1 of the Employment Rights Act 1996 ("ERA") requires certain terms to be recorded in writing. If they are not, a member can go to a tribunal under s11 for clarification. This can be risky because the tribunal may make a decision which the member does not like and, even worse, which adversely affects many other workers employed by the particular employers.

Contracts can change over time. There may have been new agreements between the worker and the employers on particular terms since the original agreement. It is often hard to know whether a contract has really been changed in this way.

In theory, contracts can only be changed by agreement between the employers and the worker. In practice, a worker's failure to object to a change, or a worker's change in behaviour, may amount to an implied agreement to the change.

Contract law is difficult and you should not make guesses where there is any uncertainty.

What terms are in the member's contract?

Different kinds of contract terms

A contract of employment is made up of many terms and conditions which set out the obligations of the employers and of the worker. Terms may be express, implied or imposed by statute.

Express terms

Express terms are those which were explicitly agreed by the employers and the worker, whether verbally or in writing. Express terms take primacy over implied terms unless overridden by statute. However certain generally implied terms can sometimes modify the application of express terms.

Written terms may be found in a variety of places, eg
→ Letter of appointment.
→ A contract of employment.
→ A statement of main terms and conditions.
→ Incorporated from other sources, eg staff manual; other works rules; collective agreements.
Verbal terms may have been agreed, eg at the interview or on starting work.

If there was a simultaneous but contradictory written and oral agreement on the same term, the written term takes precedence. However an oral agreement subsequent to a written agreement may amount to an agreed change to the contract, provided the agreement was unambiguous and can be proved.

The wording of express terms is sometimes ambiguous and it may be uncertain how it applies in practice. For example, a term may say that "overtime must be worked in an emergency". In practice, there may be a dispute as to what amounts to an emergency.

Also contracts are often unclear on precisely what hours, days or shifts the member can be required to work.

Always read the whole contract. There may be another term in the contract which modifies the effect of an express term. For example, the contract may say that the member "will be located at the Town Hall", but there may be another term somewhere else in the contract which says the member "may be required to work at any of the Council's other buildings". A term which means the member can be required to work elsewhere is known as a "mobility clause".

Some rules and policies are simply "works rules" about ways of working and behaving at work. These may not be contractual at all and can be decided by management. Rules as to smoking, clocking in, dress codes etc. may fall into this category but there is no clear dividing line.

Implied terms

Implied terms fill the gap where there is no express term on a particular point. For example, the contract does not say whether the member gets full pay when off sick.

The law implies a term, based on what is presumed to have been the real intention of the employers and the worker at the time the contract was made. The law does not imply terms because they are reasonable. The employers and worker may well have chosen to agree to unreasonable terms.

It can be difficult to work out what an implied term may be. One of the following tests may work:

1 **The business efficacy test:** The term is implied because it is necessary to give the contract business efficacy, ie to make it work. For example, it would be implied that a worker employed to be a chauffeur must have a driving licence. It is not always possible to use this test. For example, it is not necessary to make a contract work that there is full sick pay.

2 **The officious bystander test:** A term may be implied because it is so obvious that the employers and worker must have intended it. For example, if a passer-by overheard a worker and potential employer discussing a job as a chauffeur and asked whether it was necessary for the worker to have a driving licence, both worker and employer would immediately say "of course". Again this test does not always work. If the passer-by asked whether the worker would get full pay when off sick, this would start a negotiation.

3 **What has happened in practice:** A term can be implied because it is obvious from what the employers and worker have done in practice during the employment This is sometimes referred to as "custom and practice" which makes it confusing with the other type of custom and practice (below).
For example, every time the worker has been off sick, s/he has received full pay. The problem with this method is that s/he may never have been sick before.

4 **Custom and practice:** A term is implied by custom and practice in the particular workplace or across the industry. This test rarely works as it must be a well-known term which is always followed. For example: Every cleaner in the particular company always receives two weeks' full sick pay and no more.

Terms which are generally implied
This type of implied term is central to any employment relationship, eg
→ Neither the employers nor the worker must behave in a way to destroy trust and confidence.
→ The worker will obey the employers' lawful and reasonable orders.
→ The worker will use reasonable care and skill in doing his/her duties.
→ The employers will provide a safe system of work and a safe working environment. (There are also statutory rules about health and safety.)
→ The employers and the worker will co-operate with the other and not frustrate the other's attempts to perform the contract.

→ There is an implied right to be paid (unless overridden by an express contract term), but only in rare circumstances is there an implied right to work.

Occasionally this kind of implied term can modify the exercise of an express term by the employers. For example, the employers may have an express right to require the worker to move workplace to another town. The employers may instruct the member to move to a town at the other end of the country on one day's notice. Such short notice may be a breach of the implied contract term of trust and confidence.

You should be very careful in reading express terms as modified in this way. From a contract viewpoint, employers can rely on express terms however unreasonably (although if the member is dismissed, there may be an unfair dismissal issue). It is only in very extreme circumstances that the implied term of trust and confidence is broken. Members therefore should not risk resigning in the hope that they can claim constructive dismissal just because the employers have unreasonably relied on an express term. (See p118 on constructive dismissal.)

Collective agreements

Collective agreements are rarely in themselves legally enforceable by the parties to the agreement. The way it usually works is that the terms in a collective agreement may become enforceable by individual workers if their contract of employment expressly or impliedly incorporates the collective agreement. The worker may not even be a member of the union.

Examples of express incorporation would be where the member's letter of appointment, statement of main terms and conditions or contract of employment explicitly states:

"Your terms and conditions are in accordance with and subject to the collective agreements currently in force between the local authority and UNISON"; or

"Your wages will be regulated by the scheme of pay of the Scottish Joint Negotiating Committee for Local Authorities Services (Craft Operatives)".

If there are conflicting local and national agreements, it is a matter of what each say and custom and practice as to which takes priority. For example:

"During your employment with the Council your terms and conditions of employment will be in accordance with collective agreements negotiated from time to time by the National Joint Council for Local Government Services, as supplemented by agreements reached locally through the Council's negotiating Committees."

Is the particular term apt to be incorporated?

Even where the collective agreement is expressly incorporated, a particular term of the collective agreement may not be incorporated, eg because it is a collective matter regarding negotiation processes which is not suitable for incorporation into an individual's contract.

To be suitable for incorporation, a term needs to be clear, precise and appropriate for insertion, ie a term which confers rights or duties, eg pay and hours. A term which regulates the relationship between the employers and the union as opposed to between the employers and the member, will not be suitable for incorporation. However, the dividing line may not be clear. Cases have differed as to whether a redundancy selection procedure is an apt term for incorporation.

What happens when there is a new collective agreement or the collective agreement is terminated?

Once a term in the collective agreement is incorporated into the member's contract of employment, it is normally implied that the term will be varied in accordance with any newly negotiated collective agreement, although this will always depend on the facts. It is better if the contract makes this explicit, eg:

"From time to time variations in your terms and conditions will result from agreements negotiated with UNISON and these will be notified to you."

If the employers withdraw from the collective agreement, the terms incorporated from the last collective agreement will remain in the individual contracts.

Section 1 statements

Although there is no general legal requirement that a contract of employment must be in writing, within two months of starting employment, the employers must give workers written particulars of certain basic terms of employment at the very least. This right is given by section 1 of the Employment Rights Act ("ERA") and is often referred to as a "Section 1 Statement", "Statement of Particulars of Employment" or a "Statement of the main terms and conditions of employment". It is acceptable if these basic terms are included in a general contract. Under section 4, changes in terms should also be notified.

The terms which must be included are:

→ the names of the employers and employee;

→ the date continuous employment began;

→ pay; hours; overtime requirements; holiday and sick pay terms;

→ any pension term;

→ workplace and any mobility clause;

→ job title and brief description of duties;

→ notice entitlement including expiry date of any fixed term contract;

→ disciplinary and grievance procedures;

→ reference to any incorporated collective agreements;

The European Court of Justice has said that the Employment Particulars Directive requires employers to put all "essential" terms in writing, but it is unclear what else these may be.

A statutory written statement is not itself a contract although it is usually strong evidence of what the contractual position is. If it has been signed by the worker, it probably will amount to a contract in itself.

A worker who has none – or not all - of the basic section 1 terms in writing, can ask an employment tribunal under section 11 of the Employment Rights Act to make a declaration as to the terms. Where there is a dispute as to what a term is or whether it has been changed, the tribunal will declare the true position. This can sometimes involve quite complicated legal arguments.

The tribunal cannot award compensation if this is the only claim, but simply decides what the contractual position is. This procedure is therefore useful in the following situations:

→ where there is no written term at all.

→ where there is a written term, but its meaning is unclear.

→ where there was a clear written term, which the employers say that they have changed and that the member has implicitly accepted the variation (but the member denies this).

The procedure helps clarify the contractual position where there is uncertainty, but the member may not get the answer s/he wants. It is not always sensible, useful or appropriate to use the procedure to get clarification, but sometimes it is practically or tactically useful.

Remember, this procedure does not apply to all contract terms, but only those required to be put in writing under section 1.

If the employers dismiss an employee because s/he has asserted a statutory right, eg his/her right to request a declaration under section 1, this is automatically unfair. Of course employers often disguise the true reason they have sacked someone, so the member needs to be careful.

Why is the contract important?

Members frequently ask questions about their contractual entitlements or duties. The issue comes up most often in the following situations:
→ the employers are trying to change the contractual terms and conditions;
→ there is a dispute about money owed or other contractual entitlements, eg holidays or sick pay;
→ members want to know whether they have to obey certain instructions, eg to work overtime;
→ a member wants to resign and claim constructive dismissal.

Members' questions lead to two problems:
1 It is not always clear what the contract says on the disputed issue.
2 Even if the contract is clear, it is not always a good idea to insist on keeping to the contract. For example, it will not necessarily be unfair to dismiss a worker who refuses to work overtime in an emergency, even if under his/her contract overtime is purely voluntary. (See p116 for factors making a dismissal unfair in the context of variation of contract and p110 in the context of disobedience.)

Checklist for contract problems

The following checklist gives points to bear in mind when faced with a question about the member's contract of employment:
1 Check what the contract of employment says about the point in question.
→ Is the contract in writing?
→ If so, which documents is it contained in?
→ Are you sure the documents are part of the contract as opposed to general works guidelines with no contractual force? Collective

agreements, works handbooks, etc may or may not be incorporated into the member's contract. They may state explicitly that they form part of the contract or they may have become incorporated by custom and practice or not at all.

➔ If the contract is in writing:

– Are you sure the wording is absolutely clear and not ambiguous?

– Are there any other clauses which add to or modify the clause you are interested in?

➔ If the contract is not in writing, was there a verbal contract or agreement about the point in question?

– If so, can you prove it?

➔ If there was no verbal or written agreement, can the contractual position be implied

– What has happened in practice?

– Is there a clear custom and practice across the workplace or the industry?

➔ Do any terms imposed by statute apply?

2 If the contractual position is not 100% certain, the member should be told. Also consider:

➔ Seeking further advice from other branch officers or your UNISON regional officer/organiser.

➔ If appropriate, getting a declaration on section 1 terms under the Employment Rights Act. But remember that an employment tribunal may make a decision you do not like which could adversely affect hundreds of your members. You must take advice from your regional officer/organiser on this.

➔ How important is it to know the precise contractual position on this issue? The practical and legal implications of the situation may mean that the member should not insist on any contractual right anyway. On the other hand, the member needs to be careful that by going along with changes to his/her contract, s/he is not implicitly agreeing to such changes on a permanent basis.

3 Find out the underlying problem behind the member's question.

➔ If the member is concerned about a variation of terms and conditions, see p20.

➔ If the employers have asked the member to do something which is outside the member's contract, is it worth the member refusing?

→ Is there a risk of dismissal or harassment if the member refuses and is s/he willing to risk that?

→ Is this an issue only affecting the member or can there be collective action?

→ Would the member be eligible to claim unfair dismissal for refusing such an instruction and would s/he win? (See Chapter 5.) Remember, your member is now going to be out of work, so it is a very big step which needs careful thinking through. You must consult your regional officer/organiser about this.

→ As before, the member needs to be careful that by agreeing to do something outside his/her contract on a one off basis, s/he does not implicitly agree to a permanent change of his/her contract.

4 Check whether the member is getting less favourable terms and conditions as a part-timer (p281), or as a fixed-term employee (p24).

Variation of terms and conditions

The law is complicated regarding what a worker can do if the employers try to impose a change of terms and conditions. In theory, no change can be made to a contract, unless the worker agrees. In practice, the employers may just sack the member if s/he refuses to go along with the change. The member will then be out of a job and may have limited or unsatisfactory legal rights. S/he may not be eligible to claim unfair dismissal, eg due to short service or because s/he is not an employee. Even if s/he is eligible, there is no guarantee s/he will win an unfair dismissal claim or that s/he will get enough compensation to cover his/her loss of earnings.

Advice in connection with variations should be sought from your regional officer/organiser.

There is a myth that the employers only need to give 90 days notice of a change. This is not in fact true.

The following checklist is a guide to some steps to thinking through an individual member's legal position, but specialist advice is strongly recommended. The member should not delay in getting advice as s/he may lose rights by letting matters drift.

Note that it is not enough for members simply to make a written objection, stating they are working under protest. This is a good start, but it will not safeguard their position indefinitely. After a while, they will be taken to have implicitly accepted the change and this will reduce or remove their legal options.

1 Check the member's contract of employment. Are you sure you know what it means? Are the employers really changing the contract, or are they making a change that the contract allows?
Remember: contract terms may be written, verbal or implied. If written, they may be ambiguous. If unwritten, they may be hard to ascertain or prove.

2 If the contractual position is uncertain, it may be possible to go to an employment tribunal under s11 ERA for clarification. But this only works if the disputed term is one of those which must be listed under ERA sl or, if applicable, the Employment Particulars Directive.
Note that:
→ you may get the wrong decision from the tribunal and this could harm many members. It will also undermine your negotiating power.
→ there may not be enough time to get a tribunal's Judgment;
→ the tribunal does not have power under s11 to prevent a change of the contract, but a declaration may inhibit the employers;

3 Consider whether the member is eligible to claim unfair dismissal if s/he is sacked or resigns due to a contractual change? (See p96.) If not, his/her position is very weak.

4 Even if the member is eligible to make an unfair dismissal claim in such circumstances, is s/he likely to win it?
→ Did the employers adopt fair procedures in implementing the change? (Advance notice; consultation; flexibility)
→ Would the tribunal think it reasonable for the employers to impose the change? (Relevant factors include: the employers' important needs vs the impact on workers; whether there were better alternatives; whether the majority of the workforce accepted the changes and whether the changes were recommended by UNISON.)

5 Is the member willing to risk losing his/her job over this?
→ What is the likelihood of him/her winning a case and what

compensation is s/he likely to receive?

→ What are his/her chances of getting a new job?

→ Will s/he get social security benefits meanwhile?

→ Compare the problems for the member in working under the varied contract with his/her alternatives and job prospects.

6 Has the member been discriminated against in the change, directly or indirectly?

→ Is s/he covered by the SDA, RRA, DDA, sexual orientation or religion and belief regulations ?

→ Is there any indirect sex discrimination, eg introducing flexi-shifts or other changes interfering with childcare?

→ Is there any indirect race discrimination, eg introducing duties requiring sophisticated written English skills?

→ Are the changes imposed on some workers but not on others? Is this direct discrimination? For example, the employers may make an exception for a white worker unable to work flexi-shifts for health reasons, but refuse to make an exception for a black worker with equally valid reasons.

→ Have the employers introduced duties which are hard for a disabled worker to undertake?

Note that although the member may be able to claim discrimination without resigning from her job, s/he may nevertheless be victimised for doing so.

The member's options for action

1 Agree change (orally or in writing).

2 State disagreement with change and attempt to negotiate. Be very careful. Once negotiation has clearly become futile, the grievance procedure is exhausted, and the employers are still insisting on the change, a worker needs to make up his/her mind swiftly whether or not s/he accepts the change. Otherwise s/he can lose the right to do anything because s/he has implicitly agreed by his/her inaction.

3 If relevant, a claim under sl and sll ERA may clarify a disputed contractual term and add negotiating pressure on the employers. If the member is dismissed as a result, s/he may be able to claim this is automatic unfair dismissal for asserting a statutory right. There is no guarantee this will succeed.

4 Refuse to accept the change. If it amounts to a pay deduction, make a tribunal claim for an unlawful deduction. If it is a change in duties, refuse to carry out the change.

Remember: All these steps risk dismissal. The issue then becomes what legal rights the member would have if dismissed.

5 Resign and claim unfair constructive dismissal. You should seek the advice of your regional officer/organiser before giving advice on this. There are many legal pitfalls in claiming constructive dismissal, in particular:

→ Is the worker eligible to claim unfair dismissal?

→ Are you sure what the contract says and that the employers have broken it in a fundamental way?

→ Has the worker resigned quickly enough or has s/he taken too long to decide, so that the tribunal would consider s/he had already accepted the change?

→ The employers' behaviour would not necessarily be considered unfair by the tribunal.

→ The member is out of a job and may not get much compensation even if s/he wins.

6 Make a discrimination claim. This can be done whether or not s/he resigns, but it does risk victimisation or dismissal.

7 The member may also be entitled to a redundancy payment if s/he loses her job in circumstances which fit the legal definition of redundancy.

Be careful. The application of the legal definition of redundancy can be difficult and uncertain. What the member believes is redundancy may not be so. Also, if s/he has unreasonably refused an offer of suitable alternative employment, s/he would lose any redundancy pay. (See Chapter 6.)

8 If the employers impose the change by dismissing the member with correct notice and then offering a new contract on different terms, s/he may be able to accept the new contract while claiming unfair dismissal in respect of the old contract.

9 Alternatively, if the employers simply impose radically different terms of employment, this may amount to a dismissal under the law. If so, the member can claim unfair dismissal, even though s/he has remained in employment under the new terms.

10 It will be more effective if a large number of workers simultaneously bring one of the above kinds of legal action.

11 There is a right to collective consultation under s188 of TULR(C)A if the employers propose to change the contracts of 20 or more employees (see p133).

12 Collective opposition and negotiation will usually be the best bet.

Fixed term employees

In the past, many employers have tried to avoid employment rights by putting workers onto fixed-term contracts with inferior terms and conditions and waiver clauses preventing them from claiming unfair dismissal or statutory redundancy pay when their contracts are not renewed. Some workers have been employed for years with this secondary status, although for all intents and purposes, they are working like permanent employees. The EU Fixed-Term Work Directive was passed to prevent the worst of these abuses.

The Fixed-Term Employees (Prevention of Less Favourable Treatment) Regulations 2002 were brought in to implement the Directive. The DTI has produced a guide to the Regulations which can be downloaded from the DTI website (www.dti.uk/er). This guide has no legal status as such, but it is a useful reference point.

The Regulations only cover employees, but it is arguable that the Directive also protects other workers. A fixed term employee means someone who is employed under a contract of employment that will terminate on a specific date, or on completion of a particular task, or when a specific event does or does not happen. This would include:

→ employees employed on short contracts as sickness or maternity locums;

→ seasonal or casual workers, eg shop assistants employed purely for the busy Christmas period.

The Regulations do not cover workers supplied by an agency or on certain government training schemes.

An employee on a fixed-term contract must not be treated less favourably than a comparable permanent employee just because s/he is on a fixed-term contract. A comparable permanent employee is someone employed by the same employer on broadly similar work (taking account of qualifications and skills) and who is based at the same establishment, or if there is no one, then at a different establishment.

These are examples of less favourable treatment, unless the employers can justify the different treatment:

→ denying of benefits which are given to permanent employees, eg free membership of a workplace gym; season ticket loans; more paid holidays;

→ not giving fixed-term employees non-contractual bonuses, eg at Christmas;

→ reduced access to training courses;

→ exclusion from an occupational pension scheme;

→ denying promotion opportunities;

→ selecting fixed-term employees first for redundancy.

It is not unlawful to treat a fixed-term employee less favourably if the employers can justify this. The employers should consider each individual's case separately and balance the employee's own rights against business objectives. The treatment will be justified if it is necessary to achieve a legitimate objective and is an appropriate way to do so.

Another way the employers can justify different treatment is by using the "package approach", ie if the terms of the fixed-term employee's contract, taken as a whole, are at least as favourable as those of the comparable permanent employee. For example, the fixed-term employee receives higher pay but less annual leave.

Where the employee is employed on a single short contract, then s/he may only be entitled to a proportion of an annual benefit available to permanent employees. For example, someone employed on a single six month contract, may only be entitled to pay for half the cost of annual health insurance.

Fixed-term employees have the right to be informed of any available permanent vacancies. It is enough if the vacancy is contained in an advertisement which is reasonably accessible to the employee at work. Also, once a fixed-term employee has been employed for four years on fixed-term contracts, s/he will be entitled to become a permanent employee unless the employers can justify refusing this. However, employment before 10th July 2002 cannot count towards the four years.

If the member thinks s/he may have been less favourably treated under these Regulations, s/he may make a written request to the employers to supply written reasons for the treatment within 21 days. S/he can also bring a tribunal case claiming compensation and recommendations that the employers take corrective action.

It is automatic unfair dismissal to dismiss an employee because s/he has raised an issue under the Regulations in any way, eg by alleging in a grievance that the employers have broken the law (except where the allegation is false and not made in good faith), bringing a tribunal case, giving evidence or requesting a written statement. It is also unlawful to take action short of dismissal against an employee for these reasons.

The contract of employment: myths

● *Myth:*
If employers want to change the member's contract without the member's agreement, they need only write giving 90 days notice.
Truth:
Employers cannot change a member's contract without the member's agreement, however much notice they give. See p20 on variation terms and conditions.

● *Myth:*
If the employers try to change the member's contract, as long as the member writes a letter stating s/he is working under protest, s/he preserves his/her rights.
Truth:
Letters saying the member is "working under protest" do not provide indefinite protection. After a while, the law expects the member to make up his/her mind whether s/he accepts the change or not. If s/he just carries on working, s/he may well be deemed to have accepted the change as time goes by. See p22, point 2 on affirmation.

Chapter 2:

Pay and conditions

Contents

National minimum wage

Who is covered

The National Minimum Wage Act 1998 ("NMWA") introduced a national minimum wage for the first time, although previously there had been minimum pay for workers in certain industries. A "worker" means someone working on a contract to perform personally any work or services (except to a professional client or business customer). Agency workers and home workers are usually covered.

UNISON has a long history of campaigning for a decent minimum wage. In November 2004, UNISON together with the YMCA England, presented a written submission to the Low Pay Commission. The submission: "The Big Bite! Why it's time for the minimum wage to really work" is available on UNISON's website.

The rate

The rates are set by Regulations. From October 2004, the rate was £4.85/hour for adult workers aged 22 years and over, a development rate of £4.10/hour for workers aged 18–21 years inclusive, and £3/hour for those aged 16-17 years (but not apprentices).

UNISON believes these rates are too low, and in its submission to the Low Pay Commission, it recommended a target rate of £6.50/hour by October 2006. It also recommended that 18-21 year olds are paid the full adult rate, with an increase in the rate for 16-17 year olds to the development rate.

In response to the Low Pay Commission's recommendations, the government announced increases from October 2005 to £5.05 (adult rate) and £4.25 (development rate) and from October 2006, to £5.35 (adults) and £4.45 (development rate).

Calculating whether a member has been paid the minimum wage can be complicated in practice. There are special rules about what payments may and may not be added in. Benefits in kind, such as free meals or luncheon vouchers, cannot be counted towards the wage, but the value of free accommodation can be counted to a limited extent. There are complicated rules for which hours should be paid when a worker is on-call at the workplace, but not actively working at all times.

Enforcement

If a member is paid below the minimum wage, s/he can take a tribunal case for deduction from wages. It is unlawful to dismiss a worker or subject him/her to a detriment for asking for the minimum wage on his/her own behalf or on behalf of others.

In addition, the Inland Revenue has general powers of enforcement. It has issued two new Codes of Practice explaining its powers. These are available on the Inland Revenue website: http://www.inlandrevenue/gov/uk or on the helpline (telephone 0845 6000 678). COP19 is the employers' Code and COP20 is the workers' Code. In summary, if a complaint is made to the Inland Revenue on its helpline, it will contact the employers to check the pay details and will instruct the employers to make any necessary increase and to reimburse back-pay. The worker making the complaint will not be identified without permission. If the pay is not corrected, the Inland Revenue can issue an enforcement notice and, if still unpaid, a penalty notice which includes a fine. If all this does not work, it can bring a tribunal case for the individual workers concerned (if they so wish). Alternatively, workers can at any stage bring their own cases or be represented by a UNISON official in the normal way.

The Inland Revenue has no power to assist or represent workers who are dismissed because they have asked for minimum pay.

UNISON has said that, while the Inland Revenue's record on payment retrieval has been good, it should concentrate its efforts more towards low paying areas and be more proactive in its work. Although awareness of the national minimum wage is widespread, knowledge as to the statutory amount is far less well known, and the right to make an anonymous complaint even less. A common problem is spotting underpayments, because flexible hours and payment rates, make it hard for members to calculate what they are due or what they have been paid from their payslip. All this suggests you should take a proactive role in identifying underpayments for groups of workers and taking this up with employers or notifying the Inland Revenue.

UNISON reports that many employers continue to evade the minimum wage regulations or use a wide range of strategies to claw back costs, eg reducing hours, reducing sick and holiday pay, eliminating paid breaks, introducing charges for uniform. These strategies may well be unlawful and you need to take advice from your regional officer/organiser on the position.

Working time regulations

The Working Time Regulations 1998 ("WTR") were brought in to implement the EC Working Time Directive (93/104) and the Young Workers' Directive (94/33). The WTR as well as government guidance can be downloaded from the DTI's web site at www.dti.gov.uk/er/work_time_regs

As with all government guidance, it is helpful but not necessarily a definitive statement on the law. Also, it may not be completely up-to-date on any legal changes.

Who is covered

The WTR cover workers in the wide sense and not purely employees. A "worker" includes anyone working on a contract to perform personally any work or services (except to a professional client or business customer). Agency workers are usually covered. Few of the entitlements apply to the police, fire brigades, ambulance or other emergency services. The 48 hour limit on an average working week does not yet apply to trainee doctors, but is being gradually phased in. The rules for workers in the transport sectors are piecemeal and complicated as they are often covered by separate regulations.

Working time means any time during which the member is working at his/her employers' disposal or receiving relevant training. On-call time is covered while the member must be at or near the workplace (even if s/he is allowed to sleep), but not at home. However, on-call time during which the member need not be at work and is free to do other things is working time only for the periods when the member is actually doing work for the employer.

Most of the WTR rights do not apply where the member works on "unmeasured working time". If only part of the member's time is "unmeasured" the WTR do not apply to that part. "Unmeasured" time means where, due to the nature of the work, the member's time is not predetermined or the member can decide how long s/he works. Employers often try to interpret this exception widely, suggesting that it covers middle management. However, it is almost certainly confined to very high-powered self-regulating executives, and does not mean more junior managers who are forced to work limitless overtime by higher management.

The rights

The WTR grant a number of rights, some of which the member can agree to give up, others which are absolute. The member is entitled to:

1 A minimum daily rest period of 11 consecutive hours in each 24-hour period, unless working a shift pattern.

2 A weekly rest period of at least 24 hours which can be averaged out over a fortnight.

3 A minimum 20 minute rest break away from the work station during the working day if more than 6 hours is worked. This means a complete break, not simply "down-time", when the member must remain in radio contact and at the employers' disposal. The break need not be paid unless the member already has a contractual entitlement to paid breaks.

4 Night workers should not average more than 8 hours in each 24-hour period, averaged over 17 weeks. A night worker is someone who works at least three hours between 11 p.m. and 6 a.m. on most working days.

5 The employers should offer members a free health assessment before starting night work and regular free health assessments while remaining on night work. If a registered medical practitioner advises that the member is suffering from health problems caused by night work, the employers must transfer the member to suitable work off nights if possible.

6 The entitlements set out above do not apply in a number of circumstances set out in regulation 21. The circumstances include:
→ where there is an accident, risk of accident, or unusual and unforeseeable event beyond the employers' control.
→ where there is a foreseeable surge of activity, eg in tourism or postal services. This means an exceptional level of activity, not the normal fluctuation present in most industries over a working day.
→ where the worker lives a long way from work.
→ where there is a need for continuity of service or production, eg reception, treatment or care in hospitals or residential homes; gas, water and electricity production and distribution. It is the member's job which has to be continuous, not the service itself.
→ where the job needs permanent security or surveillance.
→ where the daily and weekly rest periods do not apply to shift workers when they change shifts.
→ where the above entitlements can also be modified or excluded by a collective agreement.
In all these cases, where a worker is required to work through a rest period or break, the employers must allow the worker to take an equivalent period of compensatory rest fairly soon after. In exceptional cases, where that is impossible for objective reasons, the employers must provide appropriate health and safety protection.

7 The member is entitled to at least four weeks paid annual leave. This must be taken in the leave year in which it is due and cannot be substituted by pay in lieu except on leaving.

The member can take leave by giving the correct notice, specifying the number of days to be taken. If the employers object to the timing, they must give the correct counter-notice. UNISON may agree its own notification procedure with the employers. Paid Bank Holidays can be included in the four week total unless the member's contract already gives Bank Holiday rights in addition to other holiday entitlements.

Some employers try to claim that an element of holiday pay is included in the normal weekly pay. This is often referred to as a "rolled-up" payment. It defeats the object of the WTR, which is to ensure that paid holidays are taken each year, and has been held unlawful by the Scottish Court of Session in *MPB Structures Ltd v Munro*.

Unfortunately, the Court of Appeal in England and Wales disagreed in the case of *Marshalls Clay Products v Caulfield* and has asked the European Court of Justice to decide the position. Meanwhile, the guidelines in *Marshalls Clay* as expanded by a subsequent case, are that holiday pay can be rolled up, provided:

– the provision for rolled-up holiday pay is clearly incorporated in the contract of employment

– the amount allocated to holiday pay must be clearly identified in the contract and, preferably, also in the pay-slip

– most importantly, the holiday pay must be a genuine and true addition to the pay

– records should be kept of holidays taken and steps taken to ensure the workers do take their holidays in each holiday year.

8 A member cannot be forced to work more than 48 hours/week, usually averaged over 17 weeks, though for some workers over 26 weeks. A collective agreement cannot modify or exclude the 48-hour ceiling, though in some circumstances it can extend the period over which hours are averaged. The member can personally opt out and agree to work more than 48 hours. This agreement must be in writing and can be ended by the member at any time. The member must not be subjected to any detriment because s/he refuses to work more than 48 hours.

Many workers sign an opt-out agreement because they do not realise they have a right to refuse or they may be afraid of the consequences. UNISON should ensure that all members are aware of their rights in this respect. The European Court of Justice has emphasised that consent to opt-out must be freely given by the worker. It is particularly important that workers are not pressurised by employers who present them with opt-out forms for signing on induction. The European Commission considers the UK is misapplying the scope for opt-out in the Working Time Directive, and has proposed a revision of the Directive to prevent pressure on workers to opt-out. Unfortunately the Commission has stopped short of removing the opt-out altogether. For an interesting research review on the regulation of working time in the UK and across Europe, see *Flexible working and the long-hours culture* by Patricia Leighton at 138 Equal Opportunities Review p10 (February 2005).

9 There are additional rules for young workers, ie those under 18.

10 It is unlawful to dismiss the worker or subject him/her to any detriment for taking up any rights under the WTR.

Note that it is not a straightforward issue as to how and where each of the various rights should be enforced if negotiation is unsuccessful. You should always take advice from your regional officer/organiser.

Sick pay

It is a matter of contract whether employers pay the member full pay when off sick and for how long. There are certain social security payments, subject to certain rules, ie initially statutory sick pay ("SSP") and in the long-term, incapacity benefit. SSP is paid at a low weekly rate by the employers and partially reclaimed by them from the government. For detail as to precisely how SSP works, you need advice from a specialist body such as a Citizens Advice Bureau.

Contractual rules which grant longer periods of sick pay in accordance with length of service may amount to indirect race or sex discrimination against members with shorter service, unless the employers can justify such a policy. (See p129 on length of service as a potentially discriminatory criterion.)

Unauthorised deductions from pay

Where employers fail to pay the member any money due to him/her, usually the simplest way to recover the money is through a tribunal claim for deduction from wages. The alternative is to claim for breach of contract in the county court or high court. The two rights are similar but not identical and you need specialist advice as to which is the appropriate option in any case. Speak to your regional officer/organiser about this.

A claim for deduction from wages was originally made under the Wages Act 1986, which has now been replaced by Part 2 of the Employment Rights Act 1996. A "worker" can make a claim, which includes someone employed on a contract to perform personally any work or services (except to a professional client or business customer). The claim must be made to the tribunal for an "unauthorised deduction" within three months of when the money was due. If there is a series of deductions, the time-limit runs from the last deduction in the series.

A "deduction" can mean partial or complete non-payment. For example, the member could claim:

→ For complete failure to pay holiday pay.

→ For overtime payments or bonuses which are owed.

→ For the shortfall where the employers have made a pay-cut without his/her agreement. (This may be a better option than resigning – see p20.)

→ Where the employers deducted sums to cover unauthorised telephone use, stock shortages or fraud by customers.

The employers are allowed to make deductions for certain purposes, eg tax, National Insurance, union subscriptions or where the member has agreed in writing (including in the contract) before the incident leading to the deduction arose. There is additional protection for "retail workers", eg those working in electricity showrooms, whereby no more than 10% of the member's wage can be deducted for a stock shortage in any week.

A member cannot make a tribunal claim for an unauthorised deduction, where the employers' reason for deducting was to recover an "overpayment" of wages. The legal position is complex on this and you need to take advice from your regional officer/organiser.

Equal pay

Introduction and single status

Women make up 71% of UNISON's members. Women also form 70% of the local government workforce. The 2000 New Earnings

Survey revealed that women in local government earned on average about 80% of comparable male earners, taking bonuses into account. Of 4500 female UNISON members polled in its NOP published in 2000, 78% said that equal pay was the "most important" thing the union could achieve for them. For this reason, UNISON's Employment Rights Unit deals with all equal pay cases. **If you identify a case, you must refer it to your Regional Officer/Organiser.**

The 1997 Single Status agreement in local government had two main aims – to harmonise the terms and conditions of manual and white collar workers and to create integrated, equal pay proofed pay and grading structures. To the latter end, a joint bespoke job evaluation scheme was drawn up, designed to capture the attributes of local government jobs – especially 'people' skills – which had historically been undervalued. The employers refused to agree to the national, mandatory use of the NJC job evaluation scheme or to a national pay and grading system, thereby requiring trade unions and employees in each local authority across England, Wales and Northern Ireland to job evaluate all jobs and create new pay and grading structures within the national pay spine.

So far only 20% of councils have completed the exercise. This primarily reflects the lack of funding available to councils. In contrast to the NHS, where the parallel Agenda for Change is Government funded, no extra money has been made available to local authorities. The 2004-6 agreement in the National Joint Council for Local Government Services now requires all councils to complete pay and grading reviews by the end of the agreement. While thousands of women in jobs such as home care, care assistant, school cook supervisor, teaching assistant and nursery nurse have improved their pay and grading by the agreements made so far, underfunding, problems with protection of downgraded staff and moves to make school-based staff 'term time only' continue to keep progress slow. The gender pay gap has narrowed in most councils completing Single Status, but overall unsurprisingly remains at the UK level, with over 300 councils still to complete pay and grading reviews.

For more detail on Equal Pay law and practice, it is worth reading the regular updates in the Equal Opportunities Review. You may want to get UNISON's "Getting Equal" Campaign Pack, which includes leaflets on the equal pay aspects of Best Value, Single Status and part-time working (see p314 for availability). It is also worth reading the

UNISON Briefing "Winning Equal Pay: Equal Pay developments in the UK" (April 2002), available on the website under Resources / Online Catalogue / Equalities.

You should have a copy of the Equal Opportunity Commission's excellent Code of Practice on Equal Pay. The revised Code came into force on 1st December 2003 and can be downloaded from the EOC website, together with several good practice guides.

The following checklist provides an overview on how to approach individual claims. The EOC Code also gives detailed guidance on how to conduct a general review of pay systems for sex bias. The UNISON protocol for litigating equal pay cases is available on the UNISON website under "Resources".

Legal overview

1 The law is contained in the Equal Pay Act 1970, which deals with sex discrimination in pay and contract terms. Other forms of sex discrimination are dealt with by the Sex Discrimination Act. Sometimes it is not clear whether the Equal Pay Act or the Sex Discrimination Act applies to a certain situation.

2 Race discrimination in pay or contract terms is dealt with by the Race Relations Act as are all other forms of race discrimination.

3 European law also forbids sex discrimination in pay. The law is contained in Article 141 of the Treaty of Rome and the Equal Pay Directive.

4 Men and women are entitled to the same pay if they are doing (i) like work, (ii) work rated as equivalent on a Job Evaluation Scheme, or (iii) work of equal value.

5 The member must find a worker (or "comparator") of the opposite sex employed in the same employment, ie in the same establishment or service, to compare herself with. A comparator can be employed by a different employer only if there is sufficient overall connection. There must be a single source in control of the pay of the member and her comparator. For example, in the case of *South Ayrshire Council v Morton* ([2001] 95 EOR 51, EAT), although the comparator was employed by a different education authority, the authority was within the same overall structure as the worker's own. Unfortunately, comparisons with retained staff after contracting-out are unlikely to be successful, as there is not usually a single source of pay. This is a complex point. See p154 for a UNISON test case.

6 The employers have a defence if they prove that the difference in pay is due to a genuine material factor other than sex.

What to look for

1 What are the duties which the member is actually carrying out?
→ Is there a written job description?
→ What is the member doing in practice? Can s/he prove it?
→ What proportion of time is being spent on each element of her duties?

2 Can you find a man who is paid more than the member, so that she can compare herself with him?

3 Check the man is in the "same employment" as the member (see above).

4 Are the member and her comparator doing "like work"?
→ Consider what they actually do in practice.
→ Are the jobs identical?
→ If there are any differences, are they only minor?

5 Even if the jobs are not the same or very similar, are they of equal value?
Note: this requires imagination, creative and non-stereotypical thinking.
→ Consider and compare the jobs in terms of such elements as the knowledge, skill, effort and responsibility involved.
→ Some examples of where tribunals have found jobs of equal value are:
− speech therapist / psychologist
− packer / labourer
− group personnel & training officer / divisional sales trainer
→ You could also consider whether the following jobs may be of

equal value:
- domestic assistants / hospital porters
- welfare assistants / drivers or messengers
- nursery nurses / technicians

In March 2005, UNISON agreed the biggest ever equal pay award with North Cumbria Acute NHS Trust for 1500 women working at the Cumberland Infirmary and the West Cumbria Hospital. The following job comparisons were made:

- Grade C and D nurses / Medical technical officers, spinal points 25-29
- Grade A nurse / Joiner
- Domestic supervisor / Joiner
- Lab assistant; porter; cook; catering assistant; domestic assistant; clerical officer; sewing room assistant; switchboard operator / Maintenance assistant

---

Kenefick and others v South Wales Police Authority

In March 2005, UNISON agreed settlements for six senior police women, having brought an equal value case against the South Wales Police Authority. The employers were forced to admit that five female Administration Managers had carried out work of equal value to that done by a male Paymaster. A sixth woman successfully compared her work as temporary Business Manager with that of a male Financial Accountant. Compensation between £7600 and £1900 was agreed. A seventh woman is due to have her compensation assessed later in 2005.

The employers' defence

The law about what makes a suitable defence is complicated. These are only some key points.

1 Has the member's job been rated as lower than her comparator's on a suitable non-discriminatory Job Evaluation Scheme? If so, she will lose.

2 What reason will the employers give for the pay differential? Can you find out and pin them down?

3 Is the reason significant and relevant?

4 Is the reason a neutral reason or linked with gender in some way?

5 If the reason amounts to indirect sex discrimination, can the employers objectively justify it?

For example:

– the reason the employers pay a woman less than a man is because she is a part-timer. The employers would need to prove why favouring full-timers met a real need on the part of the organisation.

– A group of women in one job, which is predominantly held by women, are paid less than a group of men in a comparable job, which is predominantly held by men. The employers would need to show objective reasons for the pay differential.

Victimisation

Watch out for victimisation. It is unlawful sex discrimination to punish a worker for raising issues about unequal pay. See p199.

Indirect discrimination in pay

Pay rules and agreements often appear neutral but their effect is to disadvantage substantially more women than men. Criteria determining levels of pay and access to bonuses often benefit men. The EOC Code on Equal Pay sets out guidelines on reviewing pay and identifying discriminatory elements.

The following are reasons for pay differentials which may disadvantage women more than men and be indirectly discriminatory:

– Inferior pay, terms and conditions for part-timers.

– Pay increments, increased holiday and sick pay entitlements, based on length of service.

– Paying more for "flexibility" and "mobility", eg unpredictable working hours, last-minute overtime, week-end working.

– Paying bonuses for jobs traditionally done by men rather than by women.

– Performance-related pay based on appraisals which tend to involve subjective judgements and reward long hours.

The employers must justify any indirectly discriminatory rule.

1 Find out and pin down the employers on what they were trying to achieve.

2 Consider whether that was a legitimate objective and a real need.

3 Would there be a non-discriminatory way of achieving the same objective?

Where part-timers' terms and conditions including pay are less favourable than those of full-timers, the Part-time Workers' Regulations may also be of assistance (see p282). The Regulations forbid unjustifiable less favourable treatment of a part-timer as against a comparable full-timer, regardless of whether either is male or female.

Legal claims and time-limits

A member considering bringing a case can find out what everyone else is paid and why, by asking the employers to answer an equal pay questionnaire. The questionnaire form and model questions can be downloaded from www.womenandequalityunit.gov.uk/pay/update_question.htm. A member needs to think carefully before sending a questionnaire because it is likely to upset the employers and the member may get victimised as a result. (See page 300 for more details of the procedure.) Another way to get more information about how pay systems work in practice is for UNISON to seek the information as part of the collective bargaining process.

If the member wins an equal pay claim, any less favourable term in her contract is modified so, for example, she is no longer paid less than the male comparator. The tribunal can award arrears of pay in standard cases for 6 years (5 years in Scotland) and interest.

The time-limit for bringing a case is 6 months from the last day the member was employed in the relevant employment. If the member worked on a series of different contracts for the same employer, the position may not be clear-cut and you should take advice. There are special rules if the member was under a mental disability (as defined in the legislation) or the employers deliberately concealed relevant information.

The statutory disputes resolution procedures may apply, requiring a grievance to be brought before any tribunal claim, and a consequent effect on time-limits. For details, see pages 57-72.

The law on discrimination against part-timers in membership and benefits of occupational pensions is extremely complex and specialist advice must be taken via your branch and regional office.

Information and consultation

The Information and Consultation of Employees Regulations 2004 (the ICE Regulations) came into force on 6th April 2005, to implement the EC Directive on Information and Consultation in the Workplace. There is detailed DTI Guidance available on its website and good practice guidance from ACAS (both available on their websites, see p314), but neither of these have legal status.

The Regulations will be phased in, initially applying to undertakings with 150 or more employees. This will be extended to undertakings with 100 or more employees from 6th April 2007 and 50 or more employees from 6th April 2008. An undertaking means a public or private undertaking carrying out an economic activity, whether or not operating for gain. It is unclear whether certain parts of the public sector carry out economic as opposed to purely administrative activities. The NHS is probably covered, but local authorities may not be. Even if they are not covered, the government is encouraging them to make similar arrangements (see DTI Guidance).

The requirement to inform and consult does not exist automatically under the Regulations. The employers may choose to initiate negotiations themselves. Alternatively, they may choose not to do anything unless a written request is made by 10% of the employees (subject to a minimum of 15 and maximum of 2500). If this happens, the employers must initiate negotiations for an ICE agreement, starting with the election of negotiating representatives (who may or may not turn out to be the trade union representatives).

Where there is a "pre-existing agreement", eg a collective agreement, the employers can choose to ask the workforce whether they endorse the request for a new ICE agreement, or would prefer to leave things as they are. A collective agreement must satisfy certain conditions in order to be a valid pre-existing agreement.

Even if the workforce vote for a new ICE agreement, the collective agreement would remain in force for other purposes.

When there is no approved pre-existing agreement, a new one must be negotiated. The employers must make arrangements for all employees to take part in the election or appointment of their negotiating representatives. Any number of representatives may be chosen, but there must be enough of them to represent all the employees from different parts of the undertaking and different sections of the workforce. The chosen reps may or may not be the union reps.

The Regulations set out the process for setting up an ICE agreement and appointing ICE representatives or for information and consultation to be carried out directly with the employees, or both. The ICE representatives need not be the same people as the negotiating representatives.

The negotiated agreement must set out the circumstances in which employers will inform and consult their employees. The subject matter, method, frequency and timing of information and consultation should be agreed. If no agreement is reached, the standard ICE procedures apply by default. Under these, the employers must give information on (1) the recent and probable development of the undertaking's activities and economic situation, (2) the situation, structure and probable development of employment within the undertaking and any anticipatory measures envisaged, particularly where there is a threat to employment within the undertaking, (3) decisions likely to lead to substantial changes in work organisation or in contractual relations.

The information must be given at an appropriate time to enable the representatives to conduct an adequate study and to prepare for consultation on categories (2) and (3). The DTI Guidance at paragraph 55 expands on what kind of information should be provided under these categories. Employers can insist that representatives do not pass on information to anyone else, or can withhold information altogether on grounds of confidentiality. This covers price-sensitive or other information which would seriously harm the functioning of the undertaking or be prejudicial to it.

Category 3 includes decisions on collective redundancies and business transfers. Employers need not consult on these matters under the Regulations if they notify the ICE representatives on a case by case basis that they will be consulting under the legislation specific to those matters, (see p133 and p155).

The DTI Guidance points out that consultation is more than simply providing information and carrying on regardless. Although ultimately it is for the employers to make decisions. there should be genuine consideration of the views of the ICE representatives and a reasoned response should be given. The employers must meet the representatives with an appropriate level of management – presumably a level capable of changing the decisions under discussion. There is no obligation on the representatives to obtain the employees' views and report back to them, but the DTI says this would be good practice.

The Regulations do not say how often or when information and consultation must take place. The DTI Guidance says it should be ongoing and regular, not solely on one-off occasions, when there is a problem. Ideally the representatives should agree frequency and timing with the employers, but a lot will depend on how and when issues actually arise.

Negotiating and ICE representatives are entitled to reasonable paid time off during working hours to perform their functions. This right does not apply to representatives paid under a pre-existing agreement. It is automatically unfair to dismiss an employee or subject him/her to a detriment for seeking paid time off or performing the functions of a representative (including candidates) or for a number of other reasons connected with these rights.

The Central Arbitration Committee (CAC) will adjudicate on breaches of the general rights in the Regulations, eg what amounts to an undertaking; whether the appointment or election of representatives is valid; whether the employers have failed to comply with the terms of a negotiated or default arrangement. In the last case, ICE representatives or if there are none, employee representatives, may apply within three months of the decision to the EAT for a penalty notice of up to £75,000. The CAC is to publish guidance on the procedure for complaining under the Regulations.

UNISON is concerned that the Regulations may lead to staff councils being set up, which undermine union recognition rights. UNISON advises:

1 Employers don't have to make any changes unless 10% of employees request it.

2 If any proposals are made, involve your Regional Officer/ Organiser straight away.

3 Pre-empt the Regulations by renegotiating your agreements to include information and consultation arrangements to cover all staff.

4 If a staff council is imposed, try to get union reps elected to every seat.

5 In areas where UNISON isn't strong enough to get recognition, you may be able to use the new rights to get an information and consultation staff council and use it as an organising tool.

For further information and bargaining advice, see the Information and Consultation factsheet at www.unison.org.uk/acrobat/B1462.pdf or on the Bargaining Conditions Zone at www.unison.org.uk/bargaining/conditions.asp.

Pay and conditions: Myths

● *Myth:*

The member can complain under the Equal Pay Act if a colleague doing work of equal value is paid more than him/her, even if s/he is of the same sex.

Truth:

Under the Equal Pay Act, the member can only compare his/her pay with someone of the opposite sex.

● *Myth:*

The member can complain under the Equal Pay Act about more senior staff getting more favourable terms and conditions eg length of holidays.

Truth:

Under the Equal Pay Act, the member can only compare his/her pay or contractual terms with someone doing like work or work of equal value.

Pay and conditions: key points

■ The National Minimum Wage Act sets a minimum wage. The entitlement can be enforced by individual members, although the Inland Revenue has general responsibilities for enforcement.

■ It is unlawful to dismiss or subject the member to a detriment for requesting the minimum wage.

■ UNISON has researched the effect of the NMWA on its members and campaigned for a higher minimum wage. (See its informative submission to the Low Pay Commission on the UNISON website.)

■ The Working Time Regulations give rights to minimum rest periods, during the day, every 24 hours, every week and annual holiday entitlements. There is also a 48-hour maximum working week unless the member opts out.

■ Various workers and industries are excluded from certain rights under the Working Time Regulations. You need to be aware of the exclusions as they affect certain UNISON members.

■ There are special rules for young workers and night workers.

■ It is unlawful to dismiss or subject the member to a detriment for taking up rights under the Working Time Regulations.

■ There is no minimum pay set by statute when workers are sick. It is entirely a matter of contract (and negotiation). However, subject to certain rules, the member should receive SSP (statutory sick pay

■ Watch out for unjustifiable discrimination where the length of contractual sick pay is linked to length of service.

■ Members can go to the employment tribunal under Part 2 of the Employment Rights Act 1996 to recover certain non-payments or deductions from their wages. Alternatively, they may claim for breach of contract in the courts.

■ Sex discrimination in pay or contract terms is covered by the Equal Pay Act and European Law (Article141 of the Treaty of Rome and the Equal Pay Directive).

■ A worker bringing an equal pay case must compare him/herself with a worker of the opposite sex, in the same employment, at the same establishment or at another establishment where common terms and conditions apply generally or to workers of the relevant classes.

■ In equal value cases, the member can compare him/herself with a worker doing a different job which requires similar skills and capabilities.

■ Employers can defend an equal pay case if they can show the difference is due to a genuine and non-trivial reason and not based on the difference of sex.

■ If there is indirect discrimination in pay, eg a female dominated group of workers is excluded from a bonus scheme, the employers must go further and must objectively justify the differential.

■ The revised EOC Code of Practice on Equal Pay is a very useful and practical guide to reviewing pay systems in the workplace to detect areas of inequality.

■ UNISON can seek information on pay statistics as part of the collective bargaining process. In individual cases, members can serve a questionnaire to gain more information about pay differentials and the reasons.

■ Where a part-timer is less favourably treated than a comparable full-timer, regardless of whether either is male or female, see also the Part-Time Workers Regulations (p282).

Chapter 3

Disciplinary and grievance procedures

Contents

Disciplinary procedures

Introduction

Small employers in non-unionised environments often follow no procedure at all when disciplining or dismissing workers. The government has therefore introduced minimum procedures which must be followed by all employers. These "statutory disputes resolution" procedures are set out later in this Chapter. In a unionised environment, it is likely that the negotiated disciplinary procedures already include the minimum steps and are far more sophisticated. Nevertheless, you need to be aware of the minimum statutory steps and the consequences of not following them.

The ACAS code

The ACAS Code of Guidance on Disciplinary and Grievance Procedures sets out good practice guidelines for the handling of disciplinary and grievance issues in employment. The latest version of the Code (edition 3, with effect from 1st October 2004) can be downloaded from the ACAS website at

http://acas.org.uk/publications.htm. When handling any disciplinary or grievance process, it is important you are familiar with what the Code says.

Although it is not against the law in itself for employers to fail to follow the Code, employment tribunals must take this into account when deciding cases. A member claiming unfair dismissal can draw the tribunal's attention to any relevant part of the Code which has not been followed. The tribunal will also check whether the employers' own procedures have been complied with. For other factors relevant to the fairness of a dismissal, see Chapter 5. When you represent a member at a disciplinary hearing, even if dismissal is not a possibility, it is important to keep in mind these principles.

There are three important principles set out by the ACAS Code:

→ It is important that workers know what standards of performance and conduct are expected of them.

→ There should be fairness and consistency in the treatment of individual workers.

→ Disciplinary procedures should not be viewed primarily as a means of imposing sanctions on the worker. They should be seen as a way of helping and encouraging improvement in the worker's conduct or standard of work.

The employers' disciplinary rules

Large and public-sector employers such as local authorities and NHS trusts often have different procedures for dealing with conduct and capability issues. Some employers use a single disciplinary procedure for either issue. The procedure usually covers:

→ The disciplinary rules, and standards of expected conduct.

→ The procedures to be followed when disciplining a worker.

The rules are usually found in the written disciplinary procedure or an employee handbook.

It is important that workers have seen and understood the rules. The employers should make appropriate efforts to translate or explain rules to workers whose first language is not English or who suffer a disability such as a visual impairment or dyslexia.

The rules will set out unacceptable behaviour in a number of areas, although obviously not every scenario can be covered. The written rule effectively serves as advance warning to the member. Employers sometimes have rules that workers will be automatically dismissed for certain offences, eg fighting at work, regardless of the circumstances. Although the employers may lay down very strict rules, employment tribunals still expect them to consider the individual circumstances of each case including:

→ Whether the member was aware of the rule and its seriousness.

→ The member's general work and disciplinary record.

→ The reason the member broke the rule on this occasion and any mitigating factors.

The disciplinary rules will normally list behaviour which is considered to be gross misconduct. Usually the list comprises examples and is not exhaustive. See p52 for the significance of gross misconduct.

The procedural steps

The employers should follow their own procedure when disciplining the member, provided it complies with the general standards of fairness set by the ACAS Code and the statutory minimum disputes resolution procedures (see below). The ACAS Code recommends the following stages:

→ When a disciplinary matter arises, the relevant manager should first establish the facts promptly, before recollections fade. A member may be asked about an event so long after it occurred that s/he cannot give a proper explanation. This can make a dismissal unfair.

→ In local authorities and health trusts, this stage often consists of investigatory or "fact-finding" interviews under the procedure. Members need to be very careful what they say in these informal meetings, as it can affect how the matter develops. (See p80 below.)

→ The manager then decides whether to drop the matter, give informal counselling or deal with it under the disciplinary procedure.

→ Minor cases of misconduct and most cases of poor performance should be dealt with through informal advice and counselling. The manager's objective should be to encourage and help the member to improve. It is important that the member understands what the problem is, what needs to be done to improve and over what period, and how his/her performance will be reviewed.

→ Where formal disciplinary action is likely, then the formal procedure should be followed.

→ The member must be informed of the allegations against him/her and the supporting evidence in advance of the disciplinary hearing.

→ The member should be advised of his/her right to be accompanied to the disciplinary hearing. (See p72.)

→ Before any disciplinary decision is taken, there should be a disciplinary hearing at which the member is given the opportunity to answer the allegations and state his/her case.

→ If disciplinary action is taken, the member should be given an explanation why and informed of his/his right of appeal.

→ Where serious misconduct is alleged it may be fair to suspend the member during the investigatory or disciplinary process, although this should be for as short a time as possible and, unless the contract says otherwise, on full pay.

→ Overall, the process should be handled without undue delay and confidentiality should be maintained. The member should be given records of the meetings and hearings,

→ Where the member has lodged a grievance against the manager bringing the disciplinary proceedings, the Code says it may be fair and appropriate to deal with the grievance first. This issue often arises where discrimination is involved. (See p75 below.)

Forms of disciplinary action

The ACAS Code recommends that no worker is dismissed for a first offence unless it amounts to gross misconduct. (See p52). Therefore the member should normally have received some warnings before dismissal. It is often thought that the law requires precisely one oral and two written warnings before a worker can be fairly dismissed. This is a myth. If the member's offence is sufficiently serious, the employers can skip the earlier warnings.

The usual stages followed would be as follows:

1 A formal oral warning. This is suitable for minor infringements. The member should be given reasons for the warning and advised of his/her right of appeal. A note of the warning should be kept but disregarded for disciplinary purposes after a specified period (often 6 months).

2 First written warning. The employers can start at this stage for more serious behaviour. The warning should set out the details of the complaint, the required improvement and time-scale, and the right of appeal. It should also state that the worker is at risk of a final written warning if there is no improvement. Again, a copy of the warning should be kept on file but disregarded for disciplinary purposes after, say, 12 months.

3 Final written warning. The member can be given a final warning, because there is no improvement within the time-scale set on the first warning, or even if there have been no prior warnings – if the behaviour is serious enough. The warning should give similar details to those required on a first warning, but additionally in this case to indicate the risk of dismissal if there is no improvement.

4 Dismissal. If the member repeats offences or fails to improve after a final warning or if s/he commits gross misconduct (see below), s/he can be dismissed. Alternatively, the member's contract may allow other sanctions such as a disciplinary transfer or demotion.

Whatever disciplinary procedure applies to the member, it is likely to set out stages similar to the above.

When deciding whether to dismiss a worker, the employers may sometimes be able to rely on the fact that the worker has several live warnings, even though these concern unrelated offences. However, employers should not normally rely on warnings which have lapsed after a specified time under the procedure.

What level of penalty is appropriate?

In imposing warnings or dismissing the member, the employers must act reasonably, taking account of all the circumstances. The following factors will be relevant:

→ The member's length of service and work record.
→ The member's job and status.
→ The seriousness of the member's behaviour.
→ Any personal mitigating factors.
→ The way similar offences by other workers have been dealt with previously.

Additional factors will be relevant depending on the nature of the offence. Some of these are set out in the unfair dismissal chapter at pp 105-116.

The ACAS Code stresses that it is particularly important not to discriminate on grounds of race, religion, sex, sexual orientation or disability during the process. (See p74 below.) Also if disciplinary action is contemplated against a trade union official, the case should be discussed with a senior trade union representative or full-time official.

Gross misconduct

Particularly serious offences are known as "gross misconduct". If a member has committed gross misconduct it is significant for two reasons. It means:

→ The employers can dismiss the member without any notice or pay in lieu. This is called "summary dismissal".

→ It may be fair for the employers to dismiss the member for a first offence, although it is still important that the employers follow fair procedures in the investigation and disciplinary hearing. However, although a dismissal for gross misconduct may be unfair due to poor procedures, it is the kind of case for which a tribunal may well award reduced compensation.

Employers tend to use the phrase "gross misconduct" very readily. You should not automatically accept this as correct. Nevertheless, certain types of misconduct would obviously fall under this category e.g. theft, sexual harassment, or physical violence. Other examples in the ACAS Code include:

→ Falsification of records.

→ Serious bullying or harassment.

→ Deliberate damage to property.

→ Serious insubordination.

→ Bringing the employers into serious disrepute.

→ Serious infringement of health and safety rules.

→ Serious negligence which causes or may cause loss or damage.

The disciplinary procedure applicable to the member will probably list examples of what the employers consider gross misconduct, although this is unlikely to be an exhaustive list.

Capability issues

Depending on the employers' procedures, a member's failure to perform to the required standard may be dealt with through the normal disciplinary procedure or through a separate capability procedure.

As with disciplinary action, ACAS advises that cases of minor unsatisfactory performance are dealt with informally. If this is unsuccessful, or the matter is too serious to be treated informally, the member should be invited to a meeting to discuss the matter as a first formal step. Following the meeting, a member who is performing unsatisfactorily should be given a written note setting out the performance problem; the improvement that is required; the timescale for achieving this improvement; a review date and any support the employers will provide to assist the member.

Many employers are reluctant to rush to disciplinary action due to poor performance and many prefer several informal counselling meetings.

Continuing poor performance by the member may be due to some underlying domestic or work problems, eg ill-health or being subjected to harassment.

The member should not normally be dismissed for a failure to meet work standards unless s/he has been given warnings and/or an opportunity to improve, with reasonable time-scales and targets. However, employers may be able to dismiss for a single error due to negligence with very serious consequences. Case law suggests this is most likely where there is a danger to the health and safety of others.

Remember that on capability issues, the Disability Discrimination Act may apply if the member is disabled. (See Chapter 10.)

Appeals

The opportunity to appeal against a disciplinary decision is essential to natural justice. The right to appeal is also set out in the new statutory minimum disputes resolution procedures (see p57). The employers' disciplinary procedure probably sets out time-limits for lodging the appeal and then for dealing with it. The Code recommends that appeals are dealt with as promptly as possible.

The appeal should be heard by someone appropriate, ideally a senior manager, who has not been previously involved in the disciplinary procedure. In small organisations it may not be possible to find such an individual, in which case the person dealing with the appeal should act as impartially as possible. Independent arbitration may be a suitable alternative if agreed by everyone concerned.

The member is entitled to be represented at the appeal hearing (p72). If new evidence arises during the appeal, the member or his/her representative should be given the opportunity to comment and it may be necessary to adjourn the appeal to investigate.

The worker should be informed of the result of the appeal and the reasons for the decision as soon as possible and this should be confirmed in writing. It should be clarified whether there are any further stages of appeal.

The member may appeal on a number of grounds, for example:
– It was unfair to believe that the worker had committed the offence or that his/her work was substandard.
– The penalty was too severe.
– Procedural irregularities.
– New evidence has come to light.

The employers' appeal procedure will set out the format of the appeal. The member may not want to appeal, feeling it is pointless. However, that is normally unwise. If the member fails to appeal against dismissal but later brings and wins an unfair dismissal claim, the tribunal will almost certainly reduce his/her compensation.

Legal time-limits

The member must be extremely careful not to miss any time limit for legal action while the appeal is being handled. The three-month time limit for claiming unfair dismissal runs from when the member's job ends, not from the outcome of the appeal. Equally if the member wants to claim that the disciplinary action constituted race, sex or other discrimination, the three-month tribunal time limit is counted from the original disciplinary warning (or termination date), but not from the appeal outcome. If the member wants to bring a tribunal case, s/he may therefore have to lodge his/her tribunal claim before the internal appeal process is completed. The tribunal office then usually decides that the tribunal process can be put on stand-by until the internal appeal is completed. For more details on time limits see p294-300.

Note that in cases where the statutory minimum procedures apply, time-limits may be extended by a further three months in specific circumstances. Unfortunately the rules are rather complicated, but it is essential that you understand them. For further detail, see p294-300.

Grievances

The purpose of a grievance procedure is to give workers a way to raise issues with the management about their working environment or work relationships. Grievances can be individual or collective. An individual grievance could, for example, concern a refusal of leave or a complaint of harassment by a colleague or manager. A collective grievance could concern the criteria for essential car-users' allowances.

An individual member bringing a formal grievance, especially if it is on a controversial subject such as discrimination, does risk upsetting his/her manager. S/he needs to be clear about what s/he is trying to achieve. Sometimes a collective method may be better. For example, the member may feel his/her manager has unfairly refused a leave request. It may be that UNISON could negotiate better arrangements on different types of leave. If different line managers are applying discretionary leave entitlements according to whether they like the worker concerned, the union could take a collective grievance to Human Resources, seeking firmer guidelines on the exercise of discretion.

The ACAS Code of Practice on Disciplinary and Grievance Procedures (see p48 above) sets out guidance to employers on handling grievances. It says employers should deal with grievances fairly, consistently and speedily.

Ideally routine complaints will be resolved informally with the member's line manager. It would be a good idea to keep notes of such a meeting. If the matter cannot be resolved informally, it should be dealt with under the employers' grievance procedure.

ACAS places a lot of emphasis on dealing speedily with grievances. Taken together with the requirements of the statutory grievance procedure (see below), UNISON should use this new opportunity to press employers to change the culture of dragging their heels over grievances.

ACAS says that on receiving a formal grievance, a manager should invite the member to a meeting as soon as possible and inform him/her of the right to be accompanied. Then, having heard the grievance, the employer should respond in writing within a reasonable time. The Code says that what is considered reasonable will vary from organisation to organisation, but five working days is normally long enough.

There should be more than one grievance stage so the member can appeal against an unsatisfactory outcome. In some procedures there is provision for an external mediator.

The member should correctly follow the appropriate procedure. Otherwise management can use it as an excuse for inaction.

Some employers have different grievance procedures for different issues, eg the normal procedure plus different procedures for bullying, discrimination or sexual harassment (see p78).

They may also have a special procedure for whistleblowing under the Public Interest Disclosure Act. (See the UNISON Guide: "Whistleblowing-Speaking out without fear", available on the UNISON website under "Policy Documents".) Even if there is no such procedure, it is crucial that the member handles any whistleblowing complaint correctly. The specialist charity, Public Concern at Work, has a useful website and helpline (see Bibliography).

It is important to note that not everything a member does not like at work can form the basis of a grievance. Grievance procedures need to be used responsibly to maintain UNISON's credibility in the workplace.

Legal time-limits

The subject matter of the grievance, if unresolved, may end up as part of a tribunal claim, eg for discrimination. Different tribunal claims have different time-limits and you need to know the relevant time-limits for the particular case. The most common time-limit is three months from the relevant incident. If the statutory disputes resolution procedures apply and the member starts a grievance promptly, the tribunal time-limit may be extended by a further three months. For further details, see pp294-300.

Note: the member must start his/her tribunal case within the normal (or, if applicable, extended) time-limit, even if the grievance procedure has not been completed.

Statutory dispute resolution

Introduction

In October 2004, the government introduced statutory minimum disciplinary and grievance procedures (known as statutory dispute resolution procedures), which employers and employees need to follow in most situations. The procedures and related rules are set out in the Employment Act 2002 and the Employment Act 2002 (Dispute Resolution) Regulations 2004.

In summary, the employers must follow a minimum dismissal and disciplinary procedure (DDP) when dismissing an employee or taking relevant disciplinary action (see below). Similarly, an employee must lodge a grievance before bringing a tribunal case for discrimination or a number of other matters.

The government was concerned about the number of cases which went to employment tribunals without any prior attempt to discuss and resolve the problem in the workplace. This was particularly so in small non-unionised workplaces. The government hoped that, by forcing employers and employees to discuss matters in disciplinary and grievance meetings, agreements would be reached and tribunal cases would be avoided. Unfortunately, all that has happened in many instances, is that non-unionised employees have been put off bringing tribunal claims altogether by the requirement to take a grievance first. Hopefully, this will be less of a deterrent where UNISON represents members, and it is already common to go through grievance procedures.

The statutory procedures were meant to be simple, but they have turned out to be a nightmare to apply, with many legal uncertainties. At the time of writing, many questions remain unanswered and the interpretation of the law may change.

What are the statutory disputes resolution procedures?

There is a statutory dismissal and disciplinary procedure ("DDP") and a statutory grievance procedure ("GP"). Both have a standard procedure, which must normally be followed, and a shorter modified procedure, which can be followed in limited circumstances. The steps of each procedure are set out in the checklist on p63. These procedures only set out the minimum steps which are required. There may be more detailed disciplinary and grievance procedures under the member's own contract of employment, which should still be followed.

Which workers do the statutory procedures apply to?

The procedures only apply to employees. This is confusing because many workplace rights, eg protection under the Working Time Regulations, apply to workers generally and not only to employees. Discrimination law also applies to non-employees, eg to job applicants and to contract workers.

When does the statutory minimum dismissal and disciplinary procedure apply?

The standard DDP applies when the employer contemplates dismissing or taking relevant disciplinary action against an employee. Relevant disciplinary action excludes warnings or paid suspension, and therefore includes action such as disciplinary demotion or unpaid suspension.

The modified DDP applies when the employer has already dismissed the member for gross misconduct and it was reasonable for the employer to have dismissed the member before speaking to him/her. The DDP applies to actual dismissal, including failure to renew a fixed term contract. It does not apply where the member resigns and claims constructive dismissal, unless that was triggered by relevant disciplinary action.

The DDP does not apply exclusively to dismissals for misconduct. It applies to dismissals for any reason, eg redundancy, capability or ill-health.

If the employers fail to follow the DDP and dismiss the member, the member can claim automatic unfair dismissal. S/he will also get additional compensation. However, s/he can only claim automatic unfair dismissal if s/he is an employee with at least one year's service. If s/he has less than one year's service, the employers can get away with not following the DDP, unless there is some other claim the member can make based on the dismissal, eg that it is discriminatory. So, for example, if a member brings a case under the RRA and proves his/her dismissal was unlawful race discrimination, s/he will get extra compensation if the DDP was not followed.

There are a number of exceptions when the DDP does not apply. These are set out in the checklist on p68. There are a number of other situations, where the employer and member are deemed to have completed the DDP, even though they have only followed some of the steps or not even started it. (See p69.) These are different from the exceptions, because there may be consequences for time-limits or, in some cases, compensation.

When does the statutory minimum grievance procedure apply?

The member must first send a grievance letter in accordance with the statutory GP if s/he wants to bring a tribunal claim for any of the matters listed in Schedule 3 to the Employment Act 2002, eg equal pay, unlawful discrimination, trade union membership and activities, unauthorised deductions from pay, minimum wage, under the Working Time Regulations, redundancy pay, notice pay, and the various detriments under section 48 of the Employment Rights Act 1996 (action short of dismissal due to pregnancy or maternity, for asserting rights to parental leave or dependant leave, under the working time regulations, for whistleblowing, for taking up health and safety issues, etc.)

There is no need to bring a grievance if the member wants to bring a tribunal case about:

— the refusal of his/her right to be accompanied
— less favourable treatment as a part-time worker

- less favourable treatment as a fixed-term worker
- refusal of dependant leave, parental leave, time-off for ante-natal care, or health and safety suspension while pregnant
- breach of the flexible working regulations (although there is a slight ambiguity on this).

The GP does not apply if the member only wants to bring a case about dismissal, since that is when the DDP should apply. However, if the member resigns and claims constructive dismissal, the GP applies and s/he must bring a grievance.

The GP does not apply to "relevant disciplinary action", unless such action was discriminatory or on other hidden grounds. If so, both the DDP and the GP apply and there are special rules.

There is some uncertainty as to whether the member has to bring a grievance under the statutory GP if his/her complaint concerns actions by a colleague rather than a manager, eg sexual harassment by a colleague. This is because the Regulations define a grievance simply as "a complaint by an employee about action which his employer has taken or is contemplating taking in relation to him". This is thought to cover a complaint about action by a colleague for whom the employer would be vicariously liable (eg as under discrimination legislation), but the point is ambiguous and as yet untested.

The modified GP applies if the member has left, where the standard grievance procedure was not previously completed, and where the parties now agree in writing that the modified procedure should apply.

There are a number of exceptions when the GP does not apply. These are set out in the checklist on p69. There are a number of other situations, where the employer and member are deemed to have completed the GP, even though they have only followed some of the steps or not even started it. (See p70.) These are different from the exceptions, because there may be consequences for time-limits or, in some cases, compensation.

It can be confusing to identify whether the DDP or GP applies, or possibly both, especially where the member has several claims. The checklist on p67 gives some common examples.

What goes into the statutory grievance letter?
There is no guidance in the regulations as to how much information needs to be put into a grievance letter. The statutory GP says only that

the employee must "set out the grievance in writing". As already stated, the regulations define a grievance as a complaint by an employee about action which his/her employer has taken or is contemplating taking in relation to him/her. It seems, therefore, that a grievance simply amounts to a written complaint.

Before the grievance meeting, the employee must inform the employer of the basis for the grievance. It is therefore sensible to write a letter which includes the complaint and its basis.

As a rough guide, the grievance should:
— set out the key facts
— contain enough detail for the employers to understand and investigate the complaint
— itemise every matter of concern to the member
— make it clear if discrimination is alleged and what kind. Include any discriminatory remarks.

It is uncertain whether it is enough to describe the factual basis of the complaint or whether it is necessary to identify the applicable legal entitlement.

Sending a questionnaire does not count as a grievance letter.

What are the consequences if the procedures are not followed?
The statutory disputes resolution procedures do not form part of the member's contract of employment. Failure by the member or employer to follow the procedures is therefore only significant if the member wants to bring a tribunal case for unfair dismissal, constructive unfair dismissal, discrimination or the various matters covered by the statutory GP (see above). If so, there are three key consequences:

1   If either the employer or member fails to comply with a requirement of the DDP or GP, non-completion of the procedure will be attributed to him/her and the procedure need not go on to be completed. If the member goes on to win any related tribunal case, the member's compensation will be increased or reduced by 10 – 50% according to who was at fault for the non-completion of the procedure. If it is automatic unfair dismissal, there is also a minimum 4 week basic award.

Note that the requirements of the procedure are essentially those set out in the checklist at pp63-66 below.

2   If the employer is at fault for non-completion of a DDP, the member can claim automatic unfair dismissal (provided s/he is an employee with at least one year's service).

3   A member who has not sent his/her employer a step 1 grievance letter, where the GP applies, will be debarred from bringing a tribunal case altogether (with the exception of breach of contract claims).

What is the effect on time-limits for starting a tribunal case?

Each employment right has its own time-limit. Normal time-limits for starting an unfair dismissal case are set out on p294 and for starting a discrimination case are set out on p295.

Where either the DDP or GP applies, the normal tribunal time-limit can be extended by three months in some circumstances. It is important to read pages p294-300 for more detail. The key points are:

1   The DDP time-limit is extended only where the procedure is still ongoing at the time the normal time-limit expires

2   The GP time-limit is automatically extended as long as the step 1 grievance letter is sent to the employer within the normal time-limit. It is irrelevant whether the GP has finished or not.

3   If the procedures are still not finished after the three month extension, there is no further extension and the member must start his/her tribunal case.

4   These extensions only operate where the DDP or GP applies. If there is any doubt whether the member's case falls within the procedures, stick to the normal time-limits.

5   For this reason, it is crucial to know the difference between situations where the procedures apply but are deemed completed, and where they do not apply at all. (See below.)

Checklist: statutory disputes resolution –
the procedural steps

The Employment Act 2002 sets out the statutory dispute resolution procedures at Schedule 2. The following checklist sets out each of the legal minimum stages. Remember that under your negotiated local procedure, you may have additional rights and requirements.

The statutory Dismissal and Disciplinary Procedure (DDP)

There is a standard DDP and a modified DDP. See p58 for which procedure should apply in a particular case.

The standard procedure

- *Step 1 letter:* The employer sends the member a letter setting out the member's alleged conduct or characteristics or other circumstances which lead him/her to contemplate dismissing or taking disciplinary action, and inviting the member to a meeting.
- Before the meeting, the employer must inform the member of the basis for the grounds in the letter. This suggests the employer must provide the evidence and information on which s/he is relying.
- The member must have a reasonable opportunity (ie sufficient time) to consider his/her response before the meeting.
- The member must take all reasonable steps to attend the meeting.

- *Step 2:* The meeting is held. The timing and location of the meeting must be reasonable.
- The meeting must be conducted in a manner which enables both employer and member to explain their case.
- After the meeting, the employer must notify the member of his/her decision and inform him/her of the right to appeal.

- *Step 3:* If the member wishes to appeal, s/he must inform the employer.
- The employer must then invite him/her to an appeal meeting. The timing and location of the meeting must be reasonable.
- The member must take all reasonable steps to attend the appeal meeting.
- As far as is reasonably practicable, the employer should be represented by a more senior manager than attended the original meeting.

- The meeting must be conducted in a manner which enables both employer and member to explain their case.
- After the appeal meeting, the employer must notify the member of the final decision.
- Each step and action under the procedure must be taken without unreasonable delay. There is no definition of how long is "unreasonable", but UNISON should take the opportunity to urge employers to deal with disciplinary action promptly, and certainly well within tribunal time-limits.
- If either party or the member's rep is unable to attend the disciplinary or appeal meeting for reasons which were not foreseeable at the time the meeting was arranged, the employer must fix a new date. If the employer fixes a new date and again, someone cannot attend for unforeseeable reasons, each party is deemed to have complied with the procedure and nothing further need be done.

Note that under the Employment Relations Act 1999, s10, a worker has a right to be accompanied to a disciplinary hearing by a work colleague or trade union official. However, this is an entitlement under a different piece of legislation with different remedies if the employer fails to allow the companion.

The modified procedure

- *Step 1:* The employer must send the member a letter setting out the member's alleged gross misconduct which has led to the dismissal and the basis for considering the member guilty of gross misconduct.
- *Step 2:* If the member wishes to appeal, s/he must inform the employer.
- The employer must then invite him/her to an appeal meeting. The timing and location of the meeting must be reasonable.
- The member must take all reasonable steps to attend the appeal meeting.
- As far as is reasonably practicable, the employer should be represented by a more senior manager than attended the original meeting.
- The meeting must be conducted in a manner which enables both employer and member to explain their case.
- After the appeal meeting, the employer must notify the member of the final decision.

- Each step and action under the procedure must be taken without unreasonable delay.
- If either party or the member's companion is unable to attend the appeal meeting for reasons which were not foreseeable at the time the meeting was arranged, the employer must fix a new date. If the employer fixes a new date and again, someone cannot attend for unforeseeable reasons, each party is deemed to have complied with the procedure and nothing further need be done.

Note that under the Employment Relations Act 1999, s10, a worker has a right to be accompanied to an appeal against disciplinary action by a work colleague or trade union official. However, this is an entitlement under a different piece of legislation with different remedies if the employer fails to allow the companion.

The statutory Grievance Procedure (GP)

There is a standard GP and a modified GP. See p60 for when each of them applies.

The standard procedure

- *Step 1 letter:* The member sends the employer a written grievance. (See p61 regarding content.)
- The employer must invite the member to a meeting. The timing and location of the meeting must be reasonable.
- Before the meeting, the member must inform the employer of the basis for the grievance. (It is simplest to include these details in the original letter.)
- The employer must have a reasonable opportunity (ie sufficient time) to consider his/her response before the meeting.
- The member must take all reasonable steps to attend the meeting.

- *Step 2:* The meeting is held. The meeting must be conducted in a manner which enables both employer and member to explain their case.
- After the meeting, the employer must notify the member of his/her decision and inform him/her of the right to appeal.

- *Step 3:* If the member wishes to appeal, s/he must inform the employer.

- The employer must then invite him/her to an appeal meeting. The timing and location of the meeting must be reasonable.
- The member must take all reasonable steps to attend the appeal meeting.
- So far as is reasonably practicable, the employer should be represented by a more senior manager at the appeal than at the original meeting.
- The meeting must be conducted in a manner which enables both employer and member to explain their case.
- After the appeal meeting, the employer must notify the member of the final decision.
- Each step and action under the procedure must be taken without unreasonable delay. There is no definition of how long is "unreasonable", but UNISON should take the opportunity to urge employers to deal with grievances promptly, and certainly well within tribunal time-limits.
- If either party or the member's companion is unable to attend the grievance or appeal meeting for reasons which were not foreseeable at the time the meeting was arranged, the employer must fix a new date. If the employer fixes a new date and again, someone cannot attend for unforeseeable reasons, each party is deemed to have complied with the procedure and nothing further need be done.

Note that under the Employment Relations Act 1999, s10, a worker has a right to be accompanied to a grievance hearing by a work colleague or trade union official. However, this is an entitlement under a different piece of legislation with different remedies if the employer fails to allow the companion.

The modified procedure

- *Step 1:* The member must set out in writing the grievance and its basis and send this to the employer.
- *Step 2:* The employer must send the member a written response.
- Checklist: disputes resolution procedures – which one applies
- The following checklist covers the most common situations

Checklist: Disputes resolution procedures which one applies

Claim	Procedure
Unfair dismissal	DDP
Discriminatory dismissal	DDP
Constructive dismissal	GP
Action short of dismissal which is discriminatory	GP. If the action is also relevant disciplinary action (unpaid suspension; demotion etc): also DDP
Discrimination case: dismissal + pre-dismissal detriments	DDP for the dismissal + GP for the other detriments.
Unfair dismissal + holiday pay	DDP for the dismissal + GP for the holiday pay.
Minimum wage claim	GP
Unauthorised deduction from pay	GP
Statutory redundancy pay	GP
Standard DDP	Relevant disciplinary action or dismissal for conduct, capability, redundancy etc
Modified DDP	Member already dismissed without any hearing. Gross misconduct. Reasonable to dispense with a hearing.
Standard GP	Constructive dismissal Discrimination and other claims
Modified GP	Member has left. Employer and member agree in writing to use modified procedure.

Checklist: exceptions to statutory disputes resolution rules

Exceptions, where the DDP does not apply

Remember that, even where the statutory disputes resolution procedures do not apply, an employer risks a finding of unfair dismissal if s/he does not follow fair procedures.

Neither the standard nor the modified DDP apply in the following situations and tribunal time-limits will not be extended on this basis:

- The worker is not an employee.
- **Constructive dismissal:** The member was constructively dismissed (although a DDP would apply to any "relevant disciplinary action" prior to the dismissal).
- **Mass dismissals:**
  - All employees of the member's description or category are dismissed and then re-engaged, eg as may happen in mass dismissals to effect a change in terms and conditions.
  - The member's dismissal was one of a number of dismissals where an employer has a duty under TULCRA s188 to consult, basically collective redundancies.
- Certain types of industrial action dismissal.
- The employer's business suddenly ceases to function because of an unforeseen event.
- The member cannot continue to work without contravention of a statutory duty or restriction, eg health and safety legislation.
- A dismissal procedures agreement applies under ERA s110.
- The modified DDP would apply, but the member lodges a tribunal claim before the employer has sent the step 1 letter.
- **Significant threat:** The member or employer has reasonable grounds to believe that starting the DDP would result in significant threat to any person or property.
- **Harassment:** The employer has been subjected to harassment and has reasonable grounds to believe that starting the procedure would result in him/her being subjected to further harassment.
- **Not practicable:** It is not practicable for the employer to start the procedure within a reasonable period. Presumably this means due to illness, closure of the business or absence, but this is untested.
- **National security.**

Exceptions where the DDP does apply but is deemed to have been followed

As the DDP is deemed to have been followed in the following situations, it is possible that time-limits may be extended (subject to the rules on time-limits).

● **Significant threat:** The DDP has been started, but the member or employer has reasonable grounds to believe that continuing with the DDP would result in significant threat to any person or property.

● **Harassment:** The DDP has been started, but the member or employer has been subjected to harassment and has reasonable grounds to believe that continuing with the procedure would result in him/her being subjected to further harassment.

● **Not practicable:** The DDP has been started, but it is not practicable for the member or employer to comply with a subsequent requirement of the procedure within a reasonable period.

● **Cancelled meetings:** On two occasions, it has not been reasonably practicable for unforeseen reasons for either the member or the employer to attend a meeting after it has been organised.

● **National security.**

● **Interim relief:** Where the member has presented an application for interim relief, having completed the disciplinary stage of the DDP, the appeal stage is deemed completed.

● Where the member appeals under an alternative industry-wide procedure.

Exceptions where the GP does not apply

Although the statutory GP does not apply in the following situations, a member should always be entitled to bring a grievance about a matter of concern. The statutory GP does not apply in these situations, and there is therefore no possibility of any extension of time-limits on this basis:

● The worker is not an employee.

● **Dismissal:** The complaint concerns a dismissal or failure to renew a fixed term contract. (However, a grievance must be brought about constructive dismissal.)

● The complaint concerns "relevant disciplinary action", ie disciplinary action, but not warnings or paid suspension. However, the GP does apply if the member believes the action was on discriminatory or hidden grounds.

- **Outside the rules:** The complaint concerns a matter which is not covered by the disputes resolution rules at all, eg refusal of dependant or parental leave, time-off for ante-natal care, health and safety suspension while pregnant; less favourable treatment of part-time or fixed term workers; breach of flexible working procedures (though there is slight ambiguity on this one).
- **Significant threat:** The member has reasonable grounds to believe that starting the GP would result in significant threat to any person or property.
- **Harassment:** The member has been subjected to harassment and has reasonable grounds to believe that starting the procedure would result in him/her being subjected to further harassment.
- **Not practicable:** It is not practicable for the member to start the procedure within a reasonable period.
- **Not reasonably practicable:** The member has left and since then, it has ceased to be reasonably practicable for the member to send a step 1 grievance letter.
- **National security.**
- **Whistleblowing:** There are special rules concerning whistleblowing where the member's disclosure concerns the treatment of him/herself.

Exceptions where the GP does apply but is deemed to have been followed

In the following situations, as the GP applies and is deemed to have been completed, an extension of tribunal time-limits is possible.

- **Collective grievance:** The member's grievance is part of a collective grievance, ie a trade union or employee representative sets out the grievance in writing on behalf of two or more employees.
- The member is following a grievance under a collectively agreed industry level GP between one or more employers or an employers association and one or more independent trade unions.
- **Significant threat:** The GP has been started, but the member or employer has reasonable grounds to believe that continuing with the GP would result in significant threat to any person or property.
- **Harassment:** The GP has been started, but the member or employer has been subjected to harassment and has reasonable grounds to believe that continuing with the procedure would result in him/her being subjected to further harassment.

- **Not practicable:** The GP has been started, but it is not practicable for the member or employer to comply with a subsequent requirement of the procedure within a reasonable period.
- **Not reasonably practicable:** The member has left, has sent a step 1 grievance letter before or after leaving, and it is not reasonably practicable to have a grievance or appeal meeting. However, where there has been a grievance meeting, the employer must still provide a written response.
- **Cancelled meetings:** On two occasions, it has not been reasonably practicable for unforeseen reasons for either the member or the employer to attend a meeting after it has been organised.
- National security.
- Where a GP applies to "relevant disciplinary action" (because it is on hidden or discriminatory grounds), if a step 1 grievance letter is sent before the appeal stage of the DDP, the parties are treated as if they have complied with the entire procedure.

Notes on the exceptions:

1 Several of the exceptions occur where it is not "practicable" or not "reasonably practicable" to have meetings and take steps. The measure of what is practicable is not defined in the legislation and legally untested. Although it probably envisages situations such as illness, absence overseas and unavailability for other reasons, it is risky to rely on a tribunal accepting a particular reason.

2 You should be particularly careful with the "harassment" exception. This exception does not occur simply because harassment has occurred in the past. It has several precise elements:
- harassment must have occurred in the past
- the member (or employer) has reasonable grounds to believe
- that following the procedure would result in further harassment.
This suggests a concept like victimisation, ie the member will be penalised (harassed) because s/he has brought / followed the procedure. It does not seem to cover a situation where the member will endure further harassment simply by virtue of the fact that s/he is still around in the workplace and has not yet resigned.

For these purposes, harassment is defined as conduct which has the purpose or effect of violating the person's dignity or creating an intimidating, hostile, degrading, humiliating or offensive environment for him/her. It will only have that purpose or effect if, taking into account all the circumstances, particularly the perception of the harassed person, it should reasonably be considered as having that effect.

The right to be accompanied to disciplinary and grievance hearings

The Employment Relations Act 1999 (section 10) gives workers a right to be accompanied at disciplinary and grievance hearings. Part 3 of the ACAS Code on Disciplinary and Grievance Procedures sets out guidelines for this right.

It is possible that the employers' own procedures negotiated with UNISON already give greater rights of representation. However the advantage of the Employment Relations Act is that it establishes some basic principles which must be followed. As explained below, it may also be useful in encouraging non-unionised employers to recognise UNISON.

Who can accompany the worker

Where a worker is invited or required to attend a disciplinary or grievance hearing and reasonably requests to be accompanied at the hearing, the employers must allow the worker to choose a trade union representative or another of the employers' workers to accompany him/her. The employers must allow a worker to take time off during working hours to accompany another of the employers' workers. The ACAS Code says that where a union is recognised in the workplace it is good practice for an official from that union to accompany the worker. However, a UNISON member is entitled to have a UNISON official represent him/her even at a workplace where UNISON is not recognised. This could provide an incentive for workers in non-unionised areas to join UNISON and a way to start the steps toward recognition with particular employers.

Note that there is no duty under the Employment Relations Act on a trade union official or work colleague to accompany the worker. Of course UNISON has its own policies regarding how and when it represents members.

How the right operates

Although the right is triggered by the worker's request, the ACAS Code (and probably your own procedures) does recommend that the employers inform the worker of his/her right to be accompanied. The worker will not have the right to be accompanied to every kind of meeting. Completely informal meetings or counselling sessions where no action is taken at all may not be covered. However, hearings resulting in an oral warning are covered, if the warning is confirmed in writing and can be taken into account for subsequent disciplinary action. Where an investigative meeting can lead ultimately to disciplinary action, then it is part of the disciplinary process and arguably the right does apply. In any event, it is likely that UNISON agreed procedures give rights to accompany or represent at such hearings.

The worker's "companion" may address the hearing, put the worker's case, sum up the case and confer with the worker during the hearing. S/he is not given the right to answer questions on the worker's behalf, although UNISON officials may have this right under the agreed procedures. The ACAS code says it is good practice to allow the companion to participate as fully as possible at the hearing, including asking the witnesses questions.

The ACAS Code encourages employers to agree a mutually convenient date for the hearing. If the chosen person cannot attend the proposed time, the employers must postpone the hearing to any reasonable time suggested by the worker within five days of the original date. UNISON will find it helpful to quote this right to a short postponement if the employers try to insist that the member should choose a different union representative because the most suitable official is unavailable. Obviously the relevant management witnesses would still need to be available.

Legal remedies if employers refuse the right

A worker can complain to an employment tribunal if this right is denied. If a worker is thinking of bringing a tribunal claim, it would be wise to check the precise wording of the right set out in the Employment Relations Act and Code. The tribunal can award compensation up to two weeks' pay (subject to the statutory maximum). You must consult your regional officer/organiser before taking any action.

If the worker is dismissed following the disciplinary action, failure to have allowed him/her to be accompanied is likely to be a key factor in deciding whether the dismissal was unfair. In addition, it is unlawful to dismiss or subject a worker to any detriment just because s/he has tried to exercise this right or has accompanied another worker.

Discrimination

Issues of discrimination can arise in several ways in relation to disciplinary and grievance procedures, for example:

→ The member is subjected to disciplinary action because s/he is black or a woman or for a reason related to disability.

→ The member wishes to lodge a grievance regarding discriminatory treatment or harassment.

→ The way the disciplinary or grievance procedure is conducted is in itself discriminatory

Discriminatory disciplinary action

The member may be subjected to disciplinary action for a number of discriminatory reasons. (See checklist on p181 for evidence relevant to proving race discrimination.) For example:

→ The member's manager is angry with her because s/he has rebuffed his sexual approaches or harassment.

→ The manager has chosen to bring formal disciplinary proceedings against a black worker for being late. However, when a white worker was equally late, the manager merely had an informal word.

→ The member is accused of inaccurate completion of time-sheets. The member is dyslexic and finds it difficult to complete forms accurately.

If the member believes s/he is being subjected to disciplinary action for discriminatory reasons, s/he needs to decide at an early stage whether to say so at the disciplinary. If s/he later brings a tribunal case for discrimination, s/he may lose credibility if s/he did not raise the issue at the disciplinary.

On the other hand, discrimination is a serious issue to raise which is likely to upset the employers. The member risks being victimised as a result of raising the issue and work relations may deteriorate badly. Although victimisation is unlawful, it can be hard to prove. The member needs to consider whether s/he has sufficient objective evidence to prove the discrimination and whether s/he wants to take on this issue. If the member does decide to raise the issue, s/he should do so in writing prior to the disciplinary hearing. Employers often say later that the issue of discrimination was never raised at the disciplinary.

Once the member raises discrimination, the employers should look into it before making a decision on disciplinary action. Sometimes employers insist that the allegation of discrimination is a separate matter. This can be a particular problem where the worker is saying that white workers have committed similar offences, but faced lesser sanctions. Employers will often refuse to look into other cases and say they are only concerned with the member. They may also resist disclosing documentation which relates to others. It is important to put pressure on the employers to look into the full situation. It is a good idea to write to the employers:

→ Stating the nature of the allegation of discrimination.

→ Stating that the employers cannot make a fair judgement on the disciplinary issue unless they look at how comparable instances are normally treated.

→ Listing the required documents.

→ If the allegation of discrimination refers to far more incidents than the particular disciplinary, requesting an adjournment while a grievance is lodged and dealt with. Paragraph 33 of the ACAS Code could be cited.

Some employers' procedures state that once disciplinary action is started, any grievance brought against the manager who started the disciplinary process must await the completion of the disciplinary process. This can be unfair and discriminatory where the issues are connected, eg the member believes the disciplinary action has been brought as a result of racial or sexual harassment. In such a case, it is very important that the issue of discrimination is thoroughly investigated before any disciplinary penalty is issued. If your local procedure is unsatisfactory in this respect, UNISON should renegotiate. In the public sector, the employers can be reminded of their general duty under section 71 of the Race Relations Act to eliminate unlawful race discrimination (see p177 for details) and the equivalent duty under the Disability Discrimination Act. This public duty is to be extended to sex discrimination.

Remember that, where the statutory disputes resolution procedures apply, if the member intends to bring a tribunal claim that the disciplinary action is discriminatory, s/he must first bring an internal grievance to that effect.

Grievances about discrimination

A member who feels s/he has suffered discrimination may wish to take out a grievance. Sadly making allegations of discrimination tends to attract victimisation by employers. The grievance can be rejected, taking several months or even years to go through each stage of the process. Meanwhile the working relationship can be deteriorating badly and the member may wish s/he had never said anything.

Victimisation is a major industrial relations problem. Although the law says that workers must not be punished for raising issues of discrimination, in reality this is all-too-often just what happens. Many Equal Opportunities Policies define direct and indirect discrimination but do not even refer to victimisation. Employers' training also often overlooks this aspect of discrimination. It is in everyone's interests that victimisation does not occur, and both employers and trade unions need to work out imaginative and effective procedures to prevent it.

As explained on p173, victimisation is hard to prove to a tribunal. Nevertheless it is important for workers individually and the union collectively that discrimination issues are raised and addressed. Tribunals disapprove of victimisation and where it is proved, often award high compensation. They also disapprove where grievances are not properly investigated. In one of the leading cases on compensation for injury to feelings, one of the factors leading to the high award was the employers' attitude to the worker's attempts to deal with matters internally:

"There were here factors which entitled the tribunal to make an award
of aggravated damages. In particular, they identified the third
appellants' conduct of the investigation of the complaints of race
discrimination. The tribunal described this as a travesty of what it
should have been. Instead of providing Mr Johnson with a remedy
for the wrongs which he had suffered, they added to his injury by
attributing all his problems to his own defects of personality. We
think this was a true case of aggravation: a case where the appellants'
actions rubbed salt in his wounds."
(1) Armitage (2) Marsden (3) H M Prison Service v Johnson. (1997
IRLR 162, EAT.)

One of the largest ever awards for injury to feelings in a sex discrimination case illustrates the same point. A Southampton employment tribunal awarded £37,300 for injury to feelings to a female paramedic who was subjected to sexual harassment and whose employers totally failed to deal with the problem. Management prevaricated and delayed over the woman's grievance and the first grievance stage had not been completed after nearly two years. The tribunal said:

"Not only did the ambulance management avoid the problem, apparently quite deliberately, but the total failure of the NHS trust to deal with the applicant's grievance at any stage ensured disillusion, stress and depression in the applicant."

Whitehead v Isle of Wight NHS Trust & ors (42 EOR DCLD 1, ET.)

A member who is thinking of raising discrimination needs to consider and discuss with the UNISON representative:

→ The level of objective evidence s/he has to back up her allegation. Be careful to explain that you are not disputing that s/he has suffered discrimination, but you want to find evidence to put pressure on the employers or convince a tribunal.

→ The likely impact on his/her future working life if s/he brings a discrimination grievance.

→ What s/he is likely to achieve from the grievance.

→ What will happen if s/he does not bring a grievance. Is her work situation already intolerable?

→ Would s/he be willing and able to bring a tribunal case for discrimination? If not, s/he is very vulnerable if his/her grievance is rejected. Note the time-limits for claiming discrimination. (See p295.)

→ Remember that if s/he is thinking of bringing a tribunal case, under the new statutory disputes resolution procedures (see page 59), s/he will usually have to have brought a grievance first.

If the member decides to raise the issue of discrimination, s/he should do so unambiguously and in writing from the outset. Otherwise there is a danger that the employers will in reality victimise him/her but deny the member had ever raised the issue of discrimination. Members often complete a grievance form by referring to unfairness or discrimination but are not explicit that they mean it is on grounds of race or sex etc. This can have three disastrous consequences:

→ The employers can decide to treat it as an ordinary grievance and use the general grievance procedure as opposed to the specialist and possibly more favourable discrimination or harassment procedure.

→ The employers may understand it as an allegation of race or sex discrimination but pretend they have not done so. If the member later wants to make a tribunal claim for resultant victimisation, s/he cannot prove the "protected act" (ie the allegation of unlawful race or sex discrimination) ever took place.

→ The statutory disputes resolution procedures may be inadequately complied with, thus barring any future tribunal claim.

Specialist procedures

If the employers do not have specialist procedures for harassment and discrimination, UNISON should negotiate them. Usually the standardised grievance procedure is unsuited to discrimination cases. There are national agreements on equal opportunities in local government and the NHS. Sexual harassment cases also require a unique procedure. The European Code of Practice on Sexual Harassment sets out guidelines for good practice in the handling of sexual harassment complaints and recommends a specialist procedure. You should obtain "Harassment: a UNISON Guide to policy and representation". (See Bibliography, p314.) There are also some interesting features on the content of sexual harassment policies in the Equal Opportunities Review at issues 36 (1991, page 9) and 46 (1992, page 32). See Chapters 9 and 12 for more detail on sex discrimination and harassment generally. All these procedures must fulfil the minimum steps set out in the new statutory grievance procedures including a right of appeal (see p65).

Discriminatory handling of grievance procedures

Employers may be guilty of further discrimination or victimisation in the way they deal with a member's grievance related to discrimination, for example by failing to investigate properly or taking an exceptionally long time to deal with the matter.

In one UNISON case, Birmingham City Council were found guilty of direct discrimination and victimisation in the way they dealt with the grievance of Mr Tang, a Chinese junior manager. It was not just a matter of an unfair or ineffective handling of Mr Tang's grievance: the grievance was handled differently from normal. Mr Tang could compare the way his grievance was handled with the way a grievance of a non-Chinese staff member was handled.

Tang v Birmingham City Council   ET 46192/1996

In July 1995, Mr Tang wrote to the Director of Social Services (Mr Evans) raising concerns about the treatment of Chinese staff in the Council, including himself. On being told that he must go through the proper procedure, he lodged a formal grievance on 21st September 1995.

After initially not responding at all to Mr Tang's letters, Mr Evans eventually commissioned a grievance investigation, but failed to use the appropriate Racial Harassment procedure. By using the wrong procedure, he was able to appoint departmental personnel officers who were of insufficient seniority and independence to investigate. Mr Evans never met Mr Tang about his grievance and the investigation did not even start until 15th March 1996. Mr Tang's legitimate grievance was eventually rejected. Under the procedure used, he had no right of appeal.

The dismissive handling of Mr Tang's grievance about race discrimination contrasted with Mr Evans' handling of a complaint made about Mr Tang by a junior member of his own staff (Ms Eschow) at around the same time. That investigation began almost immediately and Mr Evans met Ms Eschow personally. Her complaint was upheld.

In this and other matters, the tribunal found that successive managers of ever increasing seniority had behaved in a quite appalling manner towards Mr Tang on grounds of his race. The tribunal said that Mr Evans' approach to the investigation of Mr Tang's complaint was dictated by the fact that the complaint was one of race discrimination – there was a conscious or subconscious desire on the part of managers in the Social Services Department to silence his complaints. This amounted to unlawful victimisation.

Also, Mr Tang was treated as a difficult member of the Department, an attitude that was founded on his race. This was direct discrimination.

In addition, it is sometimes necessary with a disabled member to make reasonable adjustments to the disciplinary process, eg by allowing an interpreter or signer or, for someone with learning disabilities, adopting a particularly informal and unthreatening manner and process (see ACAS Code paragraph 105).

Practical tips on handling disciplinaries and grievances

The ACAS Code says that accompanying a member at a disciplinary or grievance hearing is a serious responsibility and it is important that trade union officials are trained in the role. Details of training courses can be obtained from UNISON Learning and Organising Services. UNISON has also produced a training video on handling disciplinary hearings. Training courses based on this video are delivered in most regions.

It is important to prepare fully for any hearing, to anticipate what management is likely to say and to look into all relevant details of the member's case.

Relatively informal fact-finding or investigation meetings are a common part of the pre-disciplinary procedures of many UNISON employers, especially local authorities and health trusts. What the member says at these meetings often affects the ultimate outcome of the disciplinary hearing – and indeed whether the matter proceeds to the disciplinary stages at all. Often management does not have enough evidence to proceed to a disciplinary hearing, but the member unwittingly gives too much away during an apparently informal discussion. The member is particularly vulnerable because at this stage s/he is often only vaguely aware of the nature of the allegations and weight of evidence against him/her.

Most procedures in areas where UNISON organises give the member a right of accompaniment or representation at the fact-finding or investigatory interviews. Some managers try to circumvent this by calling members into very short meetings at little notice. Even where the member is formally told of his/her right to have union representation, often s/he has not been given enough time to contact the union and find an available official. If you find management repeatedly misuses the procedures in this way, UNISON could consider informing Human Resources that a collective grievance will be taken unless members are given proper advance notice.

Once you have been contacted in advance of an investigatory interview, depending on agreed procedures, you should normally:

→ Find out as much as possible about the allegations and supporting evidence in advance of the meeting.

→ Fully interview the member prior to the meeting.

→ Advise the member that s/he should say nothing at the outset of the meeting and wait for management to give more details of the allegations. Remind the member that s/he will be stuck with what s/he says in this meeting and it can be held against him/her later in any disciplinary.

→ Listen carefully to what management say at the start of the meeting. This is often a clue to you as to how much evidence they already have and whether this matter is likely to progress to a disciplinary.

→ Once management has set out the allegations in more detail, call for a brief adjournment so that you can privately discuss with the member his/her response before returning to the meeting. The danger of allowing the member to respond immediately before you have had a private discussion is that his/her instinct will often be to deny everything. This often causes more problems.

→ If management bring up additional allegations of which the member had no forewarning at all, you should insist on a postponement of the meeting for a few days.

Do not rigidly apply the above principles and use common sense. The member should not risk appearing evasive where there is a quick simple explanation which can immediately put an end to the matter.

After the fact-finding or investigatory meeting, management may decide that the matter should go on to a disciplinary process. The member is entitled to be fully informed of the allegations and evidence against him/her in advance of the hearing so that s/he can prepare his/her case. With small employers, eg voluntary sector organisations, this might be done in a fairly informal way and there will not necessarily be any obligation for the member to set out his/her own response in advance of the hearing. In local authority and NHS trust employers, there is usually a written time-scale under the disciplinary procedure for the exchange of evidence by each side. Fairly often the steps are these:

→ The employers set out fully in writing the allegations against the member. The relevant parts of any policies and procedures which have allegedly been broken by the member are identified.

→ The employers give the member or UNISON representative a statement of their case including witness statement and documents relied on.

→ Within a specified number of days before the hearing – or after receipt of the employers' papers, the member must supply his/her own statement of case, list of witnesses and witness statements. The member should also request any documents which s/he thinks are relevant from management.

Some employers deliberately supply their case papers very late in the day so that the union has inadequate time to prepare. This is likely to be contrary to the statutory disputes resolution procedures. You should not allow it to happen and if necessary, UNISON should negotiate stricter time-scales in the procedure with safeguards if employers ignore them.

In preparing the member's case, make sure you do the following:

1 Carefully read management's case papers and discuss the details fully with the member. Make your own list of points in the member's favour. Then imagine what the employers' will say and list weaknesses in the member's case. Consider how you will try to overcome those weaknesses.

2 Do not automatically assume that the member's explanation will be adequate. Imagine you are management and look for gaps in what the member says. Be careful to do this very sympathetically. You are on the member's side. Explain that you do not want to be caught by surprise or fail to anticipate what the employers' will say. Do not role-play "devil's advocate". This can upset or alienate the member. You can explore problem areas through discussion.

3 Make sure the member's witness statement is precise and accurate. Remember the member will be held to its content and will also be cross-examined on any vague or sweeping comments. If the member intends to raise the issue of race, religion, sex, sexual orientation or disability discrimination, say so explicitly in the statement.

4 Discuss with the member what documents may be in management's possession which you need to ask for to help defend the member. Make sure you ask for these documents in writing in good time for the hearing. Ask for anything you think is relevant and helpful. Do not just assume that you are not entitled to or will be unable to get certain documents. The test is whether they are strictly relevant. If necessary, names of other workers or members of the public can be blanked out.

5 Discuss which witnesses the member needs. You should be very focused when considering witnesses. They can do as much harm as good. Consider (a) precisely what they can say to help the member, and (b) whether there are any awkward questions which management may ask them which will harm the member.

6 Once you have decided upon a good witness who is willing to help, make sure his/her witness statement is precise, accurate, factual, relevant and helpful. If the member later takes a tribunal case, the witness statements used at the disciplinary will be part of the evidence even if those witnesses refuse to come to the tribunal. This can be very useful. Therefore start each statement by explaining who the witness is.

7 Prepare your cross-examination of the management witnesses. Look for any inconsistencies or false assumptions in their statements. Identify any areas where mismanagement led to the disciplinary problem, eg unclear or inconsistent procedures, failure to pick up errors at early stages, failure to train etc.

With large employers, the procedure to be adopted at the disciplinary hearing will be set out in the written procedure. The main legal principle is that the member has access to all the evidence against him/her and an opportunity fully to answer and state his/her case. Not all procedures allow for cross-examination of witnesses, but at the very least, the member must have been shown and allowed to comment on the witness statements against him/her.

Both the member and UNISON officials should try to be calm and polite during the hearing. You should make points firmly but not angrily. Do not allow the employers to spring allegations or evidence unexpectedly on the member. You should be permitted reasonable time to confer privately with the member outside the hearing room.

It is extremely useful if two UNISON officials can attend the disciplinary hearing, although in practice this may not be feasible. While the representative speaks and cross-examines, the second official can look after the member and take notes. It is important to ensure that an accurate note is taken of the hearing. If you are relying on management's minutes, pause when any very crucial point emerges and ask if it has been noted. If you obtain very important concessions from management witnesses, make sure you note them verbatim. These may be used in any subsequent employment tribunal hearing.

The data protection act

The member may want to see his/her personnel file before any disciplinary or grievance hearing. The Data Protection Act 1998 ("DPA") gives workers access to personal data held on them and safeguards against misuse of the data by their employers. There is Guidance and parts 1 - 4 of the Employment Practices Data Code of Practice on the Information Commissioner's website at www.dataprotection.gov.uk. The Code covers:

Part 1: recruitment and selection
Part 2: employment records
Part 3: monitoring at work
Part 4: health records

The data covered by the DPA includes electronic and computerised information plus manual personnel files, provided these are ordered in a very structured way. Members have the right to see their file (or other data) if they make a written request and pay a fee up to £10. They must be shown the information within 40 days of their request and if possible, be given a hard copy to keep. They can take someone with them to inspect the data. Remember that under their own contract, members may have a right to see their own file anyway, without following these formalities. Members employed by public authorities can also ask to see unstructured personal data held about them, but this does not extend to personnel information.

There are certain exceptions to the right of access. In particular, where data reveals information about any other individual, the employers can hide the identity of that individual or if necessary, withhold the data altogether (unless the other individual consents to disclosure or it would be reasonable for him/her to consent.) This includes situations where the other individual is the source of the information, eg the author of an appraisal or reference.

Workers are not entitled to see job references given by their own employers to others. They may see references given to their current or prospective employers. Although this is subject to the rules about identifying other individuals, the Data Code of Practice encourages employers to reveal as much information as possible in these circumstances.

The DPA allows disclosure of data about other individuals in connection with actual or prospective legal proceedings. Therefore in running a discrimination case, for example, it is still possible to request comparative information regarding other workers in the vital questionnaire procedure. (See Chapter 14.)

If the member finds inaccurate information on his/her file, s/he can ask for it to be changed or a corrective statement added. If the employers refuse and there is potential harm as a result, s/he can seek the intervention of the Information Commissioner. If there is actual harm, s/he can also go to Court.

The freedom of information act

The Freedom of Information Act 2000 and the Freedom of Information (Scotland) Act 2002 came into effect on 1st January 2005. The Freedom of Information Act applies to public authorities in England, Wales and Northern Ireland, UK government departments, parliament and the Welsh and Northern Ireland assemblies. For UNISON's Bargaining Support Guide, see www.unison.org.uk/acrobat/B1803 or download from the website under Resources/Bargaining.

The Freedom of Information (Scotland) Act applies to Scottish public authorities, the Scottish Executive and Scottish parliament. It is similar to the Freedom of Information Act ("FIA") 2000, but gives slightly better rights. There is a briefing on the Scottish Act at www.unison-scotland.org.uk/briefings/foibrief.

Schedule 1 of the FIA lists the public authorities to which it applies and this list is updated every October. Some authorities are listed by category and others are precisely described. The list includes central and local government, the health sector, the education sector and the police. There is useful guidance, including a full list of authorities covered, on the website of the Department for Constitutional Affairs at www.foi.gov.uk. There is also a detailed guidance booklet which can be downloaded from the website of the Campaign for Freedom of Information at www.cfoi.org.uk.

All public authorities must produce a publication scheme, which sets out what kinds of information the public authority will proactively make available, how it can be accessed and the cost. Very often these schemes are published on the authorities' websites. The scheme must be approved by the Information Commissioner.

A member of the public can request any information held by the public authority, whether or not it appears on the published scheme. "Information" is wider than "data" covered by the Data Protection Act 1998. It covers information which is recorded in any form, including paper records, handwritten notes, computer information, information on audio cassettes and videos. Information which is in the knowledge of the authority but unrecorded is not covered.

A request should be in writing, state clearly what information is required, and state the name of the applicant and an address for correspondence. The request can be sent to the authority's Freedom of Information officer, if it has one, or otherwise to the chief executive. The authority must respond as soon as possible and no later than 20 working days after receiving the request. The response must either provide the information or explain why it has not been provided, quoting an exemption under the FIA.

There are two categories of exempt information: information which is absolutely exempt and information which is exempt if the authority can prove the public interest in keeping it exempt is greater than the public interest in its disclosure. Absolute exemptions include information contained only in court documents, personal data about the applicant (because there is a right of access under the Data Protection Act) or about another individual, if disclosure would breach the Data Protection Act, and information whose disclosure would be a breach of confidence at common law. Public interest exemptions include information covered by legal professional privilege and information whose disclosure is likely to prejudice commercial interests. It is advisable to look at the full list of exemptions before making a request.

The authority may charge a fee, but it cannot charge (except for photocopying and post) for requests costing less than £450 to answer (£600 for requests to central government) at the rate of £25/hour. If it costs more than these figures to search out the information, the authority can either charge or refuse to supply the information altogether.

If a request is refused, there is a right to apply for an internal review of the decision. If the review also fails, the Information Commissioner can be asked to review the decision.

A worker who is employed by a public authority may be able to use the FIA to get relevant information, which s/he cannot get in any other way. The FIA does not place restrictions on how the information supplied under it may be used, although certain types of confidential information may be exempt from disclosure. However, if the information sought by the worker concerns him/herself, s/he must apply under the Data Protection Act, which involves a different procedure (see above).

Disciplinary and grievance hearings: myths

● *Myth:*
If a member is dismissed for gross misconduct, the employers need not follow fair disciplinary and dismissal procedures.
Truth:
If the member is guilty of gross misconduct, the employers are entitled to dismiss for a first offence. However, under unfair dismissal law, they should still hold a fair disciplinary hearing prior to dismissal.

● *Myth:*
A worker cannot be fairly dismissed for ordinary misconduct unless s/he has previously received one verbal and two written warnings.
Truth:
It depends on the employers' disciplinary procedure, but usually if an offence is serious, employers can skip some of the warning stages. See p51.

● *Myth:*
If the UNISON rep is very nice to the employers at the disciplinary, this will prevent the member getting dismissed.
● *Myth:*
If the UNISON rep is aggressive towards the employers at the disciplinary, this will prevent the member getting dismissed.
Truth:
The UNISON rep should always be calm and polite. Being aggressive will antagonise the employers and be counter-productive. On the other hand, being friendly will not in itself put any pressure on the employers not to discipline the member. The important thing is to put strong arguments and evidence to the employers, so that they find it hard to justify disciplinary action.

Disciplinary and grievance hearings chapter: key points

- There are statutory minimum disputes resolution procedures setting out minimum steps for disciplinary and grievance procedures. A member may be unable to take a tribunal case for discrimination or other workplace matters, if s/he has not brought a grievance first.

- You should also be familiar with the procedures set out in the policies agreed between management and UNISON, which may provide additional rights.

- Ensure the procedures are not abused or side-stepped by the employers.

- The ACAS Code of Practice on Disciplinary and Grievance Procedures sets out basic principles of fair practice and natural justice which should form part of the procedures.

- In particular, disciplinary procedures should be seen as a way of helping and encouraging workers rather than imposing sanctions.

- There should not normally be dismissal for a first offence.

- Even on allegations of gross misconduct, fair investigative and disciplinary procedures should be followed.

- Grievances can be individual or collective. Members need to decide what they are trying to achieve.

- Workers have a legal right in relation to their employers to be accompanied to disciplinary and grievance hearings. This includes the right of members to be accompanied by a union official, even where the union is unrecognised.

- Discrimination may be relevant to disciplinary action or the subject of grievances.

- Be very careful not to miss legal time-limits while taking out grievances or appeals. The new statutory disputes resolution law will extend time-limits in some circumstances. Make sure you know the precise rules.

- Representation on disciplinary or grievance hearings is a serious matter. Allow time to prepare fully and in detail. Try to anticipate what management will say and deal with it.

- Members can get access to information held on them under the Data Protection Act.

- Members can get information held by public authorities under the Freedom of Information Act.

Chapter 4:

Dismissal overview

Contents

Rights on dismissal

Members may come to you when they have been dismissed. At first they may just enquire about a reference or notice pay as they may not realise they have other legal rights. However, dismissed members may have a variety of legal rights depending on their eligibility to make claims and the evidence they may have. The following checklist should help you identify the next steps and any legal claim the member may have.

■ Ask the member for the facts surrounding the dismissal, including dates and the current position.

■ Obtain all relevant documents in the member's possession, for example all dismissal and warnings letters; all other documents relating to the dismissal; minutes of disciplinary hearings and witness statements used; the disciplinary and grievance procedures; the member's contract of employment; pay-slips etc.

■ Check whether the correct disciplinary procedures have been followed. These will normally be set out in the disciplinary or grievance procedures or the member's contract.

■ Also check whether the compulsory statutory dismissal procedure applies, and if so, whether it has been followed. (See Chapter 3.)

■ Check whether the member has lodged an internal appeal. If not, ensure this is done within the correct time-scale (usually set out in the procedures).

■ Check the employers' reasons for the dismissal. Usually these are set out in the dismissal letter. If the employers announced the member's dismissal at the end of the disciplinary hearing, the minutes may also record any reasons given.

■ Ask the member's response to these reasons. Does the member think they are fair? Has the member received warning letters in the past?

■ Does the member think the employers had a hidden agenda? Could the true reason be a form of unlawful discrimination, eg dismissal due to race, religion or belief, sex, sexual orientation, pregnancy or disability. Does the member believe the employers wanted to dismiss him/her for a particular reason which would amount to one of the automatically unfair dismissals, eg for trade union activities or for insisting on breaks under the Working Time Regulations? (See p101 for a fuller list of automatic unfair dismissals).

■ Of course even if the member believes this is the case, s/he will still have to prove the connection. However, it is important to find out early if the member thinks this is an issue, so that you can fully look into it.

■ Check whether the member can bring an employment tribunal claim for unfair dismissal. (For more detail see pages 95.)The relevant considerations are:

– Is the member eligible to claim? (See p96.)

– What are the member's chances of success?

– How much compensation may the member get?

– What is the deadline for starting a tribunal claim? (See p294.)

– Have you told the member what the deadline is? Is it in writing?

– Ensure that the regional officer/organiser knows about it in enough time to assess the case and if necessary ensure that the claim is lodged in time.

■ Check whether the member can bring an employment tribunal claim for race, sex or disability discrimination, or for discrimination on grounds of religion, belief or sexual orientation. (For more detail see Chapters 8 - 11.) Consider:

– Is the member covered by the legislation and is s/he eligible to claim?

– Would the employers have dismissed the member if s/he had been of a different race, religion, belief, sex or sexual orientation? If not, this is direct discrimination.

– Has the member been dismissed because s/he has raised issues of race, religion or belief, sex, sexual orientation, or disability discrimination? This may be victimisation.

– Has the member been dismissed or selected for redundancy for an indirectly discriminatory reason, eg inability to work flexi-shifts due to childcare?

– Has the member been dismissed or selected for redundancy for a reason related to his/her disability?

– What are the member's chances of success?

– How much compensation may the member get?

– What is the deadline for starting a tribunal claim? (See p295.)

– Have you told the member what the deadline is? Is it in writing?

– Who is going to ensure that the claim is lodged in time?

– Have you told the member about the questionnaire procedure and time-limits? (See pages 300.)

– Who is going to write the questionnaire and ensure it is sent to the employers within the time-limits?

■ Has the member received the correct notice or pay in lieu? (See p92.)

– Check the member's statutory minimum notice entitlement.

– Check whether the contract requires the member to be given longer notice.

– Have the employers denied notice is due on the ground that the member was dismissed for gross misconduct? Are the employers correct that it was gross misconduct?

– Have you told the member about the time-limits for claiming notice pay?

■ Is the member entitled to pay for holidays not taken?

■ Has the member received pay to the termination date plus any outstanding pay or overtime, plus his/her P45?

■ If the member was made redundant, has s/he received the correct redundancy pay? (See pages 125.)

■ Can anything be done immediately to secure a good open reference?

■ Overall, what does the member want to do? Is s/he interested in legal possibilities?

■ Check the date of dismissal. Is it clear or ambiguous? (See p294.)This is relevant to time-limits for internal appeals and for tribunal claims.

■ Make sure you and the member are clear about time-limits and have agreed further action. You should especially ensure that the regional officer/organiser is keyed in to assist with decision-making at an early stage.
■ Ensure you are complying with UNISON policy before advising on any tribunal cases.
■ Further action. (See checklist on p301.)

Wrongful dismissal

Wrongful dismissal and unfair dismissal are two completely different things. Unfair dismissal is a right given by parliament not to be unfairly dismissed. Wrongful dismissal is a right under the contract of employment. It has nothing to do with fairness. It simply means that a worker has been dismissed in a way that the contract does not allow. Almost always it means the worker has been dismissed without the correct contractual notice. In more unusual cases, it means the worker has been dismissed in some other way which the contract says is not allowed, for example, without following a mandatory disciplinary procedure. This is rare though.

Notice

The member's contract will normally set out how much notice s/he is entitled to. If a member is not allowed or required to work notice, s/he should be paid in lieu. The member's notice must not be less than the minimum set by law in section 86 of the Employment Rights Act, ie
■ One week's notice if s/he has been continuously employed for one month or more but less than two years.
■ One week's notice for each whole year of continuous employment of two years or more, but less than twelve years. For example, a worker employed for five years eleven months, would be entitled to at least five weeks' notice of dismissal.
■ Twelve weeks' notice for continuous service of twelve years or more. For example, a worker employed for sixteen years would be entitled to at least twelve weeks' notice.
If the member is dismissed for gross misconduct, s/he is not entitled to any notice. Employers often use the words "gross misconduct". This does not mean that they are correct. Gross misconduct is usually offences like fighting or theft. (See p52.)

If the member is not paid his/her notice entitlement, s/he can bring a claim in the county court or, preferably, in an employment tribunal. The tribunal time-limits are the same as for unfair dismissal. (See p294.) S/he should bring a grievance first (see p57 on the statutory disputes resolution procedures).

Resigning

A member who resigns must give the length of notice set out in the contract of employment. Under section 86 of the Employment Rights Act, s/he must give at least one week's notice if employed for at least 1 month, and more if the contract requires. If s/he is resigning due to the employers' fundamental breach of contract (see p118), s/he need not give any notice.

Dismissal: myths

● *Myth:*
Employers can't just dismiss someone for no good reason.
  Truth:
It is almost impossible to stop employers dismissing a worker if they want to. The only question is whether the worker has any legal rights.
If the member is not eligible to claim unfair dismissal (particularly if s/he does not have 1 year's service), the employers can dismiss him/her for any reason, however unfair. However, you do need to check there is no unlawful reason for the dismissal which does not need 1 year's service, eg discrimination or automatic unfair dismissal.

● *Myth:*
Casual workers have no employment rights and cannot do anything when they are dismissed.
  Truth:
The word "casual" is not a legal term. If in fact the worker meets the eligibility requirements for any legal right, including unfair dismissal, s/he will be able to claim. See p96 for unfair dismissal and p161 for race discrimination.

Chapter 5:

Unfair dismissal

Contents

Policy

This Chapter sets out the law on unfair dismissal, explaining which members can bring a claim and what factors make a dismissal unfair. You must consult with your regional officer/organiser about the possibility of commencing an unfair dismissal claim.

Unfair dismissal law

Who can claim

Not all workers can claim unfair dismissal. They must meet the strict eligibility requirements set out in the legislation. In summary:

- The member must have been an employee.
- S/he must have been employed for one year with the relevant employers. (Although there is no minimum service requirement for most of the automatically unfair dismissals set out below.)
- S/he must be below the normal retirement age for similar workers with the same employers, or below 65 if there is no normal retirement age. A retirement age which discriminates between men and women will not apply. Note that the 65 year ceiling was unsuccessfully challenged as discriminatory against men. (See *Secretary of State for Trade and Industry v Rutherford & ors* [2004] IRLR 892; 135 EOR 25, CA, although the case is to be appealed to the House of Lords). There may be some modification to this requirement once age discrimination law is introduced (by December 2006).
- S/he must have been dismissed by the employers.

Is the member an employee?

A self-employed worker is not entitled to claim unfair dismissal. Unfortunately it is often unclear whether a worker is in reality an employee or self-employed. Employers often try to avoid employment responsibilities by calling workers self-employed and even making them pay their own tax, when in all other ways they are treated and behave as employees.

There is no clear legal test to decide whether a worker is an employee or self-employed. The label and tax position are relevant but they are not decisive. The courts also take into account the degree of control by the employers, the benefits offered and, most importantly, whether there is an obligation on each side respectively to offer and accept work.

Length of service

For ordinary unfair dismissal, the member must have been continuously employed for at least one year with the employers as at the termination date. Workers employed on a succession of fixed term contracts with the same employers can add the contracts together. It does not matter if during the year, the member has been on paid or unpaid leave, for example due to sickness or holidays, or if s/he was absent on ordinary or additional maternity leave or parental leave. However, if the member leaves the job for a while and is taken on again later, this usually breaks his/her continuous service and s/he must start counting the year again.

If the member's service appears to be broken, it is important to get specialist advice on the position. There are special rules which may nevertheless preserve the member's continuous service as if s/he had continued to be employed throughout the gap. For example:

– **Temporary cessation of work:** The member's break in employment was due to a temporary cessation of work. This is where the employers dismiss the member or the member leaves because there is no work available, but the member is taken back when work resumes. The break in employment must be short relative to the periods when the member is employed.

This rule would probably cover a member working in a school, who is dismissed at the end of each Summer term and taken on again at the start of each Autumn term. Under this rule, the member's service would be counted as if s/he had continued to be employed through the Summer holidays.

– **Custom or arrangement:** Although the member was dismissed and later re-engaged, s/he was regarded as continuing in employment by custom or arrangement. For example, a teacher who is only employed during school terms, but on the understanding that s/he will continue to be employed at the start of the next term.

– **Reinstatement:** Where the member was dismissed but has been reinstated following a tribunal case, ACAS conciliation, compromise agreement or under the statutory disputes resolution procedures.

– **Strikes:** Where the member has participated in a strike, continuous service is not broken, but unlike in the other situations listed above, the days of absence are deducted from the start of the total length of continuous service.

There are also some other grounds which do not break the member's service. All these rules can be difficult to apply in practice.

Has the member been dismissed?

To claim unfair dismissal, the member must have been dismissed. The law considers that the following situations amount to dismissal:

1 **Termination by the employers:** The employers terminate the contract of employment, with or without notice. There is no dismissal until a termination date is specified – or can be calculated.

2 **Expiry and non-renewal of a fixed-term contract:** The member is employed on a fixed term contract which runs out. If the employers fail to renew the contract, they are taken to have dismissed the member.

3 **Forced resignation:** The member is forced to resign. This is where the employers have said that if the member does not resign, s/he will be dismissed. Usually this is said verbally and can be hard to prove.

A forced resignation is not where the member feels s/he has to resign because s/he is being treated so badly by the employers.

4 **Constructive dismissal:** The member resigns due to the employers' fundamental breach of contract, for example a significant pay-cut or a breach of the implied term of trust and confidence.

It is not possible for members to dismiss themselves, whatever the employers say. For example, employers sometimes tell members that if they arrive back late from holiday, they will be taken to have dismissed themselves. It is important that a member arriving back late immediately goes to work. If the employers refuse to take the worker back, they have dismissed him/her.

In all the above situations, a member who wishes to claim unfair dismissal must still meet the other eligibility criteria for bringing a claim and must still prove the dismissal is unfair.

If the member voluntarily resigns (except in constructive dismissal situations) or agrees to leave, s/he cannot claim unfair dismissal. The member needs to be very careful. Some situations are ambiguous and can lead to legal difficulties later. For example:

– A member who volunteers for redundancy may be taken to have agreed to leave rather than to have been dismissed. The case-law is divided on this and it will very much depend on the surrounding facts.

– A member who agrees to early retirement may well be taken to have agreed to leave.

– A member who negotiates a compensation package during the same conversation in which s/he is informed of his/her dismissal, may appear to have agreed to leave in return for a payment.

Temps, casuals and contract workers

Members have many different working arrangements and they work under a variety of labels, many of which have no technical legal meaning. Workers on fixed term contracts and other so-called casual workers may surprisingly have unfair dismissal rights if they meet the above eligibility criteria. In particular, consider:

1 Despite the label and tax arrangements, is the member an employee?

2 Has s/he at least one year's unbroken service leading up to the termination date? Shorter contracts can be added together provided there is no break between them or no break which counts, bearing in mind the special rules mentioned above.

3 Has the member been dismissed? This includes failure to give him/her a new contract when the existing contract runs out.

There is no reason why a member employed on a series of short contracts should not prove unfair dismissal if the employers suddenly refuse to give a new contract. The following case is a good example:

University of Glasgow v Donaldson and another

(1995) 522 IRLB 522, EAT

Ms Donaldson was employed by the University of Glasgow under a one-year fixed term contract to work on an externally funded project. Her contract was renewed annually for the five year duration of the project. When the project was completed, her contract was not renewed

The EAT considered her dismissal unfair, particularly because there had been virtually no consultation with the University regarding the possibility of alternative employment. Reasonable efforts should have been made to consult and offer any suitable vacancy.

Sometimes where there are mass redundancy or transfer situations, the rights of contract workers can be overlooked. As well as unfair dismissal rights, they may also have discrimination claims if applicable.

What makes a dismissal unfair?

Unfair dismissal law is set out in section 98 of the Employment Rights Act. Members who have been unfairly dismissed bring their cases in employment tribunals. The employers usually start and they must prove to the tribunal the reason why they dismissed the worker.

After hearing all the evidence, the tribunal must decide whether the dismissal was fair or unfair.

The employers' reason for dismissal must fall into one of these categories:

— Conduct.
— Capability or qualification.
— Redundancy.
— Statutory restriction.
— Some other substantial reason.

There are two key ways that a dismissal can be unfair:

1 It was not fair for the employers to have dismissed the worker for that reason.

2 Poor procedures were followed in dismissing the worker

Procedural unfairness and statutory procedures

Under the Employment Act 2002 (Dispute Resolution) Regulations 2004, employers must follow minimum procedural steps when dismissing an employee. These are set out in a statutory dismissal and disciplinary procedure (DDP). It is likely that the member's own contractual disciplinary procedure covers the minimum steps and adds further requirements. Nevertheless, you want to be sure that this is the case, since failure by the employers or the member to follow any of the requirements of the statutory procedure is very significant.

If the member is an employee with at least one year's service, s/he can claim unfair dismissal when s/he is dismissed. If the employers failed to follow the minimum procedural steps, the dismissal will be automatically unfair. On the other hand, if the member refuses to cooperate with the procedure, s/he will have his/her compensation reduced. Full details of the minimum procedure and when it applies is set out on pages 57-72.

The employers may follow the minimum statutory steps but fail to comply with some further requirements set out in the member's own disciplinary procedure or with key requirements of the ACAS Code. This will not be enough in itself to make the dismissal unfair, unless the tribunal thinks the employers would not have dismissed the worker had they gone through those extra steps. If the tribunal thinks there was, say, a 50% chance that the employers would have reached the same decision had they followed these other fair procedures, the member will win but his/her compensation will be reduced by the same percentage (50%).

Other general factors

The tribunal must take account of the size and administrative resources of the employers. For example, the tribunal would expect more formal procedures from a local authority than from a small voluntary sector organisation.

The employers should treat workers consistently. For example, it would be inequitable to dismiss one worker for an offence when they did not dismiss another worker who committed a similar offence on another occasion. However, there may be good reasons for the apparent difference in treatment, for example, that one worker has a better disciplinary record than the other or there were mitigating circumstances.

A tribunal must apply the band of reasonable responses test. This means that to win a case, a worker must show that no reasonable employer would have dismissed in those circumstances. If a tribunal thinks it would have been reasonable for the employers either to dismiss the member or not to dismiss the member, then the dismissal will be fair.

Automatic unfair dismissal

As explained above, it is automatic unfair dismissal for employers to dismiss a member without going through the steps of the statutory DDP. To make this claim, the member needs one year's service.

There are also certain reasons for dismissal which are automatically unfair. For these, one year's service is often unnecessary. Often it is hard to prove these reasons as employers hide their true motives. The difficulties in proving the employers' true motivation is similar to the difficulties of proof encountered in discrimination cases.

Except where indicated below, a worker does not require any minimum service in order to claim automatic unfair dismissal.

New laws are often extending the list of automatically unfair dismissals. The general pattern is that as new rights at work are introduced, they are protected by making it automatically unfair to dismiss someone for claiming those rights.

The most common types of automatically unfair dismissal are:

■ Failure to follow the DDP where it applies. One year's minimum service is required for this claim.

■ Due to pregnancy or maternity or a related reason.

■ For redundancy, if the member is on maternity leave and there is a suitable available vacancy which she is not offered.

■ For taking up statutory rights to parental leave, time off for care of dependants, paternity leave or equal treatment as a part-timer.

■ For taking up rights under the Flexible Working Regulations or the
■ Fixed Term Employees Regulations.

■ For asserting certain statutory rights, eg seeking a statement of terms and conditions; seeking pay-slips; objecting to unlawful deductions from wages.

■ For taking up health and safety issues in a reasonable way where there is no health and safety representative; for taking steps to protect yourself or others in circumstances of imminent danger.

■ For taking up issues as health and safety representative.

■ For membership or non-membership of a trade union or for trade union activities; for making use of the union's services at an appropriate time; because the union raised a matter on the member's behalf; for refusing an inducement to relinquish union membership or to opt out of having any terms and conditions negotiated by the union on his/her behalf.

■ For exercising the right to be accompanied to a disciplinary or grievance hearing, or for accompanying someone else in accordance with his/her right to be accompanied.

■ For not declaring a spent conviction (with certain exceptions). One year's minimum service is required for this claim.

■ In connection with rights under the Working Time Regulations or the minimum wage.

■ For absence on jury service, unless the absence is likely to cause substantial injury to the employers' undertaking and the member unreasonably fails to apply for his/her service to be excused or deferred.

■ Shop workers, for refusing to work Sundays.

■ For being a trustee of an occupational pension scheme.

■ For whistleblowing, provided the member has gone about it the right way. There are strict rules on this in part IVA of the Employment Rights Act 1996. The member can only go to external bodies in limited circumstances and should usually try to resolve matters internally first. Whistleblowing includes taking up concerns in good faith about matters such as dangers to health and safety (of the member, colleagues or the public), fraud, assault or serious bullying. (For more detail, see the website of Public Concern at Work, Bibliography p314.)

■ In some circumstances, due to the transfer of an undertaking. (See p150.) One year's minimum service is required for this claim.

Action short of dismissal

It is also unlawful to take action short of dismissal against a member for many of the reasons set out above. For example, this may take the form of disciplinary action or failure to give promotion, as the following UNISON case illustrates.

L B Hackney v Adams [2003] IRLR 402, EAT

Ms Adams was employed by the Council as an Administration Support Manager. She was a UNISON Shop Steward. In May 2000, she was interviewed for the post of office manager in the Social Services Department, which would have been a promotion for her. She was by far the best candidate and was told immediately that she would get the job. In June 2000, the Council withdrew the offer, allegedly on grounds of her sickness record, lack of flexibility and inexperience in certain fields.

The Employment Tribunal found none of the Council's reasons convincing and decided that the offer was withdrawn because of Ms Adams' trade union activities. It awarded £5000 injury to feelings. The Council appealed the decision on compensation, saying the award had been too high.

The Employment Appeal Tribunal refused to overturn the award. It said there were no grounds for awarding lower levels of compensation for injury to feelings in cases involving discrimination on trade union grounds than would be awarded in race or sex discrimination cases. In each case, it is a question of looking at the effect of the discrimination on the particular individual. Although injury to feelings is a more obvious and likely consequences from race or sex discrimination, some workers discriminated against on trade union grounds may feel deeply hurt by that affront, particularly where union membership is an important feature of their lives.

Different types of unfair dismissal

Overview

As already explained, unfair dismissal cases fall into four main categories: conduct, capability, redundancy and some other substantial reason such as reorganisation or adverse publicity. Conduct and capability dismissals can be for many different reasons. For example, conduct dismissals could concern dishonesty, violence or disobedience. Capability dismissals could concern inadequate skills for the job or ill-health. Some issues could be treated as misconduct or incapability, depending on the employers' viewpoint, for example alcoholism or intermittent sickness absences.

There are certain overriding principles which affect the fairness of most dismissals. In particular:

■ The minimum statutory disciplinary procedure must be followed where it applies. Failure to follow other fair procedures will only be relevant if it would have made a difference to the employers' decision.

■ There are good practice guidelines set out in the ACAS Code for disciplinary and grievance hearings. (See p48.) This concerns (1) fair procedures surrounding the process leading to dismissal (2) fair warnings except for gross misconduct prior to dismissal.

■ The employers should correctly follow their own procedures.

■ The employers must prove there is a substantial reason for dismissal and the tribunal must decide that it is fair to dismiss for that reason, taking all factors into account.

■ The size and administrative resources of the employers are relevant.

■ There should be no discrimination.

In addition, tribunals have come to expect that certain types of issue should be treated in certain ways by the employers. Below are some examples of common reasons for dismissal and special considerations which may apply. It is impossible to cover every kind of situation which may arise.

Conduct dismissals generally

Examples of different types of misconduct are set out below. Employers should only dismiss for a first offence if it is gross misconduct (see p52). The tribunal is not there to decide whether the member in fact committed the offence. Instead, the tribunal decides whether it was reasonable for the employers to have dismissed the member in the circumstances. The employers must:

1 Actually believe the member committed the offence.

2 Have carried out a reasonable investigation including informing the member of the evidence against the member and asking his/her comments.

3 Have reached a reasonable conclusion on the evidence that the member committed the offence. If the evidence does not support that conclusion, the dismissal will be unfair.

The reasonableness of the dismissal will also be affected by:

→ The seriousness of the offence and the worker's job.

→ Whether the member has received previous warnings.

→ The member's length of service and work record.

→ Any mitigating factors.

Common reasons for dismissal

For ease of reference, these are set out in alphabetical order.

Absenteeism

The employers' policies may specify that monitoring, disciplinary action and dismissal take place automatically when a member's absence level hits a specified number of days. Nevertheless, tribunals still expect employers to consider each case on its individual circumstances and not to follow their rule slavishly.

Employers should properly investigate the reasons for the absences and ask the member for an explanation. This may reveal an underlying medical problem. The member should be told what improvement in attendance is expected and warned of the risk of dismissal if that does not happen. If there is no improvement, factors relevant to the fairness of a dismissal will be:

■ The member's length of service and general work record.

■ The effect of his/her absences on the employers.

■ The chances of the member's attendance improving in the future.

■ The availability of any suitable alternative work which would solve the problem.

■ The reasons for the absences. There may be underlying issues such as temporary domestic difficulties; sickness or disability (see Sickness absences, below); harassment at work (which may also raise discrimination issues) – see Chapter 12.

Abusive language

The seriousness of this offence and the fairness of any dismissal depends very much on the context. You need to consider:

■ What exactly was said and is this in dispute? If so, were there witnesses?

■ Was there any element of threat or disobedience? If so, this raises other issues.

■ What is the relative status of the people involved? Obviously it is more serious to swear at someone senior or junior than at a colleague.

■ What is the normal language and atmosphere of the workplace? Is this kind of language generally accepted?

■ Has the member ever been warned about unacceptable language? Is there any written policy on this which the member has seen?

■ Was the conversation in private or in front of the public, patients, clients or other workers? The latter would be more serious as it could undermine the person suffering the abuse or damage the employers' image.

■ Is the incident symptomatic of a deeper problem, eg a personality clash; a refusal to accept managerial authority; a breakdown in work relations; a pattern of harassment by either party?

It will usually help the member if:

→ This was a one-off incident in the heat of the moment.

→ The member has apologised (although it is a difficult tactical decision whether to make a damaging admission).

→ There are mitigating factors, eg stress, tiredness, illness, problems at home or at work, provocation.

→ S/he has long service and a clean disciplinary record.

Occasionally the complaint is because the member has accused a colleague or manager of being racist. This can quite wrongly be taken as abuse and the member can be pressurised to substantiate what s/he said or withdraw. In this context, you need to be aware of the law of victimisation under the Race Relations Act (see p164). There are similar issues under the Sex Discrimination Act, Disability Discrimination Act, sexual orientation regulations and religion and belief regulations.

Alcohol

According to the circumstances, this may be a conduct or a capability issue. It is important to check any guidelines in the employers' own procedures.

Alcohol dependence should probably be treated as a medical condition falling under the capability or sickness procedure. Employers should take medical advice as to whether there is any underlying health problem, eg severe depression and also on the prospects of treatment and recovery from the dependency. Where there is a medical problem, related misconduct such as lateness and poor performance, should be tolerated to a greater extent than otherwise.

Even where it is a medical issue, there could come a point where the employers could fairly dismiss. Relevant considerations would be:

■ The nature of the member's job and the extent to which performance is affected.

■ The member's prospects of recovery and in what time-frame.

■ Whether the member refuses to undergo treatment.

■ Whether the member's alcoholism could endanger his/her own health and safety or that of others due to the nature of the workplace, and whether there is no alternative safer job to move the member to.

A single incident of drinking is more likely to be treated as a conduct issue. It may be that the member has brought alcohol onto the premises or arrived at work drunk. Factors relevant to the fairness of any dismissal would be:

■ The employers' alcohol policy and whether it was made known to the member.

■ How the employers generally respond in similar situations.

■ Any health or safety issues.

■ The actual or potential consequences of the member's drinking.

■ Whether the member had committed similar offences in the past and whether s/he had been warned.

■ Any mitigating factors.

If the Disability Discrimination Act applies, the member would have additional protection. (See Chapter 10.) Note that alcoholism in itself is not covered by the DDA, but any resultant disease, eg kidney damage, or any underlying cause, eg manic depression, may well be covered.

Breach of procedures

Employers should not automatically dismiss a worker for breach of procedures. As in all dismissals, they should investigate the particular circumstances of each case. Relevant factors are:

■ Were the procedures clearly set out and made known to the member?

■ Have the procedures been applied consistently as between workers? (If not, there may also be the possibility of unlawful discrimination.)

■ If procedures are new or have changed, was the member made aware of their existence, their seriousness and how to use them?

■ Was it a major or a minor breach of procedure?

■ How important were those procedures to the employers' operation?

■ What were the consequences, actual or potential, of the breach?

■ What were the member's reasons for the breach? Was it a mistake, carelessness or deliberate?

■ Has the member indicated a willingness to learn and improve in the future?

■ Is there any allegation of dishonesty? If the employers have this in mind, it is essential they inform the member and give him/her the chance to answer.

■ Is this a one-off breach or have there been previous similar incidents for which the member has been warned?

■ The member's length of service and general work record.

■ Has there been a full investigation and opportunity for the member to state his/her case?

Dishonesty, particularly theft

Members tend to think that the purpose of a tribunal where they have been dismissed for dishonesty is to clear their name. This is not so. The tribunal is not a criminal court and it looks at the matter quite differently. It can be a fair dismissal if the employers genuinely and reasonably believed the member committed the offence, even if long after the dismissal, the member is found not guilty by a criminal court.

The most important case on this is *British Home Stores v Burchell* (1978 IRLR 379, EAT), which sets out the three stages listed under "conduct dismissals" above, ie

1 The employers must genuinely believe the member committed the offence.

2 They must hold that belief on reasonable grounds.

3 Having carried out a proper and adequate investigation.

Where the employers believe that one of several workers must have committed the offence but are unable to narrow it down, it may be fair to dismiss all the suspected workers. Obviously for such drastic action the employers would need to prove they had done everything possible to pinpoint the blame and also that it was reasonable to consider each worker in the group equally likely to have committed the offence.

However serious the offence, it will be unfair to dismiss if the member has not had the opportunity to state his/her case. As with any type of gross misconduct, the employers must still follow fair procedures in conducting the investigation. (See p53.)

It is not enough for the employers to follow fair procedures. It must also be fair to dismiss in the circumstances, taking account of the type of the general factors listed under "conduct dismissals" above. In the workplace, dishonesty often consists of offences such as over-claiming expenses, deliberately inaccurate time-sheets, and clocking offences. Workers often see helping themselves to small items of the employers' property as "perks", but this can also be regarded as dishonesty unless it can be proved that the employers were aware it was happening and ignored it, or knew that many workers did it, but singled out the member unjustifiably or for discriminatory reasons. Unfortunately tribunals can regard dishonesty over quite small amounts very seriously, especially if the member is in a position of responsibility or has been previously warned.

It may or may not be fair to dismiss the member for out of work misconduct or even criminal convictions. It will depend on the type of dishonesty and how it could affect the employers, eg because of adverse publicity or undermining the worker's supervisory authority at work.

If the police have become involved and the member may be subjected to criminal proceedings, s/he needs specialist advice as soon as possible. S/he needs to be careful what s/he says to the employers as this may be used against him/her in a criminal case. On the other hand, refusing to speak to the employers could lead to a fair dismissal. This is a tricky situation. In criminal matters your branch has a form CR which should immediately be filled in and forwarded as indicated on the form.

Disobedience: refusal to obey a management instruction

This covers a wide range of situations. Whether or not it is fair to dismiss a member for refusing to follow a management instruction is not necessarily dependent on whether the instruction was within the member's contractual obligations. Unfair dismissal is more about the reasonableness of each side and the procedures followed.

Where a member has been dismissed for refusing to follow a management instruction, the following factors are relevant:

■ Whether the instruction was within the contract of employment. Note that although this is relevant, it is not the only factor.

■ Whether the contract was clear and unambiguous on that point. (See Chapter 1 on contracts.)

■ The reasonableness of the employers in issuing the instruction.

■ The reasonableness of the member in refusing the instruction.

■ Whether each side explained their reasons to the other and whether there was any attempt to compromise by either side.

■ Whether the member was warned of the consequences (ie dismissal) of continuing to refuse.

■ The consequences for the employers of the member's refusal.

■ The member's length of service and general work record.

You need to be very careful if a member asks your advice in advance as to whether to obey a management instruction or not. For example, if a member asks you whether s/he has to work overtime on a particular day as management have required, the answer is not "What does your contract say?" The contractual position is relevant, but it is not the final word. The relevant considerations would be:

■ What does the member's contract say?

■ Why does management want the member to work overtime on this occasion? Is it something very urgent? Is the member the only one who can do it?

■ Is the member unable to work overtime on this occasion for any very strong reason? Has s/he explained this to management? What did management say? Did the member offer a compromise?

■ Is the member willing to risk being dismissed over this?

■ If s/he is dismissed, is s/he eligible to claim unfair dismissal, would s/he win and how much compensation would s/he receive?

■ If the member agrees to an instruction which is outside his/her contract, there may be a risk that s/he impliedly agrees to a change in his/her contract. (See p20.) It may be important to write a note stating that this is a one-off agreement.

■ Does UNISON have a collective policy on how members should respond in such circumstances? Bear in mind that even if UNISON does not wish members to agree non-contractual obligations, the individual member may be vulnerable to dismissal. Is there any collective solution or room for negotiation?

There may be other special factors which are legally relevant. For example:

→ It is automatically unfair to dismiss a member for refusing to work in circumstances of serious and imminent danger to him/herself, to work colleagues or to members of the public.

→ There are special (and complex) rules regarding whistle-blowing under part IVA of the Employment Rights Act. It is automatically unfair to dismiss the member for refusing to cover up unlawful behaviour by the employers, provided s/he has followed correct procedures. See also the website of Public Concern at Work (Bibliography p314).

→ It is unlawful victimisation to dismiss the member because s/he has refused to carry out an act of race, sex or disability discrimination.

Lateness

Only in extreme cases would it be fair to dismiss a member for a first offence. However, it may be fair to dismiss for persistent lateness once a series of warnings have been given. Relevant factors would be:

■ The member's length of service and work record generally.

■ The number of prior warnings regarding lateness.

■ The degree to which the member is late and the reasons.

■ Whether the member makes up the time at the other end of the day.

■ The consequences for the employers of the member's lateness.

■ Is there a written policy regarding lateness which has been brought to the member's attention?

■ Is management consistently applying the lateness policy? (There may also be a discrimination issue if, eg, management discipline black workers when they are late but merely have a word with white workers.)

■ Are there underlying issues causing the member's lateness? For example:

- Health reasons. (This could also lead to rights under the Disability Discrimination Act. See Chapter 10. Note that the DDA covers certain illnesses and injuries as well as "disabilities")
- The member is afraid to come into work because s/he is suffering sexual harassment. (This could also lead to a sex discrimination claim. See Chapters 9 and 12.)

Negligence

It may be fair to dismiss a member for a single error due to negligence, where the actual or potential consequences could be extremely serious, even if s/he has no prior warnings. In the key case on this, *Alidair Ltd v Taylor* (1978 IRLR 82, CA) a mistake by an airline pilot justified a fair dismissal.

Poor work

The ACAS Code on Disciplinary and Grievance Procedures sets out useful guidance at paragraphs 11-12 and 19-20. Also check the employers' own capability procedure. Employers should not normally dismiss for a first offence unless it is gross negligence with potentially very serious consequences, especially to health and safety. Apart from this, where the member is not performing to the required standard, employers should give warnings and an opportunity to improve, with reasonable targets and time-scales. They should identify the nature of the problem and provide the member with training and support.

Where employers have identified poor performance, it is often a good strategy (depending on the facts) for the member to ask the employers for guidance on their procedures where they are unclear or for training, and to demonstrate a willingness to learn.

The test is not whether the member is actually incompetent. The employers need only prove that they genuinely believed the member was incompetent and they reached that belief on reasonable grounds following a proper investigation. This is similar to the test on misconduct.

Persistent poor performance may be a symptom of some underlying problems, for example

→ Domestic problems.

→ Harassment at work, eg sexual harassment. (See Chapters 8-12 on discrimination.)

→ Illness or disability. (See Chapter 10 on the Disability

Discrimination Act. Note that the DDA also covers certain illnesses. The DDA requires employers to take positive steps to help.)

Redundancy
See Chapter 6.

Reorganisation
Dismissals due to reorganisation may be fair if the employers follow fair procedures. However, existing workers should normally be retained or red-circled where they have the necessary skills or could be trained for new jobs or there are suitable vacancies. Reorganisation often overlaps with redundancy. See Chapter 6 regarding unfair redundancy dismissals and the obligation to consult the union on collective redundancies including in reorganisation situations.

Sickness absence
Genuine sickness absences should be dealt with differently from other issues of conduct or capability. It is important to note from the outset that as well as unfair dismissal law, the Disability Discrimination Act may apply more often than you expect. The DDA does not only protect workers who have a "disability" in the conventional sense of the word. It can often cover members with long-term illnesses or injuries, such as back injury or depression. The advantage of the DDA is that it requires employers to take more positive steps and to be more flexible and patient than they would otherwise be. It also applies to a wider spectrum of workers. (See Chapter 10.) See also p256 if the member is suffering from stress.

From an unfair dismissal point of view, there are two key issues:
→ Have the employers followed fair procedures in consulting with the member over the medical issues?
→ How long should the employers be expected to wait before dismissal?

Fair procedures would normally involve the following steps:
1 The employers should find out the correct medical position regarding the effect and likely length of the illness. Usually this should be from the member's GP or specialist, and the employers will probably also want the member to see their own doctor or Occupational Health Service. Unfortunately with some employers, Occupational Health can

be under severe pressure from management to give the answers that the employers want. You want to see all letters and memos which go between managers and Occupational Health and if necessary, ask for an independent doctor, who should be chosen and instructed jointly.

2 The member's own GP is probably best placed to advise on the member's overall health, a specialist may give most accurate advice on a particular condition, but Occupational Health will be more familiar with the working environment.

3 The employers must get the member's consent to obtaining medical reports. If the member refuses consent or to visit Occupational Health, s/he increases the risk of a fair dismissal. Under the Access to Medical Reports Act 1988, the member must sign a written consent before the employers can obtain a report from the member's own doctor. The member is asked to indicate on the consent form whether s/he wishes to see the report before it is sent on to his/her employers. This is a good idea, as s/he is entitled to make amendments to the report with the doctor's consent or otherwise attach his/her own comments. It is advisable for the member to see his/her doctor before signing the consent form, to discuss what the doctor will put into the report and explain the relevant issues.

4 After the employers have received the relevant medical reports, they should discuss the matter with the member. The member should be given the opportunity to comment on the reports of the employers' doctors. The discussion should include when the member thinks s/he will be able to return, the employers' views on how long they can wait and whether there is any suitable alternative employment or other steps which the employers can take to facilitate the member's return. If the DDA applies, the employers may be required to take particularly proactive steps in seeking alternative work, allowing a phased return, acquiring specialised equipment or offering training. However, the member also needs to be reasonable and cooperative.

5 Discussions should be held at suitable intervals during the member's illness to see how s/he is progressing. Although disciplinary warnings will be inappropriate, the member should be told if there comes a stage when dismissal may be an approaching possibility.

6 How long employers are expected to wait will depend on:
– How long the member is likely to be off and the extent of the envisaged recovery.
– The effect of the member's absence on the workplace and how easy it is in terms of cost and skills to cover his/her absence
– Whether suitable alternative work is available or other steps can be taken to ease the member's return.
– Whether the DDA applies.

Unauthorised absence

Unauthorised absence is viewed very seriously by tribunals, so members must be extremely careful. As always, the employers must fairly investigate and listen to the member's explanation. Obviously the reason for the absence will be a relevant factor and where there is a good reason, eg personal or family sickness, the member should be ready to produce evidence to corroborate his/her story.

The following situations may apply:

■ The member overstayed leave. If this is due to illness or travel difficulties, it is important that the member provides evidence. The member should have kept in touch with the employers as far as possible to explain the situation. Some employers state in advance that if a worker overstays leave, s/he will be taken to have dismissed him/herself. Legally this is not possible and it is crucial that the member presents him/herself for work as soon as s/he returns. Note that restrictions on the length of leave may amount to indirect race discrimination for members whose families are based in other countries. (See p169.)

■ The member's absence may be due to a family emergency. As well as the employers' own rules for compassionate leave, there are statutory minimum entitlements to dependant leave and parental leave (see p277 and 274).

■ The member may be refusing to work in circumstances of serious and imminent danger to him/herself or others. It would be automatically unfair to dismiss the member for this reason.

■ The member may be sick or disabled. (See Sickness absence, above.)
For intermittent absences, whether authorised or not, see Absenteeism above.

Variation of contract

The legal position when employers attempt to vary a member's contract without the member's consent is complex. See p20. Whether or not it is fair to dismiss a member for refusing to go along with a change in his/her contract will depend on a number of factors including:

■ Whether the contract allows the change.

■ The impact of the change on the member and the member's reasons for objecting.

■ Whether the employers had powerful reasons justifying their need to make the change.

■ Whether the employers followed fair procedures including consulting with the member and UNISON and whether they attempted any compromise.

As well as the individual right to claim unfair dismissal, if the employers are changing terms and conditions of 20 or more employees, UNISON has the right to be consulted under s188 TULR(C)A (see p133).

Violence

Fighting or violence at work is usually gross misconduct and employers can dismiss for a first offence. Even so, the employers must still carry out a fair investigation and allow the member to comment on the evidence and state his/her case. In some workplaces, employers may have tolerated violence in the past and it would be unfair to act inconsistently without prior warning. Other relevant factors would be the relative status of the parties involved and whether there were any wider safety issues, for example due to the location where the fight took place. The employers should also consider mitigating factors such as who started the fight, length of service, previous good record and provocation. There have been many cases where a black worker has been provoked into fighting by racist abuse. Employers should be aware of this as it can also amount to unlawful race discrimination.

Unfair dismissal checklist

- Check whether the member is eligible to claim unfair dismissal:
- Is the member an employee.
- Does s/he have one year's continuous service? (Except for most automatic unfair dismissals.)
- Is s/he below normal retirement age? (See p96.)
- Has s/he been dismissed? (This includes failure to renew a fixed term contract and constructive dismissal.)
- Is the dismissal for an automatically unfair reason? (See p101.)
- Is the dismissal unfair?
- Was it a fair reason to dismiss?
- Was the statutory minimum procedure followed
- Were other fair procedures followed? If not, are the employers likely to have made a different decision had they gone through those procedures?
- For fair procedures, take account of (as appropriate):
- The employers' own procedures.
- The ACAS Code on Disciplinary and Grievance Hearings.
- The size and administrative resources of the employers.
- Whether there was proper investigation and full consultation with the member.
- Was it a fair reason to dismiss?
- Did the employers genuinely believe on reasonable grounds following reasonable investigation that the member was incapable or guilty of the misconduct?
- Have the employers been consistent in their treatment of similar offences with other workers? (Always consider this if the member belongs to a commonly discriminated group as it may also raise issues of race, religion, sex, sexual orientation or pregnancy discrimination etc.)
- Had the member received previous warnings or was it gross misconduct or gross negligence?
- Were the employers' policies clear and made known to the member?
- Have the employers considered the individual circumstances of the member's case?
- What was the member's length of service and general work record?

- How serious was the offence and what were its implications?
- Are there mitigating factors or underlying issues?
● As well as this chapter, also read chapter 3 on disciplinary and grievance procedures.
● If the member has been dismissed, s/he needs advice on:
- His/her rights to an internal appeal, time-limits, procedure and tactics.
- Any unfair dismissal, discrimination or other legal claim s/he may have plus time-limits.
- The chances of success on any legal claim and what the tribunal can award.
- What help UNISON can offer and who will take the next steps.
- Remember that other parts of employment law may also apply, eg
- The proactive duties on employers towards sick, injured or disabled workers under the DDA.
- The law against race, religion, sex, sexual orientation or disability discrimination or harassment.
- Laws granting and protecting members who assert their rights to certain entitlements, eg the right to parental and dependant leave; the right not to work in dangerous circumstances; rights under the Working Time Regulations.
- Discuss with the member whether there may be an underlying motive for the employers disciplining or dismissing him/her.

Constructive dismissal checklist

There are many myths about constructive dismissal. In reality, it is full of dangers and members should be very careful before they resign. More often than not, members who decide to resign find themselves out of a job and deprived of their rights. In particular, a member may successfully prove s/he was constructively dismissed (ie her contract was broken), but fail to demonstrate that the dismissal was unfair.

The following is a brief summary of the key legal issues and dangers.

Overview
● Constructive dismissal is where the member has resigned in circumstances which the law would regard as a "dismissal". This is important because a worker who resigns cannot normally claim

unfair dismissal, redundancy pay or other legal rights which arise on dismissal.

● Constructive dismissal occurs when the reason for the member's resignation is that the employers have broken his/her contract in a very serious way. This is called a "fundamental" or "repudiatory" breach of contract. For detailed rules, see below.

● If the member wants to claim unfair dismissal, s/he still needs to fulfil the other eligibility requirements, eg the necessary minimum length of service.

● A member who is constructively dismissed may not necessarily prove that her dismissal was unfair. Constructive dismissals may be fair or unfair. In the following cases, for example, tribunals said the worker had been constructively dismissed but the dismissal was fair:

– A worker who resigned because she was demoted with loss of pay because she was unable to do her original job, but could do the demoted job.

– A worker who resigned because of a cut in her hours and pay due to her employers' serious financial crisis.

– A managing director who resigned due to loss of job satisfaction when half his duties were reallocated for reasons of efficiency, though he was unaffected financially.

Note that every case depends on its facts. Do not generalise from these examples. The tribunal will consider:

– Why the employers broke or changed the member's contract.

– The effect and seriousness of the employers' breach on the member.

– Whether good procedures were followed, eg advance notification, consultation and constructive discussion.

● Even if the member wins her unfair dismissal case, s/he may not get a new job easily and his/her compensation may not cover all his/her losses. The compensation and remedies on unfair dismissal cases where the member was constructively dismissed are the same as for any other type of unfair dismissal case. See p291. Note that:

– Compensation may be significantly reduced if the only reason the tribunal thinks the dismissal was unfair is because of poor procedures.

– Although a tribunal can order reinstatement, it cannot insist that the employers take the member back.

–   If the member resigned over not getting an expected promotion or job on restructuring, the tribunal cannot insist on him/her being reinstated to the desired post.

● The member should consider the alternatives, individual and collectively, legally and practically, to resigning.

The detailed rules

Before a member even gets onto the question of fairness, s/he needs to prove her resignation amounted to a constructive dismissal. This involves several difficult stages:

● The employers must have broken the contract in a serious or fundamental way, not a minor way. Sometimes it is hard to know whether a tribunal would consider what has happened sufficiently serious.

● The employers may have broken a concrete contract term , eg by cutting pay, reducing hours or changing duties or location.

Be careful. It may not be clear what the member's contract says on the particular point, so for example it may be uncertain whether the change in hours is within the contract or breaking it. See p20.

● The employers may have broken one of the generally implied contract terms which exist in every contract. The most well-known of such terms is the employers' contractual duty not to destroy the member's trust and confidence. For example, the employers refuse to investigate a member's complaint of sexual harassment.

Note that this type of constructive dismissal is particularly hard to prove. Tough or unsympathetic management; unfair behaviour; bringing disciplinary proceedings which the member feels unjustified; will not necessarily be seen as serious enough to destroy all trust and confidence in the employment relationship.

● Once the employers have broken the contract, the member needs to decide fairly quickly whether or not to resign. If s/he leaves it too long, s/he will be taken as having accepted what the employers have done. It then becomes too late to resign.

There are no fixed rules on how quickly the member must resign though s/he may be able to wait until the outcome of negotiations or a grievance. S/he cannot keep open her right to resign indefinitely simply by stating s/he is "working under protest". On the other hand, s/he must be careful not to resign prematurely.

● Before bringing a case for constructive dismissal, the member will usually have to bring an internal grievance. (See Chapter 3 on the statutory disputes resolution procedures).

● UNISON would not normally be able to agree to represent a member who resigns and claims constructive dismissal where either UNISON has advised against the course taken or has not even been consulted.

Unfair dismissal: myths

● *Myth:*
Employers sometimes claim if the member is late back from holiday (or in other circumstances) that s/he has dismissed him/herself. Employers say this so the member cannot claim unfair dismissal or any other employment rights resulting from a dismissal by the employers.
 Truth:
Under the law, it is not possible to dismiss yourself. If the employers will not let the member back, they have dismissed him/her. See p98.

● *Myth:*
Employers sometimes say the member will have dismissed him/herself if s/he refuses to agree to a new contract or new terms and conditions.
 Truth:
Under the law, it is not possible to dismiss yourself. If the member refuses to agree the change, the employers may choose to dismiss him or her. See p20 regarding unilateral variation.

● *Myth:*
A member who has been dismissed for dishonesty, often wants to claim unfair dismissal in the tribunal in order to "clear my name".
 Truth:
If a member is dismissed for dishonesty, the employers need not prove the member was actually guilty of the act of dishonesty. They need only prove they reasonably believed after a reasonable investigation that the member was guilty of the dishonesty. Therefore, even if the member was in fact innocent, s/he may lose his/her unfair dismissal case. See p108.

● *Myth:*
Members believe they cannot be dismissed while off sick.
Truth:
There is no reason why not, as long as the employers follow fair procedures and have fair grounds for dismissal. See p113.

● *Myth:*
The member cannot claim unfair dismissal if s/he works on a fixed-term contract, just because it expires and is not renewed.
Truth:
Failure to renew a fixed-term contract is a dismissal in law. If the member meets the other eligibility requirements for unfair dismissal, s/he will be able to claim. See pp96-99.

● *Myth:*
A worker who pays Schedule D tax and is referred to by the employers as self-employed, is not an employee and cannot claim unfair dismissal.
Truth:
This is not necessarily so. Whatever the label and tax position, it depends on the reality of the employment relationship. See p96.

● *Myth:*
The member can claim constructive dismissal when in fact s/he has been dismissed.
Truth:
Constructive dismissal refers to the situation where the member resigns due to his/her employers' fundamental breach of contract. See p118.

● *Myth:*
If the employers treat the member unpleasantly and even unfairly, s/he can resign and claim constructive dismissal.
Truth:
Unpleasant treatment is not enough. The employers must have broken the member's contract in a fundamental way. This can include breaking the implied term of trust and confidence. However, in order to have broken the implied term of trust and confidence, the employers must have done more than be unpleasant or a bit unfair. They must have behaved in an extremely bad way. See p120 for more detail.

Chapter 6:

Redundancy

Contents

The definition of redundancy

The definition of redundancy is set out in section 139 of the Employment Rights Act, but it has been the subject of much case law. There are three types of redundancy. A member is redundant if s/he is dismissed

1 Due to a closure of the whole business; or

2 Due to closure of the particular workplace where the member was employed; or

3 Because of a reduction in the overall size of the workforce or because the employers want fewer employees to carry out the type of work the member is doing.

The test is not whether the employers need fewer workers, but whether they want fewer workers. There may be just as much work to be done as before, but for economic or other reasons (eg the acquisition of labour-saving machinery) the employers decide they want fewer workers to do it.

The definition of redundancy can be difficult to apply in borderline situations. It can be most uncertain where the employers retain the same overall numbers in their workforce, but delete some jobs and create others.

For example, if a local authority employer decides to reduce its employed plumbers from 8 to 6 workers, but to increase its electricians from 7 to 9 workers, there will be the same total number of employees. However, two plumbers will have been dismissed for redundancy. This is because a job as a plumber is obviously different from a job as an electrician and the local authority requires fewer plumbers.

On the other hand, a Hospital may decide it needs fewer night nurses and more day nurses. Are the excess night nurses redundant? Or is the job simply that of a nurse (whether working days or nights), so that no "nurses" are redundant? A mere change in the member's terms and conditions within the same job does not mean there is a redundancy situation. In this example, it may depend on whether a "night nurse" is a distinct job compared with a "day nurse" in terms of skills and functions.

A similarly borderline situation is where a manual job becomes computerised. If a finance worker's job, formerly done completely with paperwork, becomes entirely done on computer, is it a different job, so that the original job is redundant? Probably not. It is probably the same job, now done in a different way.

A member who is dismissed to make way for another worker, whose job is redundant, is dismissed for redundancy. This is often called "bumping".

Depending on the legal situation, the employers' policies and the industrial relations context, it may or may not suit a member to argue that his/her job is redundant.

Redundancy pay

Statutory redundancy pay

A member who is dismissed for redundancy is entitled to statutory redundancy pay provided that s/he is an employee with two years' continuous service with the particular employers. Continuous service within local government or within the National Health Service may be added together. Statutory redundancy pay is often quite low. It is worth the member knowing this if s/he is assuming s/he will receive a substantial sum.

The member must be careful not to leave the job prematurely if s/he wishes to get this pay. The member must not leave before s/he is given notice of dismissal with a clear termination date.

If the member wishes to leave before the notice expires, s/he must either get the employers' agreement that s/he may do so and will still be given the redundancy payment (s/he should get this in writing), or s/he must follow the correct procedure under section 142 of the Employment Rights Act. Section 142 requires notices and counternotices within a strict time-scale.

If the member unreasonably refuses an offer of suitable alternative employment with the employers or associated employers, s/he will lose the redundancy pay. To have this effect, the offer must fulfil the following criteria:

1 It must be made before the old job ends and start immediately or within four weeks of the end of the previous employment.

2 The offer need not be in writing, but it must set out the terms of the new job in enough detail to show the member how it differs from the old job.

3 The member can try out the new job for a maximum of four weeks, even if s/he is absent through sickness or otherwise during that time. If s/he remains beyond the four weeks, s/he will lose his/her entitlement to the redundancy pay. However, an offer of a different job, will attract another four week trial period. The four weeks can only be extended for the purpose of retraining, in which case there must be a written agreement specifying a new date when the trial period will end.

4 The offer must be "suitable" in terms of factors such as its hours, pay, status and location.

5 The "reasonableness" of the member's refusal will tend to depend on personal factors such as health or childcare responsibilities if extra travelling or longer hours are involved. It is very hard to predict whether a tribunal will consider a worker's refusal unreasonable. Tribunals often expect workers to be willing to undertake extra travelling, for example, although this will depend on the nature and status of the job and general location. If travel is the issue, it's a good idea for the member to work out exactly what would be involved in time and expense, and even to try it out for a few weeks.

How statutory redundancy pay is calculated

There is a ready reckoner available from the Department of Employment and reproduced in many employment law textbooks. The calculation is according to age, number of whole years' worked and gross pay at the termination date, ie

– One and a half weeks' pay for each complete year of service after reaching the age of 41.

– One week's pay for each complete year of service between the ages of 22 and 40 inclusive.

– Half a week's pay for each complete year of service between the ages of 18 and 21 inclusive.

– Years below age 18 are not counted and a maximum of 20 years is counted in all. In the last year before retirement age, the payment is reduced by 1/12th for each completed month. l   the member would be entitled to receive a pension payment within 90 weeks of leaving the job, the amount of the redundancy pay may in some circumstances be reduced or excluded by the employers. The member would need to take specialist advice if this happens.

– Unlike for unfair dismissal purposes, unbroken service with different employers but within the health service or within local government can be added together.

– The pay is subject to a gross weekly maximum which is increased annually (£280 from February 2005). In local authority and National Health Service schemes, there may be contractual entitlement to actual gross weekly pay. You should clarify this with your regional officer/organiser.

Contractual and voluntary redundancy pay

Some employers have more generous contractual redundancy pay. This may carry its own rules regarding the effect of refusing alternative offers. Voluntary redundancy packages may also be offered.

Unfair redundancy dismissals

A member who is dismissed for redundancy may be able to claim that his/her dismissal is unfair. The eligibility requirements for claiming unfair dismissal are set out on p96. The member should remember that a voluntary redundancy may not amount to a dismissal for the purposes of claiming unfair dismissal.

A tribunal will rarely challenge the fairness of the employers' decision to make redundancies in the first place. That is usually considered the employers' prerogative. But a tribunal may think it unfair to have selected the particular member for redundancy or that unfair procedures were followed. The employers will probably already have an agreed redundancy procedure with UNISON. They do not have to follow that procedure, but they would need very good reasons for failing to do so.

The following steps should be taken by fair employers:

■ The employers should notify UNISON and individual workers of the possibility of redundancy and the process.

■ The employers should consult UNISON on the possibility of avoiding redundancies altogether. (See below on collective consultation.)

■ It can be unfair if the employers failed to call for volunteers or failed to take up offers from volunteers. However, the employers may justifiably say that the wrong people volunteered and it was important to retain a balanced workforce with the requisite skills.

■ The employers should choose an appropriate pool for selection. The correct selection pool is usually a group of workers with similar skills and jobs, but there is no absolute definition as to what pool is appropriate.

■ The employers should use clearly defined selection criteria, which can be objectively measured. The employers are fairly free to choose whatever criteria they wish, as long as these are rational, objective, nondiscriminatory and can be fairly applied. The employers usually consult UNISON regarding appropriate criteria, but UNISON will have its own policy on how much to get involved. It is difficult to challenge the criteria later if the union has agreed them. On the other hand, UNISON may think it is important at least to prevent the employers adopting discriminatory criteria (see below).

■ The employers must apply the criteria fairly, objectively and without discrimination to each worker. In many cases, the employers should consult each worker individually regarding the assessment of the criteria.

■ The employers must consult individual workers regarding the possibility of alternative employment. Generally speaking, redundant workers should be offered any suitable vacancies (although they will not have priority over disabled workers needing redeployment).

Remember that, subject to any extensions under the statutory disputes resolution procedures, the time-limit for claiming unfair dismissal is three months from the termination date. (See p294)

Redundancy and discrimination

You should watch out for signs of discrimination in the redundancy selection or redeployment process.

Direct discrimination (race, religion or belief, sex, being married, sexual orientation, disability)

Direct sex discrimination occurs if the member is chosen because s/he is of a particular race, religion, belief, sex, sexual orientation, or is disabled, married or pregnant. Warning signs could be:

→ The member scores lower on the selection criteria than you would expect, taking account of objective evidence as to his/her skills, experience or competence.

→ A disproportionate number of, say, black workers or women are selected for redundancy. Note that the fact that the employers have retained some black workers does not mean they have not discriminated against those they chose to dismiss.

Victimisation

Victimisation occurs if the member is selected for redundancy because s/he has complained about race, sex, pregnancy, religion, belief, sexual orientation or disability discrimination. Warning signs could be:

→ The member complained about such discrimination relatively recently.

→ There is some evidence that the employers were upset about the complaint.

→ One or more managers making the redundancy selection decision are aware of the member's complaint.

→ There are other examples of less favourable treatment by the employers since the complaint.

→ The member is selected for redundancy when you would not have expected that to happen given his/her work record and the selection criteria used.

Indirect discrimination (race, religion or belief, sex, being married, sexual orientation)

Many selection criteria are vague and it is unclear how they are measured. Words such as "flexibility", "co-operation" "personal effectiveness", may mean a number of things, measurable in a number of ways. Unless these elements are clear, they allow for direct or indirect discrimination.

Indirect race or sex discrimination, in particular, is a serious risk in the chosen selection criteria. An indirectly discriminatory selection criterion is one which would disproportionately exclude women or men or one racial group etc, and which the employers cannot justify using. (See pp169 and 196 for the definition of indirect discrimination and pp179 and 202 for lists of potentially discriminatory criteria.) The following are examples of potentially discriminatory selection criteria. Whether they are in fact discriminatory will depend (1) on the particular facts and jobs concerned and the workforce profile, and (2) on whether the employers can justify using those criteria (see p00.)

Criteria:

■ **Full-time working.** A criterion which screened out part-time workers would usually adversely affect women. Most tribunals would consider it unjustifiable. It may also contravene the Part-time Workers Regulations (see p282).

■ **Length of service or Last In First Out ("LIFO")**. This is often a popular criterion because it seems fair and objective. Unfortunately in many workforces it can have the effect of disproportionately targeting women and black workers who often have the shortest service – women due to childcare, black workers due to repeated discrimination costing them jobs in the past.

■ **Flexibility.** What does this criterion mean? If it means willingness to work late, week-end and flexible hours, this would discriminate against women due to childcare. Mobility and attendance record may also discriminate against women. Willingness to work certain shifts, eg on Fridays, Saturdays or Sundays, could discrimination against certain religious groups.

■ **Disciplinary record.** UNISON branches have started to monitor disciplinary action in certain local authority employers and it is clear that in many authorities, black workers are disproportionately the subject of disciplinary action due to direct discrimination. It is difficult to find evidence to prove that in individual cases, a black worker has been disciplined on grounds of race, but the statistical pattern reveals widespread direct discrimination. It would therefore be unjustifiable indirect discrimination with such employers to allow disciplinary records to count against workers in redundancy selection. You need to know in advance whether there has been disproportionate disciplinary action against black members so you can prevent this criterion being adopted. (It would also suggest other collective action by the union, so this is an area which you should ensure is monitored. See p177.)

■ **Customer complaints.** Black workers can attract more complaints from the public than white workers due to racism. This is a very unreliable selection criterion.

■ **Appraisals.** Members may have suffered direct or indirect discrimination in their appraisals, which could then be held against them a second time in a redundancy selection exercise. As with disciplinary action, this is an area where black workers are particularly discriminated against, but find it hard to prove individual cases. Again it is recommended that UNISON branches monitor appraisals where these carry measured ratings, and take necessary preventative action. (See p177.) It is too late once members have been selected for redundancy on these criteria.

■ **Tests.** Tests can potentially discriminate for several reasons: they may benefit those with longer service who have greater experience at the job; they may require good English; they may be culturally biased. It is not always obvious what is wrong with a test until the results show that certain groups have done noticeably less well. If employers insist on using selection tests; they should at least agree to discount the results if it turns out that any racial or other group disproportionately scores badly.

■ **Contract workers.** It is common that workers employed on fixed term contracts are made redundant first on mass redundancy exercises. Many of these workers may have been employed for years on very similar terms and conditions to so-called permanent workers. It is possible that women or black workers are disproportionately represented amongst this group. It may also contravene the Fixed Term Employees Regulations to select workers unjustifiably, purely because they are on fixed term contracts. (See p24.)

■ **Working with others.** How can this be safely measured? It carries the risk of workers being penalised due to the racist assumptions or behaviour of others, hostility towards religious practices, homophobia, or innocent cross-cultural misunderstandings.

■ **Personal effectiveness.** This is a vague term which is hard to measure objectively and may well lead to race or gender-related disadvantages both in the member's ability to perform the job and the reactions of others towards the member.

Disability

A disabled worker may be discriminated against in the redundancy process in a number of ways, eg:

■ The employers no longer want to employ a disabled worker.

■ The employers unconsciously underestimate the worker's abilities when assessing him/her against selection criteria.

■ Selection criteria are applied which the worker is unable to comply with for reasons related to his/her disability.

■ Inadequate reasonable adjustments are made to re-deploy the member. (See p212.)

Examples of selection criteria which might discriminate against disabled workers (unless the employers can justify applying them to the member):

■ **Attendance.** The member may have a higher absence record due to his/her disability or related treatment.

■ **Length of Service.** The Disability Discrimination Act is relatively new and many disabled workers may have achieved employment with its assistance only recently.

■ **Flexibility.** The employers may be measuring flexibility in the past or requiring multi-skills in the future. Due to his/her disability, the member may be unable to do as wide a variety of tasks.

■ **Co-operation.** This may be measured by a worker's willingness to do a variety of tasks as asked or to work overtime. The member may be less flexible due to the restrictions caused by his/her disability.

■ **Working with others.** A member may be less able to work with others due to the effects of his/her disability or the reactions of others towards him/her.

■ **Personal effectiveness.** This is a vague term which is hard to measure objectively and may well lead to disability-related disadvantages both in the member's ability to perform the job and the reactions of others towards the member.

Maternity leave

A woman whose post is made redundant while she is on maternity leave must be offered any suitable available vacancy, however inconvenient to the employers. Failure to do this is automatic unfair dismissal. See also Chapter 13 regarding pregnancy and maternity law generally.

Time-limits

A member who wants to claim that s/he has been subject to discrimination in his/her selection for redundancy must bring a tribunal claim within three months of his/her redundancy selection. S/he may at that stage still be in employment, for example in the redeployment pool, or s/he may be making an appeal. Either way, s/he cannot delay lodging his/her tribunal claim.
If the statutory disputes resolution procedures apply (see p57), time-limits may be affected.

Trade union consultation on collective redundancies

There are statutory rules as to how and when consultation must take place on collective redundancies. This is quite separate from member's individual rights not to be unfairly dismissed. In this context, "redundancy" has a wider meaning than for individual rights (set out at p123 above.) It means dismissals for any reason not related to the individuals concerned, eg reorganisation as well as redundancy dismissals. It also covers where the employers propose to:

1 substantially vary the contracts of 20 or more employees

2 dismiss 20 or more employees in order to offer new contracts on different terms

3 redeploy 20 or more employees in a redundancy situation.

The following UNISON case established employers' obligations to consult in the latter situation.

Hardy v Tourism South East [2005] IRLR 242, EAT

Sarah Hardy was one of 26 workers employed by Tourism South East at its Tunbridge Wells office. On 30th January 2004, the employers announced they were closing the office. They anticipated 12 redundancies, with the remaining staff being redeployed. The employees would have to apply for the vacancies, which would be on different job descriptions and based at another office.

In the employment tribunal, Mrs Hardy complained that the employers had failed to inform and consult the workforce, contrary to section 188 of the Trade Union and Labour Relations (Consolidation) Act. The employers accepted they had not carried out any consultation under s188, but said they were not required to do so because, since they expected most of the staff to be redeployed, they were not proposing to dismiss 20 or more employees as s188 requires.

The tribunal decided that the employers had not breached s188. With the assistance of UNISON's Employment Rights Unit, the case was successfully appealed to the Employment Appeal Tribunal.

The EAT said that redeployment can amount to a dismissal, if the terms of the redeployment are so different from those of the old contract, that it amounts to the withdrawal of the old contract and offer of a new one. On the facts of this case, it was clear that the employers were proposing to terminate the old contracts. This was because the employees would have to apply for new jobs, in new locations and with fresh job descriptions. The appeal was therefore allowed and Mrs Hardy's claim succeeded.

The rules are set out in section 188 of the Trade Union and Labour Relations (Consolidation) Act 1992 as amended by the Collective Redundancies and Transfer of Undertakings (Protection of Employment) (Amendment) Regulations 1999. Employers must consult with the trade union, or if there is none, with correctly elected employee representatives. Consultation must be with the representatives of any workers who may be affected by the proposed dismissals or measures taken in connection with them. Consultation should be undertaken by the employers with a view to reaching agreement and should include ways of avoiding or reducing the number of dismissals. The European Court of Justice has said this means the employers must negotiate.

The employers must provide written information on:

→ The reason for the proposed redundancies.

→ The numbers and descriptions of workers whom it is proposed to make redundant.

→ The total number of workers employed at the establishment in question.

→ The proposed selection method.

→ The manner in which dismissals are to be carried out.

→ The proposed method of calculating redundancy payments.

Timing of the consultation

The information should be provided before the employers have settled on any rigid plan and in good time for meaningful consultation. As a minimum:

– Where it is proposed to make 100 or more workers redundant at one establishment, consultation must begin at least 90 days before the first dismissal takes place.

– Where it is proposed to make at least 20 but less than 100 workers redundant, consultation must begin at least 30 days before the first dismissal.

Dismissal notices cannot be issued until consultation is completed.

Employers sometimes try to avoid or reduce their consultation obligations by arguing that the workers they propose to dismiss are not concentrated in one "establishment". It is therefore important to know what an "establishment" is. This is not defined in the TULR(C)A. It is for the tribunal to decide what is an "establishment", using common sense and looking at the facts of the case. Relevant factors would include: geographical separation, permanence, exclusive employees, managerial and administrative independence of different areas.

In an old case, the EAT found that different house-building sites operating from one base could be one establishment. *(Barratt Developments (Bradford) Ltd v UCATT* 1978 ICR 319.)

In *Rockfon A/S v Special arbejderforbundet i Danmark acting for Nielsen & Ors* (1996 IRLR 168), the ECJ decided the meaning of "establishment" under the Collective Redundancies Directive. They said it meant the unit to which the redundant workers had been assigned to carry out their duties. The unit did not need independent management. The ECJ did not clarify what "assigned" or "unit" meant, but the main principle to emerge was that the ECJ was keen to secure a result which encouraged consultation. Unfortunately Danish law is worded differently from UK law and this case is not helpful here.

Following *Rockfon*, the EAT found that branch offices of an insurance company were separate establishments because each was a separate costs centre and each had its own staff assigned to it under its own branch manager. *(MSF v Refuge Assurance plc & another* [2002] IRLR 324.) This case goes against the spirit of Rockfon because it made consultation less likely.

If there is a transfer covered by the TUPE regulations at the same time as the redundancies, there are similar (though not identical) rules on trade union consultation regarding these. (See p155.)

Remedies for failure to consult

If the employers fail to consult, UNISON can bring a tribunal case for a declaration that the employers have not consulted. The tribunal may award compensation to each affected worker for the protected period ie the length of consultation there should have been. This is called a "protective award". The purpose is to punish the employers for not consulting, not to compensate individual workers for their loss. Therefore, the amount will be affected by the seriousness and degree of the employers' failure to consult. The tribunal's starting point will be to consider the 90 day maximum award and reduce it only if there are appropriate mitigating circumstances.

UNISON must bring the tribunal claim before the last of the dismissals takes place in respect of which the complaint is made, or within three months afterwards.

Redundancy: myths

● *Myth:*

When mass redundancies are made, the first to go can be workers employed on fixed-term contracts. When the contracts expire on the relevant date, they simply need not be renewed. Those workers will have no rights.

Truth:

Failure to renew a fixed-term contract is a dismissal in law (see p98). Depending on whether they are an employee and their length of service, these workers may be able to claim unfair dismissal (p95), breach of the Fixed-Term Employees Regulations (p24) or indirect race or sex discrimination, if the contract workers are disproportionately of one race or sex.

● *Myth:*

The member cannot be made redundant because there is still as much work to do.

Truth:

Redundancy occurs when the employers decide they want fewer employees doing a particular type of work, even if there is still as much or more work to be done. See p123.

CHECKLIST: REDUNDANCY

● The member is entitled to reasonable time off to look for alternative employment.

● Check whether the member is entitled to statutory or contractual redundancy pay and whether s/he may lose it by unreasonably turning down an offer of suitable alternative employment.

● Check the member is aware of the tribunal time-limits and what steps to take next if s/he has not received his/her redundancy pay. (Note that some contractual agreements may need to go to the county court, but the member would need specialist advice.)

● Check whether the member received notice or pay in lieu.

● Can the member claim unfair dismissal?

● Is s/he eligible to claim?

● What are his/her chances of success?

● How much compensation would s/he receive? (The redundancy pay will be set off against his/her award and the claim may have little value if the member quickly gets a new job.)

● Have you advised the member on the tribunal time-limits and what steps to take next?

● Has the member been selected for redundancy for any of the automatically unfair reasons?

● Has the member been subjected to direct discrimination on grounds of race, sex, marital status, pregnancy, sexual orientation, religion or belief, disability?

● Has the member been victimised, ie selected for redundancy because s/he previously complained of race, sex or disability discrimination etc?

● Are any of the redundancy selection criteria potentially indirect discrimination, eg full-time working, flexibility, disciplinary action, length of service?

● Has UNISON been monitoring relevant statistics on the workforce so you are aware in advance of what criteria may be discriminatory?

● Would the employers be able to justify the discriminatory criteria? How does each criterion benefit them?

● Have part-timers been unjustifiably selected for redundancy contrary to the Part-time Workers Regulations or the Fixed Term Employees Regulations?

- If the member is disabled, have any of the selection criteria disadvantaged him/her for a related reason? Has s/he been assisted to find redeployment?
- If the member was on maternity leave, has she been offered any suitable available vacancy?
- Was UNISON correctly consulted on collective redundancies?
- See also the general checklist regarding rights on dismissal in Chapter 4.

Chapter 7:

The transfer of undertakings regulations

Contents

Introduction

The Transfer of Undertakings (Protection of Employment) Regulations 1981 (commonly referred to as "TUPE") were introduced to protect workers' rights on the transfer of the business in which they are employed. The TUPE Regulations were brought in to implement the European Acquired Rights Directive – sometimes known as the Business Transfers Directive. This is one of the main areas other than sex discrimination, family friendly and working time laws, where decisions of the European Court of Justice ("ECJ") influence UK law. The case-law and legislation is constantly changing in this area, so there can be great uncertainty as to the legal position in any work situation. The TUPE Regulations are to be amended with effect from 1st October 2005. At the time of writing (April 2005), the government is consulting on the final wording of the revised Regulations. As far as possible, the anticipated changes are indicated in the text below.

In recent years, workers have increasingly found themselves with new employers through no choice of their own. It is common for hotels and restaurants to change hands, multi-nationals to buy and sell businesses and large organisations to contract out services such as cleaning, catering and maintenance. Many local authorities and NHS Trusts have been at the forefront of this trend, issuing contracts to private companies for core services such as rent collection and long-term patient care. The current fashion is for Public Private Partnerships and Private Finance Initiatives ("PFI"), whereby contractors agree to build hospitals and other facilities in return for lengthy contracts to provide maintenance and other services in the new buildings. For more detail on this, see the PFI page on UNISON's website (click "Resources", then "Documents Database", then "PFI".)

The TUPE Regulations are necessary to protect the interests of workers employed on the contracted out services. If the Regulations do not apply, the workers may be made redundant with no obligation on the new contractor to take them on. Theoretically the Regulations require the contractors to take on the old workers and maintain the same terms and conditions. In practice, there are two big problems with the TUPE Regulations:

→ Do they apply at all to the transfer in question?

→ Assuming they do apply, are they sufficient to protect the worker?

The key legal principles and difficulties are set out below, but specialist advice would always be necessary in this area. In terms of jargon, the organisation selling the business or granting a contract is known as the "transferor". The purchaser of the business or company winning the contract is known as the "transferee".

Is contracting out a good idea?

Contracting out, in all its variations, is rarely beneficial for the member. There are legal and practical consequences of moving from a public sector to a private sector employer. Even where the TUPE Regulations apply, they cannot indefinitely protect members against the effect of having less sympathetic employers. The new employers often operate a two-tier system, bringing in newly recruited workers on different terms and conditions. Obviously this makes the new employers see the transferred workers as less desirable to retain in the long-term.

The UNISON and Low Pay Unit submission to the Low Pay Commission in October 2002 reported on the effect of contracting out in driving down wages.

Well-organised union opposition can reduce the number of services contracted out by the employers. There are alternatives even within PFI, for example DFB-only projects (Design, Finance and Build). There is also the Retention of Employment (ROE) Model which has been tested by UNISON and the Department of Health in some NHS PFI Schemes in England. Under ROE, ancillary staff in cleaning, catering, laundry, portering and security services remain NHS employees, although they are managed by the private sector. Supervisors, managers and other groups of staff may still be transferred. The practical and legal consequences of ROE remain to be tested. There is a UNISON Briefing and Negotiating Guide on the website under Resources / PFI. The Guide: "The Private Finance Initiative – Retention of Employment Model". It was written in 2003, so you need to ascertain the up-to-date position. There is also the revision to the Department of Health's PFI Guidance: "Fair treatment of staff and observing TUPE" on www.doh.gov.uk under Procurement and Proposals / PPP / PFI.

Public Sector Transfers

If staff transfers are inevitable, then it is important that the TUPE Regulations do apply and are followed. The government has said it is committed to ensuring that transferred workers are treated fairly and it has issued two important documents:

→ A Code of Practice on Workforce Matters in Local Authority Service Contracts. This was issued on 13th February 2003. It is available at Annex D to ODPM Circular 03/2003. This is available on the ODPM website, www.odpm.gov.uk, though extremely hard to find. Once on the site, try searching "Circular 03/2003". The one you want is about number 24 on the list and is called "ODPM Circular 03/2003: Best Value Performance Improvement – with 2004 addendums".

→ The Cabinet Office Statement of Practice on Staff Transfers in the Public Sector. (January 2000.) This is available on www.civilservice.gov.uk/publications/staff_transfers/publications_an d_forms/pdf/stafftransfers.pdf.

The Code of Practice applies where a local authority transfers employees to a private or voluntary sector contractor. At the time of writing, it is being extended to include the NHS, civil service and maintained schools. Check your regional office for the precise position if needed. Best value authorities under the Local Government Act 2003 are required to monitor compliance with the Code and to confirm in their annual Best Value Performance Plans that individual contracts comply with the requirements in the Code. The Audit Commission oversees this process. The enforcement of the Code is by way of a clause in the contract between the contracting authority and the contractor.

The Cabinet Office Statement of Practice applies to the NHS and central government as well as local authorities. However, it is only a policy statement and is not enforceable in itself except in respect of local authorities (and others if covered), which are required by the Code of Practice to apply the principles set out in the Statement of Practice. With other employers, it is still a useful document for UNISON because it puts pressure on employers and contractors to take steps which ensure TUPE applies.

The rest of this Chapter sets out the general law under TUPE and then indicates what the Code of Practice or Statement of Practice say on the matter. Remember:

→ The Code of Practice applies to local authorities and is being extended to cover the NHS, civil service and maintained schools. It is enforceable against the contractor by those authorities.

→ The Statement of Practice provides good practice guidelines for the public sector, but is only enforceable by authorities covered by the Code.

UNISON has written an excellent guide to the law with practical negotiating `tips: "UNISON Guide: Best Value Code of Practice on Workforce Matters in Local Authority Service Contracts in England and Police Authority Service Contracts in England and Wales (July 2003)". It is available at www.unison.org.uk/acrobat/13612.pdf.

The law

Is the transfer covered by the regulations?

The TUPE Regulations apply when an "undertaking" or part of an undertaking is transferred. The transfer may take place by various means, eg sale, franchise, granting a contract or taking back a service in-house. The undertaking must consist of an identifiable economic entity, which is transferred in a recognisable form. These are examples where the TUPE Regulations have applied in contracting-out situations:

→ The transfer of hospital cleaning services from one contractor to another.

→ A college's termination of a catering contract in order to provide catering services itself.

→ The transfer of a grant by a public body, eg a local authority, from one advice agency to another.

The Cabinet Office Statement of Practice covers the following types of situation that may involve transfers of staff:

→ Public Private Partnerships, including contracting-out, market testing, PFI, privatisation, other outsourcing exercises.

→ Second and subsequent generation contracting where staff transferred out of the public sector on the first contract.

→ Reorganisations and transfers from one part of the public sector to another.

Unfortunately, not every grant, transfer or release of a contract will be covered by the Regulations. Each case depends on its particular facts. There are two legal stages:

1 Is there an identifiable economic entity prior to the transfer?

2 Has the entity been transferred in a recognisable form?

An identifiable economic entity

The undertaking must be a stable economic entity. This is obvious where, for example, an entire hotel is bought by a new company. But it is less obvious where a local authority contracts out one of its many in-house services. A particular problem occurs where, prior to the transfer, the relevant activity was carried out by an imprecise number of staff, who were also involved on other work.

The ECJ has defined an economic entity as "an organised grouping of persons and assets ... which pursues a specific objective." The entity need not own any tangible assets, but it must be something more than an activity. In a labour-intensive undertaking such as catering or cleaning, there would need to be a dedicated workforce, management structure, operating methods and resources. The size does not matter – one cleaner and his/her cleaning operation could amount to an entity.

The entity must be stable and not short-term such as a building contract. Non-commercial ventures are covered by the Regs, eg charities, voluntary sector organisation and NHS trusts.

Has the entity transferred in recognisable form?

The overall test is whether the business in question retains its identity after transfer. This is indicated in particular by the continuation or resumption of its operation by the new employers. The greater the similarity between the business run before and after the transfer, the more likely it is to satisfy this test. So for example, a take-away fish and chip bar which is sold to be converted to an up-market clothes shop, would be a mere sale of assets (the building) and not of an undertaking. However the business need not be identical before and afterwards in the way it is run.

There are many borderline situations. For example, in one case a hospital shop selling flowers, chocolates and magazines, was sold and converted to a general grocery with longer opening hours. This was considered a different business, so TUPE did not apply.

Case-law has set out certain guidelines in deciding whether or not the same business is transferring. It is helpful if the transferee takes over the transferor's buildings, equipment, customer base or employees, but no single factor needs to be present in every case. In weighting the factors, the type of undertaking must be taken into account. The tribunals must take a purposive approach when they assess the situation, ie remember that the purpose of the TUPE Regulations is to protect workers. These are the relevant factors:

→ The type of business or undertaking concerned. Its size is irrelevant.

→ Whether the business's tangible assets, such as buildings and equipment, are transferred. It is not essential that ownership (as opposed to use) of assets is transferred. If the business solely comprises services, transfer of assets will not be important.

→ The value of the intangible assets, eg goodwill, at the time of transfer and whether they are transferred.

→ Whether or not the majority of employees are taken over by the new employers. This is particularly important in labour- intensive businesses, but not essential. If employees are not taken on by the new employers, it is relevant to consider why not. (See below.)

→ Whether customers are transferred.

→ The degree of similarity between the activities carried on before and after the transfer.

→ The period, if any, during which those activities are suspended.

There has been much legal uncertainty regarding the significance of whether the transferor's employees have been taken on by the transferee. In the *Süzen* case (*Süzen v Zehnacker Gebaudereinigung GmbH Krankenhausservice* [1997] IRLR 255, ECJ), the ECJ seemed to say that in a labour-only undertaking, TUPE would not apply unless the new employers took on the majority of the staff in terms of numbers or skills. This disastrous decision would allow unscrupulous contractors to avoid TUPE by cynically refusing to take on any of the old employees. However this case goes against a whole number of earlier ECJ decisions, for example the *Spijkers* case (*Spijkers v Gebroeders Bedik Abattoir CV* [1986] CMLR 296, ECJ), which say that all factors should be considered and no single one is decisive.

After initial uncertainty, UK courts and tribunals have decided to follow the earlier and more numerous ECJ decisions. In particular, the Court of Appeal has said that the importance of Süzen has been overstated. (*ECM (Vehicle Delivery Service) v Cox* [1999] IRLR 559, CA.) Following this, UNISON has successfully won two cases, one in the Court of Appeal, one in the Employment Appeal Tribunal on the basis that transfer of employees is not the overriding factor. Where no employees are taken on by the transferee, it is also relevant to consider the reasons for that decision. Both cases were reported and are summarised on pp147-148 below. In the *Cheeseman* case, the EAT set out very useful guidelines summarising the legal state of play.

Süzen is problematic for labour-only contracts. However, the ECJ has said that catering contracts are based essentially on equipment rather than labour. An important factor is therefore whether the transferee uses the same catering premises and equipment as the transferor.

In some situations, the entity before the transfer is divided on transfer to two or more new contractors. For example, a refuse collection service initially supplied by one contractor for the whole Borough may be put out for tender separately as North and South of the Borough. Nevertheless, if the two parts add up to the previous whole service, there can still be a transfer in a recognisable form.

Public sector transfers: the code and the statement of practice

As explained below, the revised TUPE Regulations should ensure all service provision changes are covered. In addition, the Statement of Practice on Staff Transfers in the Public Sector (see p142 above) tries to ensure that the contracting process in the public sector is carried out in a way which means legally staff will transfer. It makes the following key recommendations:

→ At the earliest appropriate stage in the contracting exercise, the public sector contracting authority should state that staff are to transfer. Staff and recognised unions (or if none, staff representatives) should be told in writing of the intention that staff will transfer and TUPE should apply.

→ Potential bidders would then be invited to tender and told in the Invitation to Tender letter of the intention that staff transfer and TUPE apply. Bids not based on TUPE should be rejected unless one of the limited exceptions set out in the Statement of Practice applies. Exceptions include new projects; contracts mainly for the provision of goods; contracts where service functions are to change significantly.

→ Where one of these exceptions does apply, the cost of redeployment and redundancies must be taken into account when assessing the bid.

RCO Support Services Ltd and another v UNISON and others [2002] IRLR
401, CA

Ainslee Hospital NHS Trust ran two in-patient hospitals three miles apart in
Liverpool: Walton and Fazakerley. Initial Hospital Services Ltd held the
contract for cleaning Walton. There was a team of staff which had been
permanently dedicated to cleaning particular wards and theatres for many
years. The team operated established systems with the medical staff and
received specialised training.

Walton closed its in-patient wards and transferred patients, doctors, nurses,
equipment and furniture to new wards at Fazakerley. RCO took over the
cleaning contract at Fazakerley, where it was already based.

RCO also held the catering contract at Fazakerley. The Trust had provided an
in-house service at Walton, employing six chefs and a larger number of
support staff. The Trust continued to employ the chefs at a new facility at
Fazakerley, but some of the support staff were made redundant.

A number of the cleaning and catering staff brought a tribunal case.
UNISON also brought proceedings for failure to consult.

The employment tribunal decided that TUPE applied. It said that both the
cleaning and the catering operations were economic entities which had been
transferred to RCO. The core business of the domestics moved to
Fazakerley, ward for ward, theatre for theatre. It was no more than a change
of location for the same business carried on by a different firm. The nature
of the business was such that there would be few tangible or intangible
assets, so this was not an important factor. The point was that the
customers remained the same (the Trust and the patients in the local
community) and there would be same kind of cleaning requiring the same
skills as before. The situation was similar on the catering contract.

RCO and the Trust appealed. They argued that, following Süzen, there was
no TUPE transfer because there was neither a movement of significant
assets nor had the majority of the workers moved across. The EAT rejected
the appeal, stressing again that all factors must be taken into account. EAT
said there was a real danger that if Süzen was taken too literally, "the basic
objective of the Directive would be jeopardised in relation to perhaps the
most vulnerable of all classes of worker, those with only relatively simple
and commonly available skills, which on that account, the incoming
contractors could readily choose to supply by way of others in the labour
market."

The Court of Appeal also confirmed the tribunal decision. Again it stressed
that all factors must be taken into account. Where none of the previous

workforce is taken on, a tribunal should look at the context in which the employers' decision was made. There was significantly more to this case than Initial losing a contract and RCO winning a contract covering the same activities in a different location. There had been a distinctive and organised structure for cleaning and catering at Walton which was replicated at Fazakerley on the moving on the inpatients' services.

Cheeseman and others v R Brewer Contracts Ltd [2001] IRLR 144, EAT
In 1995, Onyx won the contract for responsive maintenance of Teignbridge District Council's let-out housing stock. It acquired the use of the Council's offices, yard and equipment, and took on the fourteen employees who had done this work for the Council. On re-tender in 1998, Brewer won the contract. Brewer did the same work in much the same way, but did not take on any of the workers. No tangible or intangible assets were passed from Onyx to Brewer. Brewer used their own premises, van and workforce.
Mr Cheeseman and other workers who were not taken on brought a tribunal case against Brewer. The employment tribunal said that TUPE did not apply. Again following Süzen, the tribunal said that neither significant assets nor the majority of workers had been transferred. Mr Cheeseman and the others appealed.
The EAT said that the tribunal was wrong to have made the failure to take over the workforce the decisive factor. No single factor should be looked at in isolation. The tribunal also adopted the wrong approach by failing to ask the two separate questions ie, (1) what was the economic entity and (2) did it transfer in the same form. The answer to the first question could affect a tribunal's assessment of the second.
Here, UNISON was arguing that:
1 there was an entity, which consisted of an organised grouping of wage earners who were specifically and permanently assigned to a common task, ie the responsive maintenance contract.
2 the entity transferred. The work continued at the same level for the same client (the Council) in respect of the same housing stock and in very much the same way.
The EAT allowed the appeal and returned the case to the employment tribunal to apply the law correctly. The EAT also set out very useful guidelines on the factors applicable in the two-stage assessment process, summarising the case-law to date.

The revised regulations – service provision changes

By introducing the revised Regulations in October 2005, the government wants to end the uncertainty in many situations as to whether TUPE applies to a transfer. A particularly uncertain area is that of service provision changes in these situations:

→ A service such as cleaning, catering, security or refuse collection is contracted-out or out-sourced, whether by the public or private sector.

→ The service is retendered and reassigned to a new contractor.

→ The service is brought back in-house.

The new Regulations will provide that, where service provision change takes place, if prior to the change, certain employees were assigned to an organised grouping whose principal purpose was to carry out the service activities, then those employees must be treated as if TUPE applies.

As at the time of writing (April 2005), the government envisages that, subject to certain specified exceptions, service provision changes will be comprehensively covered by TUPE. It will not matter that the new employers will carry out the service in a different or novel way, eg by computerisation. The main difficulty will be where there was no organised grouping previously. For example, a courier service was previously undertaken on an ad hoc basis by staff in individual departments, but there is now to be a centralised courier service with a dedicated group of staff serving all departments.

The government anticipates that the impact of the new Regulations will be felt principally in the private sector, because it simply reflects the policy already set out for the public sector in the Cabinet Office Statement of Practice (above).

The legal effect of TUPE

Which workers are protected?

TUPE protects workers employed by the transferor immediately before the transfer or those dismissed in advance for a related reason. It is irrelevant if the member is off work eg due to sickness, holiday or maternity leave, at the time of transfer. S/he is still covered.

It sometimes happens that, before the transfer, the member was working partly on the transferred area of work and partly on other work for the transferor. If so, whether the member transfers will depend on all the facts, especially how much time the member worked on the transferred area of work.

The employers may try to "cherry-pick" employees by moving them around immediately before the transfer, so that any unpopular worker is moved to the activity to be transferred. The law won't allow the artificial use of temp assignments and will look at the reality of where the member was employed immediately before the transfer.

Dismissals

It is automatically unfair dismissal to dismiss a worker for a reason "connected" with the transfer, unless the dismissal is for an economic, technical or organisational ("ETO") reason entailing changes in the workforce. If the ETO reason applies, the worker may still be able to claim ordinary unfair dismissal on the normal basis. Either way, the worker must be an employee with one year's continuous service to gain protection.

It is a question of fact whether a dismissal is connected with the transfer. Dismissals at the time of the transfer are assumed to be connected unless the employers prove otherwise. Dismissals before the transfer or some time afterwards may also be connected. There is no fixed period afterwards within which a dismissal will be "connected". The widespread idea that there is a one-year protected period is a myth. Obviously, the longer after a transfer the dismissal occurs, the harder it is to show a connection. You want to show that the employers always held a secret intention to dismiss or that they still want to equalise terms and conditions with their existing staff.

Many contractors try to phase in changes over a period of time, so that they are not obviously connected with the transfer. They will not always get away with this. In one case, (*Taylor v Connex South Eastern Ltd*, EAT 5.7.00), an accountant was dismissed for refusing to agree changes to his terms and conditions two years after the privatisation of British Rail in 1996. The Employment Appeal Tribunal found the dismissal automatically unfair as, despite the lapse of time, the attempt to change Mr Taylor's employment contract was due to a desire to equalise terms and conditions of all staff, which was still connected with the 1996 transfer.

The ETO exception can severely limit TUPE protection, but it is important to remember that the reason must entail a change in the workforce, ie a change in the overall numbers or in job functions. Employers cannot dismiss simply to change terms and conditions.

If a member is dismissed in connection with the transfer and wishes to claim unfair dismissal, s/he must bring his/her tribunal case within three months of the dismissal. (See p294 on unfair dismissal time-limits.) Depending on what has happened, the case may be against the old employers or against the new employers. This requires specialist advice.

Changing terms and conditions

The new employers stand in the shoes of the old employers for most purposes. TUPE transfers the contractual terms and conditions and all rights, duties and liabilities under the contract, for example wages owed. Continuous service is also preserved on transfers.

The position regarding occupational pensions is complex (see below) and you should ask your regional officer/organiser about this.

If the new employers try to change any terms and conditions without agreement, such changes will not be legally effective. Even an agreed change, if connected with the transfer, may not be binding. If the new employers sack workers for refusing to agree to a change, this will usually amount to automatically unfair dismissal. (Although see the general problems in claiming automatic unfair dismissal set out above.)

The government intends to simplify and clarify the position in the October 2005 Regulations as follows:

1 Variations where the sole reason is the transfer are void ie ineffective.

2 Variations where the reason is connected with the transfer, but are for an ETO reason, are effective provided they are agreed between the parties. (If they are not agreed and the employees are dismissed as a result, see the position on unfair dismissal (above).)

3 TUPE will have no bearing on variations for reasons unconnected with the transfer, even though made at the same time. (For the normal rules on unilateral variation, see p20.)

Unfortunately the protection is not as clear-cut in practice as this all sounds. UNISON brought the key case on this aspect of TUPE: *Wilson v St Helens BC; British Fuels Ltd v Baxendale & Meade* (1998 IRLR 706, HL) It suggests that terms and conditions are retained only if the transferee takes over the worker directly from the old employers, without any intervening dismissal and re-engagement. If the worker was dismissed by the old employers and taken on afresh by the new employers, on different terms and conditions, s/he cannot afterwards insist on the old terms and conditions. All s/he can do is make any available unfair dismissal claim.

It is therefore usually in the interests of the transferring authority as well as the members that the latter are taken on by the new contractors with no intervening dismissals. This is exactly what the Cabinet Office Statement of Practice encourages.

Pensions

This is an exceptionally complicated area. It is important for branches to get details of the transferee's pension proposals at the earliest possible stage. **Any problems or uncertainty should be referred immediately to the regional officer/organiser,** who can seek specialist advice. This book does not provide a full guide.

Although terms and conditions generally transfer under TUPE, the position regarding pensions is different. The Acquired Rights Directive allows member states to determine whether to force new employers to provide a comparable pension provision. The only exception is regarding benefits paid as compensation for premature retirement, eg the payment of an immediate unreduced pension where a member is made redundant over the age of 50. These do transfer.

There is detailed guidance on pensions in Annex A to the Cabinet Office Statement of Practice entitled "A Fair Deal for Staff Pensions". (See p142 for the status of the guidance.) Annex A states the new employers should provide a broadly comparable pension scheme with a bulk transfer option.

The Code of Practice deals with pensions at 4 and 10, and also requires local authorities to apply the principles set out in Annex A. As an alternative, contractors with local authorities can enter into an admission agreement to allow workers to remain in the Local Government Pension Scheme after transfer. This is normally only possible in the NHS if the new employers are a non-profit making organisation.

In all cases, branches should seek to ensure that NHS or local authority employers sign up to the relevant guidance in annex A.

The Pensions Act 2004 and the Transfer of Employment (Pension Protection) Regulations 2005 introduced a minimum occupational pension entitlement to transferred employees who had such an entitlement with their employers before the transfer. Unfortunately there is no requirement that the post-transfer pension is equivalent to the original scheme. In the public sector, the government has said it will continue to follow the more generous policy set out in Annex A.

UNISON's Pensions Unit continues to monitor how transfers are operating in practice and welcomes updates from branches and regions in this respect.

Public Sector Transfers: The code and the statement of practice

For local government employees and others who are covered, the Code of Practice requires contractors to confirm their obligations to protect employees' terms and conditions when they transfer.

But even where TUPE applies, its protection may be inadequate, as explained above. To win contracts, companies may tender on an unsustainable economic basis without making future redundancies or cutting pay. In an attempt to avoid this, the Statement of Practice says the contracting authority should ensure it is satisfied that bidders' proposals fully meet the requirements of TUPE.

New joiners

UNISON lobbied hard for legislation to help prevent a two tier system whereby new employees were employed on less favourable terms and conditions than transferred employees. The government states in the Code of Practice:

→ Overall, new employees must be employed on no less favourable terms and conditions (apart from pensions) than those of transferred employees. Unfortunately this does mean that they can have different terms and conditions, some being more favourable and some being less favourable.

→ New joiners must be offered pension provision, which may be either membership of the local government pension scheme, membership of a good quality employer pension scheme or membership of a stakeholder pension scheme with an employer contribution. It is a pity that stakeholder pensions are one of the options because they may offer lower pension benefits.

→ The contractor will consult trade union representatives (where the union is recognised) on the terms and conditions to be offered to new joiners. This should be a genuine dialogue. The intention is that contractors and trade unions should be able to agree on a package of terms and conditions, in keeping with the terms of the Code.

Equal opportunities and discrimination

It is unfortunately possible that the new employers will not take on staff or will treat them less favourably due to their ethnic origin, sex or disability. The legislation forbidding discrimination on these grounds is wider than unfair dismissal legislation and does not require one year's service.

UNISON's "Getting Equal" Campaign Pack (Bibliography, p314) contains a leaflet on the equal pay issues which may arise with privatisation. UNISON brought an important test case (*Lawrence v Regent Office Care Ltd*) concerning the effect of a transfer on equal pay claims.

Lawrence v Regent Office Care Ltd [2002] IRLR 822; 110 EOR 27, ECJ
In the original case, Ratcliffe v North Yorkshire County Council, the council's Direct Services Organisation reduced the pay of catering assistants (who were almost exclusively female) in order to compete successfully on a compulsory competitive tendering exercise. Three women successfully brought an equal pay claim, comparing themselves with male council workers, who had been rated equivalent on a job evaluation scheme.
Since then, some of the women were transferred to a private sector employer, which reduced their pay. In the Lawrence case, they claimed equal pay under Article 141. The Court of Appeal asked the ECJ to rule whether the women (now employed by a private company) can still compare their pay with male Council staff.
Unfortunately the ECJ decided that although Article 141 is not limited to situations where men and women work for the same employer, it does not cover a situation like this, where the pay differences cannot be attributed to a single source.
Arguably this goes against the spirit of the TUPE Regulations , but the ECJ insisted on seeing the local authority and its contractors as acting independently for the purposes of equal pay law.

TUPE and trade unions

Collective agreements

TUPE transfers any collective agreements in force at the time of the transfer so that they are effective between the union and the new employers. Pre-transfer recognition carries over to new employers, where the undertaking transferred maintains a distinct identity from the transferee's undertaking. This does not in itself prevent the new employers derecognising UNISON, but the general rules on union recognition help safeguard the future position.

If terms of a collective agreement are incorporated into the contracts of individual workers, then these are protected in the usual way as individual contractual rights. (See p15.)

Trade union consultation

There are statutory rules as to how and when consultation must take place on transfers. These are set out in the Collective Redundancies and Transfer of Undertakings (Protection of Employment) (Amendment) Regulations 1995 as amended by the 1999 Regulations of the same name. Employers must consult with the trade union, or if there is none, with correctly elected employee representatives. Consultation must be with the representatives of any workers employed by the transferee or transferor who may be affected by the transfer or measures taken in connection with it. This includes workers who are not employed in the undertaking to be transferred, but who are affected by the consequences of the transfer.

Regulation 10(2) sets out the nature of information which must be provided to UNISON in sufficient time before a relevant transfer to enable consultation to take place. This includes:

→ Confirmation of the transfer and when it will take place.

→ The reason for the transfer.

→ The legal, economic and social implications of the transfer for the affected workers.

If the employers fail to consult, UNISON can bring a tribunal case for a declaration that the employers have not consulted. The tribunal may award compensation to each affected worker up to 13 weeks' pay for each. The amount will be affected by the seriousness and degree of the employers' failure. UNISON must bring the claim within three months of the Transfer. It is likely that under the October 2005 Regulations, a claim will be able to be brought against either the transferor or the transferee. This threat will encourage both parties to ensure consultation takes place.

If there are to be collective redundancies at the same time as the transfer, there are similar (though not identical) rules on trade union consultation regarding these. (See p133.)

TUPE: Myths

● *Myth:*
The TUPE Regulations apply to all contracting-out situations.
Truth:
Not necessarily. See p143 onwards.

● *Myth:*
Where the TUPE Regulations apply, it is automatically unfair to dismiss a worker in connection with the transfer.
Truth:
It is not automatically unfair to dismiss the member if the dismissal was for an economic, technical or organisational reason entailing a change in the workforce. In that case, the member can only claim ordinary unfair dismissal, if it was unfair for other reasons. Also note that the member needs one year's service as an employee to make an automatic or ordinary unfair dismissal claim.

● *Myth:*
After a TUPE transfer, the new employers cannot change the terms and conditions of the transferring employees for one year.
Truth:
The law is rather complicated. (See p151-52.) There is no special one year protected period. The new employers are not supposed to change terms and conditions for reasons connected with the transfer at any stage. However, they may be able to change terms and conditions for unconnected reasons, again at any stage. (See position on unilateral variation of contract where TUPE does not apply, p20.)

TUPE: Key points

- The TUPE Regulations should implement the European Business Transfers Directive. European law is therefore influential.
- The 1981 TUPE Regulations are to be revised by 2005 Regulations, with effect from 1st October 2005.
- The Regulations protect the rights of employees when there is a relevant transfer.
- Legally it may be hard to decide whether the transfer is covered by TUPE. However, contracting out, changing contractors and taking a service back in-house can be covered.
- There is a 2-stage test: (1) is there an economic entity? (2) has it transferred in a recognisable form?
- Under the 2005 Regulations, it is intended that virtually all service provision changes are covered, provided there was an organised group of employees supplying the service before the transfer.
- Even where TUPE applies, there are practical disadvantages to transfers and UNISON may wish to campaign against them.
- The government has issued a Statement of Practice on staff transfers in the public sector to encourage good practice in local authorities, the NHS and central government.
- It has also issued a local authority Code of Practice, which will be enforceable by the authorities. The Code is being extended to cover NHS, maintained schools and the civil service. The Code incorporates the principles of the Statement of Practice and has additional content.
- The Code requires new joiners to be employed on no less favourable terms and conditions than transferring employees.
- Where TUPE applies, it preserves terms and conditions and continuous service, although the position on occupational pensions is complex.
- It is automatically unfair to dismiss an employee with 1 year's service for a reason connected with the transfer unless it is an ETO reason entailing a change in the workforce. In the latter case, it may still be ordinary unfair dismissal.
- There may be discriminatory consequences of a transfer. It may also affect equal pay comparisons.
- The employers must inform and consult UNISON where its members may be affected by the transfer.

Chapter 8:

Race discrimination

Contents

Legal framework

The law against race discrimination in employment and other areas is
set out in the Race Relations Act 1976 ("RRA").

A "Code of Practice for the elimination of racial discrimination and
the promotion of equal opportunity in employment" came into effect
on 1st April 1984. The Code was made by the Commission for Racial
Equality ("CRE") under section 47 of the RRA. The Code lays down
guidelines for good employment practice but it is not legally enforceable in itself. However, a tribunal must take into account any relevant
provision of the Code in reaching its decision. The Code is also a useful tool for negotiating with employers. The CRE has just completed a
consultation on revising the Code.

In 2000, the European Council issued a Directive on Equal Treatment
Between Persons Irrespective of Racial or Ethnic Origins. This is usu-
ally known as the "Race Directive" or the "Race Discrimination
Directive". Although the RRA had already existed for many years in
GB, the Directive made the law more beneficial in a few areas, eg the
definition of indirect discrimination and harassment, and the change

in the burden of proof.

The Directive explicitly applies to discrimination on grounds of race, ethnic origin or national origin, but not nationality or colour. Unfortunately the government decided to implement the Directive by regulations made under the European Communities Act rather than primary legislation. Such regulations can go no further than what is required by EU law. As a result, race discrimination law is more limited in certain respects where it applies to nationality and, arguably, colour. Fortunately the tribunals are tending to ignore the latter and assume that discrimination linked to colour is also race discrimination. Certain public bodies have additional positive duties introduced by the Race Relations Amendment Act 2000 (see p177).

The commission for racial equality

The CRE is the organisation set up under the RRA with overall responsibility to work towards the elimination of race discrimination. As well as its policy and educational functions, it runs some individual tribunal cases.

Which workers are covered

There is no minimum service requirement under the RRA. The RRA protects amongst others:

→ Job applicants.

→ Employees.

→ The self-employed working on a contract personally to execute any work.

→ Work-trainees.

→ Contract workers. Under the RRA, "contract worker" has a special meaning. The RRA covers discrimination by a "principal" against an employee of another organisation who is provided under a contract. This would probably cover:

– Discrimination by a local authority against an employee of a contract cleaner or caterer.

– Discrimination by an NHS trust against an agency employee supplied to work for the trust under a contract between the trust and the agency.

What does 'race' mean?

Section 3 of the RRA says that employers must not discriminate in connection with someone's colour, race, nationality, national origin or ethnic origin. Case-law has decided that Jews and Sikhs fall into the meaning of "ethnic origin" but Muslims do not.

The RRA does not cover discrimination against purely religious groups. However sometimes religious groups can gain some protection from the RRA if the discrimination against them amounts to indirect race discrimination against people of a certain "racial" group. For example, certain dress requirements may indirectly discriminate against women of Pakistani national origin.

Since December 2003, there has been a specific law against religious discrimination under the Employment Equality (Religion or Belief) Regulations 2003 (see Chapter 11). These are structured in the same way as the RRA, Sex Discrimination Act and Employment Equality (Sexual Orientation) Regulations.

Vicarious liability

As a general rule, the employers are automatically responsible for any discrimination by one worker or manager against another in the course of employment. This is so even if the top people in the organisation did not know what their junior managers were doing. This is called "vicarious liability".

The employers cannot escape responsibility by dealing promptly with the discrimination once they find out, eg in a harassment case, by sacking the perpetrator. The employers will still be responsible for the harassment that has already happened - although they will avoid additional liability for mishandling the issue once it comes to light.

Employers often do not realise that they can be held legally responsible for discrimination carried out by one manager or worker against another, even if they did not know about such discrimination and did not approve of it. This is a powerful incentive for employers to take effective preventative action.

The employers' only defence will be if they had taken all reasonably practicable steps to prevent such discrimination ever occurring. In practice, employers can rarely use this defence. It means operating an equal opportunities policy very actively indeed. Paper policies are not enough.

When may discrimination happen?

Unlike the law on unfair dismissal, the RRA does not only cover dismissal situations. In section 4 it forbids discrimination in a whole range of employment situations. In summary, employers must not discriminate against a worker:

→ When choosing whether to employ him/her.
→ When choosing whether to promote him/her.
→ In the terms and conditions offered to a worker or on which s/he is employed.
→ In offering training opportunities.
→ In access to benefits and services generally.
→ By dismissing him/her.
→ By subjecting him/her to any other detriment, eg disciplinary action, racial abuse or harassment. (See Chapter 12 on harassment.)

Because discrimination (whether direct, indirect or victimisation) can occur at so many points, you need to be constantly alert to the possibility.

In some circumstances it is unlawful to discriminate against a worker once s/he has left employment, eg by supplying a discriminatory reference.

The definition of unlawful discrimination

Overview

There are four kinds of unlawful discrimination under the RRA: direct discrimination, indirect discrimination, victimisation and harassment. Each of these words has a very precise legal meaning, which is different from its meaning in natural every-day language. You need to remember this.

Summary of legal definitions

The following is a summary. For more detail of each definition, see the remainder of this Chapter.

Direct discrimination: s1(1)(a)

This is where the member is treated differently because of his/her race. For example, the employers fail to recruit the member because s/he is black. There is no defence to direct discrimination. You should always ask the "but for" question, ie

"If the member was of a different race (but for the member's race), would the employers have treated him/her the same way?"

Indirect discrimination: s1(1A) or s1(1)(b)

This is where the member fails to get a job or is selected for redundancy or is otherwise disadvantaged:

→ because of a particular requirement, condition, provision, criterion or practice applied by the employers; and

→ that requirement etc.. would particularly disadvantage others of the member's racial group; and

→ the employers cannot justify applying the requirement etc.

For example, the member is Italian and she is rejected from a job because she cannot speak fluent English, even though her English is quite good. A requirement for fluent English would disproportionately exclude workers from non-English-speaking countries. Whether or not it is justifiable would depend on the nature of the job.

Victimisation: s2

This is where the member is punished or treated less favourably because s/he has complained about race discrimination in some way, eg in a tribunal, formally or informally, on his/her own behalf or on behalf of someone else.

For example, the member brings a grievance regarding race discrimination by her manager. Shortly afterwards she is made redundant.

The employers can defend a case of victimisation if the member's complaint of race discrimination was false and made in bad faith.

Harassment: s3A

This is where, on grounds of race, ethnic or national origins, the harasser engages in unwanted conduct with the purpose or effect of violating the member's dignity or creating an intimidating, hostile, degrading, humiliating or offensive environment.

Several types of discrimination

More than one type of discrimination may have taken place. For example, a member complains about racist practices by his/her employers. Shortly afterwards, s/he fails to gain promotion. This may be:

1 Direct discrimination in respect of the original racist practices.

2 Direct discrimination or victimisation in respect of the failure to get promotion.

The member may also have suffered discrimination on more than one ground. For example a black woman may be subjected to racial and sexual harassment at the same time, or may have failed to gain promotion because she is a woman and because she is black. You need to consider the facts to see whether they clearly indicate one ground is dominant or whether they are consistent with both grounds being present.

A focused approach

The Macpherson Report following the murder of Stephen Lawrence, made the concept of "institutional racism" well-known. Regrettably this concept cannot be used when writing a tribunal race discrimination claim. The RRA only deals with the more limited concepts of direct discrimination, indirect discrimination and victimisation
When considering whether there is a tribunal case under the RRA, you should focus on these four questions, in the order set out:

1 What are the incidents of bad treatment about which the member is complaining? These are the potential "acts of discrimination". For example, refusal to promote or giving a disciplinary warning. If the member complains generally about lack of career progression, you need to identify the specific acts of discriminatory treatment by the employers, eg refusal of a specific promotion application; refusal to give a specific overtime opportunity; failure to offer training.

2 On what date did each act of discrimination occur? (This is very important for time-limits. See p295.)

3 Who carried out the act of discrimination? (It may not always possible to identify the decision-makers.)

4 What type of discrimination (direct, indirect or victimisation) does each act seem to be? It may be more than one type.

Direct discrimination

Direct discrimination is the most obvious form of discrimination. The formal definition is in RRA 1976 s1(1)(a) :

"A person discriminates against another if on racial grounds he treats that other less favourably than he treats or would treat other persons."

This introduces the central idea of comparisons. Ideally the member would find another worker of a different race who has been treated differently or better by the employers in comparable circumstances. For example:

■ A black and white worker with the same or equivalent experience and qualifications apply for a job. The white candidate is successful.
■ A black and a white worker get into a fight. The black worker is dismissed, the white worker is only warned.

If the member does find a comparator, the employers will probably try to provide an "innocent" explanation as to why they treated the white worker more favourably. For example, they may say that the black worker started the fight or had a worse disciplinary record.

It is not always possible to find an exact comparator. Even so, a less precise comparison will still be a useful indication of how the employers might have treated the member if s/he were white. For example: A black worker is sacked for sleeping on duty. Last month, a white worker only received a warning for unauthorised absence from work (an equivalent or more serious offence).

Obviously the bigger the differences between the member's circumstances and those of the comparator, the easier it is for the employers to explain away the different treatment.

It is not necessary to have a comparator to win a direct discrimination case – it is just harder to prove that the employers' behaviour is discriminatory as opposed to merely unfair. The crucial legal question is the "but for" question ie,

"But for" the fact that the member is black, would the employers have promoted (warned, dismissed etc.) him/her?

The employers' motives

The employers' motives are irrelevant. What matters is what the employers do. Obviously it is easier to prove discrimination where the employers display racial prejudice or stereotyped attitudes, but it is not essential that this is present. Direct discrimination is still unlawful even if the employers believe they have a good reason, eg commercial or workforce pressures. Employers may not recruit a black worker for any of the following reasons, but in each case it would still be unlawful direct discrimination:

– Fear of loss of business due to customer disapproval.
– Junior white workers will not accept a black manager.
– It is a dangerous location where the worker may be subjected to racial attack.

A manager may not be personally prejudiced and may even act with good intentions, but if s/he treats a black worker differently from how s/he would treat a white worker in the same circumstances, s/he has directly discriminated. Discrimination may even be unconscious, as recognised by the House of Lords in the case of Nagarajan v London Regional Transport (1999 IRLR 572, HL):

"All human beings have preconceptions, beliefs, attitudes and prejudices on many subjects. It is part of our make-up. Moreover, we do not always recognise our own prejudices. Many people are unable, or unwilling, to admit even to themselves that actions of theirs may be racially motivated. An employer may genuinely believe that the reason why he rejected an applicant had nothing to do with the applicant's race. After careful and thorough investigation of the claim, members of an employment tribunal may decide that the proper inference to be drawn from the evidence is that whether the employer realised it at the time or not, race was the reason why he acted as he did ..... Members of racial groups need protection from conduct driven by unconscious prejudice as much as from conscious and deliberate discrimination."

There is no defence to direct discrimination. Different treatment, whatever the motive, is inexcusable. However there are some limited exceptions for genuine occupational qualifications or requirements (see p175).

Tang v Birmingham City Council ET 46192/1996

Mr Tang, a UNISON member, won his case of race discrimination against Birmingham Council.

Mr Tang was a Chinese Information Manager. He requested 5 days special leave to care for his sick wife. His line manager (Mr Downer) granted only 3 days, despite a certificate from Mr Tang's doctor confirming that Mr Tang needed to remain at home with his wife for a week. In the same period, Mr Tang's own secretary, who was white, was granted 8 days special leave to visit her sick mother in Paris.

The tribunal found that Mr Downer treated Mr Tang differently to his white colleagues in his handling of applications for paternity and special leave. This was on racial grounds. There were also many other incidents of discriminatory treatment against Mr Tang.

Evidence of direct discrimination

The following types of evidence help prove direct discrimination:

■ **Racist remarks.** These help to prove the employers held hostile or stereotyped views, which make it more likely that the member was less favourably treated on racial grounds. Employers usually deny the remarks and they can be hard to prove. Especially if there are no witnesses, it is important that the member complained about the remarks at an early stage and is precise and consistent about what was said. Note that you can still prove race discrimination even if no racist remarks were made.

■ **Comparators.** Usually the most helpful evidence in a direct discrimination case is to show that the employers treated a white worker differently or better in similar circumstances. The comparison need not be identical.

■ **Extremely unfair or irrational treatment of the member.** Even if there is evidence of discriminatory attitudes by the employers, it is important also to discredit their reasons for treating the member this way on this occasion. On the other hand, unfair treatment of the member is not enough on its own to prove discrimination, because the employers may treat everyone unfairly regardless of race. However, if there is other evidence that the treatment was on racial grounds, or that the employers usually treat workers fairly, this will help.

■ **Statistics and patterns.** It is helpful to prove that the employers disproportionately discipline, dismiss, recruit or promote certain racial groups and not others. This is one reason why monitoring is so important. (See p177.) But the fact that the employers disproportionately discipline black workers does not mean that the member has been discriminated against in the particular case.

■ **Poor equal opportunities procedures.** Failure to follow any relevant provision in the CRE Code of Practice or poor equal opportunities procedures or practices generally are helpful background evidence, but not enough on their own. You still need to prove the member would have been treated differently on the relevant occasion had s/he been white.

■ **The employers' explanation.** It is crucial to pin down the employers' explanation for the relevant treatment of the member. If the employers cannot provide a satisfactory explanation of their treatment, or why they treated the member differently from any comparator, the tribunal may well conclude there has been race discrimination.

To prove discrimination, you need an enquiring mind and a willingness to investigate details. There are checklists for promotion (p184), disciplinary/dismissal (p181) and redundancy (p128). There is also the special questionnaire procedure under the RRA which can help you obtain the level of evidence you need (see p300).

Indirect discrimination

There are now two definitions of indirect discrimination. The original definition of indirect discrimination is set out in section 1(1)(b) and still applies to discrimination related to nationality and, arguably, colour. There is a slightly different definition under section 1(1A) where discrimination relates to race or ethnic or national origins. "Race" probably includes colour (see comments on p161).

Indirect discrimination under s1(1)(b) occurs when the employers apply a requirement or condition which the member cannot comply with and which proportionally fewer of the member's racial group than others could comply with.

Indirect discrimination under s1(1A) occurs when the employers apply a provision, criterion or practice which puts the member at a disadvantage and which puts or would put others of the same race or national or ethnic origins at a particular disadvantage.

Unlike direct discrimination, there is a defence to indirect discrimination if the employers can justify applying the requirement or condition. Under s1(1A), the employers must show the provision, criterion or practice is a proportionate means of achieving a legitimate aim.

An example of indirect discrimination under either definition is this: Some employers insist that job applicants speak fluent English. This would particularly disadvantage and disproportionately exclude candidates born in non-English speaking countries. The employers may be able to justify the requirement if the job is to teach English, but it would probably be unjustifiable for a manual job.

It is important to identify indirectly discriminatory practices in the workplace, but individual cases can be hard to run due to the technicalities of the legal definition.

Hidden requirements, criteria and practices

In everyday working practices and policies, there are countless hidden requirements, criteria and practices which disadvantage certain groups of workers. These requirements often create unnecessary barriers to true equal opportunities for getting jobs, promotion and improvement in pay and conditions.

Some requirements, criteria or practices with adverse effects are unavoidable and it is not unlawful for employers to impose requirements etc which they can objectively justify. However, many requirements and practices cannot be justified once challenged.

Discriminatory requirements, criteria and practices are often hidden and members may not themselves notice them. When a black or minority ethnic member brings a grievance to you, you need to consider whether any hidden discriminatory requirements or practices have caused the problem. More generally, employers' systems and policies, existing and new, need to be carefully examined for their effects.

Discriminatory requirements, criteria and practices may be imposed in a whole range of working situations. On p179 is a list of requirements etc which, unless justifiable, often have a discriminatory effect on black or foreign-born workers. (Many such requirements also affect other disadvantaged groups and particularly women.) Pages 184 and 128 give examples of requirements to be wary of in promotion and redundancy situations.

Sometimes employers adopt a preference which is discriminatory, but it falls short of a requirement. Under the s1(1)(b) definition, the law only prohibits discriminatory requirements which operate as a complete bar as opposed to a preference. However, this would not be a problem under s1A, which refers to "practices".

Can the member meet the requirement / is s/he at a disadvantage?

Indirect discrimination occurs where a worker is disadvantaged or cannot meet a particular requirement at the time it is imposed. This should not be taken too literally and includes the following situations:

■ **A worker physically cannot comply with the requirement.** For example: a requirement that workers be over 6' tall would disadvantage people from certain countries.

■ **A worker cannot meet the requirement at the time it is imposed.** For example: a requirement that workers have lived in a certain borough for 3 years or that they possess an English Language CSE. It is irrelevant that the particular worker debarred by this requirement is capable of acquiring the CSE in the near future or that s/he could easily move to the borough and live there for 3 years. What is relevant is that s/he could not meet the requirement at the time it mattered ie, to get the job or avoid dismissal.

■ **A worker cannot consistently with his/her cultural/community obligations meet the requirement.** For example: a requirement to be clean shaven or to wear a short-skirted uniform. In theory Sikhs could shave their beards and Muslim women could wear the uniform, but in practical terms they could not do so.

A worker who simply prefers not to meet the requirement, but is not unable to do so in the senses set out above, cannot claim indirect discrimination. For example: a man wishes to have a beard because he thinks it suits him, but not for any cultural/religious reason.

Can other of the same racial group meet the requirement/Are other disadvantaged?

It is not sufficient that a particular worker cannot meet a requirement. It is also necessary to show that many other workers of the same racial group would have the same difficulty. But it is not necessary to show that a requirement excludes all members of the relevant racial group. You need only show that the requirement excludes proportionally more workers of that racial group than others.

For example: a requirement that workers hold British qualifications would not exclude all workers of non-British nationality, but would bar more of them than workers of British nationality.

Is the requirement or practice justifiable?

Many requirements and conditions are imposed in everyday working life which adversely affect minority ethnic workers. However, many of these requirements are necessary and cannot be challenged. If the employers can prove that it was "justifiable" to impose the requirement, then it will not be unlawful.

The meaning of "justifiable" has been set out in case-law. In summary:

→ It is not enough for employers to say that they considered their reasons for imposing the requirement / condition adequate. The requirement must be objectively justifiable regardless of race, not simply justifiable in the personal opinion of the particular employers.

→ The requirement must serve a real business need of the employers, eg administrative efficiency, hygiene, safety or significant economic savings.

→ Whether there is sufficient justification will depend on the facts and circumstances of the particular case. The more people from a particular racial group are adversely affected by a particular requirement, the better justification the employers must provide.

Requirements should be kept to the minimum necessary for the employers' needs. Where there is a fairer way of achieving the same end, the requirement is unlikely to be justifiable.

Under the section 1(1A) definition, the employers must show that applying the provision, criterion or practice is a proportionate means of achieving a legitimate aim. This seems to reflect the above principles, which apply to the original section 1(1)(b) definition.

Action

Do not just wait for members to complain to you about indirect discrimination. You should be alert to policies and practices which ought to be challenged.

■ Consider access to opportunities such as acting-up, overtime, pay bonuses, training and promotion. Are these governed by indirectly discriminatory criteria?

■ Check there is no indirect discrimination in recruitment, promotion and redundancy procedures. (See pp184 and 128).

■ Ensure that a variety of work practices are monitored so that indirectly discriminatory criteria can be identified and avoided for redundancy selection criteria. (See p128.)

■ Where you identify criteria and practices which may indirectly discriminate, UNISON would want to negotiate with the employers to change them. Research indicates that employers impose many discriminatory criteria without realising, or without even considering whether the criteria are necessary.

Victimisation

Under the RRA "victimisation" has a specific meaning, which is different from the normal meaning of the word. Employers must not victimise a worker by punishing him/her for raising the issue of race discrimination. Section 2 states that a worker must not be less favourably treated because s/he has done a "protected act" or because the employers think s/he has done or may in the future do a protected act. The protected acts include:

→ Taking a tribunal case of race discrimination.

→ Bringing a formal grievance about race discrimination.

→ Making an informal allegation of race discrimination, verbally or in writing.

→ Giving evidence for a colleague who is bringing a tribunal case or grievance about race discrimination.
→ Doing anything else by reference to the RRA, eg contacting the CRE.

Examples of victimisation:
– A worker is sacked because s/he brings a grievance complaining about race discrimination in a recent failed promotion attempt
– A worker is transferred because s/he complains that work colleagues are making racist remarks.

The employers' only defence is if the worker's allegation of race discrimination was false and it was made in bad faith. As long as the worker genuinely believes s/he was discriminated against, it is unlawful to victimise him/her.

Evidence of victimisation

Victimisation is extremely common and you should be careful not to miss it. The law provides important protection, but you must remember that it may be hard to prove. The member needs to prove:

■ **S/he did a protected act.** If what triggered the victimisation was only a verbal allegation of race discrimination, this can be hard to prove. Another common problem is if the member wrote an ambiguous letter or grievance form referring to "unfair treatment" or even "discrimination" but not to "race discrimination". The employers may have understood it as an accusation of race discrimination and victimised the member as a consequence, but later they will say they never understood the race issue had been raised. To prevent this difficulty, if you are advising a member who is considering raising an allegation of race discrimination, ensure s/he mentions it unambiguously in writing first.

■ **The discriminator knew of the protected act.** There must be some connection between knowledge of the member's allegation of race discrimination and less favourable treatment of the member as a result. It is helpful to prove that the person victimising the member was upset about the protected act and changed his/her attitude towards the member thereafter. However, as a matter of law, the victimiser need not have been consciously influenced by knowledge of the protected act.

■ **A connection between the protected act and the subsequent victimisation.**
– Legally it does not matter how much time passes between the protected act and the victimisation, but it is easier to prove a connection if the two events are close together.
– Compare the treatment of the member before and after s/he did the protected act. For example, before s/he complained of victimisation, the worker was allowed to work through lunch-breaks and leave early on Fridays; afterwards s/he was not.
– Compare the treatment of the member with that of other workers. For example, other workers are allowed to leave early and make up their time during lunch-breaks.

Action
Victimisation is an industrial relations issue as well as a legal issue. Many employers with policies against direct and indirect discrimination have not even thought about how to avoid victimising a worker who makes an allegation of racism.

An employment tribunal in Birmingham has commented: "Perhaps the question of victimisation has not been sufficiently publicised and yet it is a very important part of the Act. Indeed a very important part of race relations philosophy, and as a matter of public policy employers should be made more aware of their responsibilities in this connection."

You should ensure that a definition of victimisation is included in your employers' equal opportunities policy and that it is included in any legal training. You should give some time to think about how it can be prevented in practice.

Harassment
There is a specific offence of harassment under section 3A of the RRA, where it is on grounds of race, ethnic or national origins. If harassment is on other grounds, it must be brought within the definition of direct discrimination.

Under s3A, a harasser harasses the member if:
– on grounds of race or ethnic or national origins;
– s/he engages in unwanted conduct;
– which has the purpose or effect;
– of violating the member's dignity or creating an intimidating,

hostile, degrading, humiliating or offensive environment for the member;

– *and* it should reasonably be regarded as having that effect, taking account of all the circumstances, including in particular the perception of the harassed member.

This definition is replicated in the other discrimination legislation (although a slightly expanded definition will be brought into the SDA from October 2005). For further detail on harassment cases generally, see Chapter 12.

Some permitted race discrimination

Genuine Occupational Qualifications (GOQs)

This is another area where there are two legal definitions. The following definition of Genuine Occupational Qualifications applies where discrimination is on grounds of colour or nationality.

It is permitted to discriminate where being of a particular racial group is a GOQ for a job. Such discrimination may only occur in selecting who to offer a job, promote, transfer or train. It does not allow discrimination in the terms of the job or in access to benefits, facilities or services, or in dismissal or any other detriment.

GOQs are set out specifically and interpreted in a restrictive way by the courts. The categories are set out below, although the exact wording of the RRA should be referred to in any case.

It is not necessary for all the job duties to fall within the GOQ categories; it is enough if only some of the duties are covered. However, employers may not use the GOQ defence if they already have employees of the relevant racial group who could cover the relevant duties without undue inconvenience.

The categories

Being of a particular racial group is a genuine occupational qualification for a job only where it is:

■ For authenticity in drama or other entertainment.

■ For authenticity as an artist's or photographic model.

■ For reasons of authenticity where the job involves working in a place where food or drink is sold to the public in a particular setting.

■ The job holder provides persons of that racial group with personal services promoting their welfare and those services can most effectively be provided by a person of that racial group.

Genuine Occupational Requirements (GORs)

In relation to discrimination on grounds of race or ethnic or national origins, the exceptions are not limited to the specified categories. It is an exception where being of a particular race or ethnic or national origin is a genuine and determining occupational requirement and it is "proportionate" to apply it in the particular case. This is intended to be a very limited exception and should only apply where it is appropriate and necessary for the worker to be of a particular race, ethnic or national origin.

Special needs

It is permitted to discriminate in order to provide persons of a particular racial group access to facilities or services to meet their special needs in regard to education, training or welfare.

Positive action

Where within the previous 12 months, the proportion of workers of a particular racial group doing a particular kind of work was comparatively small, the employers may

→ Offer training exclusively to that racial group.

→ Exclusively encourage workers of that racial group to apply for jobs.

Note that the employers are not obliged to undertake any positive action. They are also not allowed to discriminate at the point of selection for a job.

Statutory disputes resolution procedures

If the member is an employee and wishes to bring a tribunal case against his/her employer for race discrimination, the statutory disputes resolution procedures will apply. If s/he wishes to complain about dismissal, the statutory minimum disciplinary and dismissal procedure (DDP) will apply. If s/he wishes to complain about anything else, including constructive dismissal, s/he must bring an internal grievance before starting a tribunal claim. There are a few exceptions, for example, if s/he has been subjected to harassment and fears that going through a grievance will cause him/her to be subjected to further harassment. For full details of the rules, exceptions and effect on time-limits, see p57 onwards.

Section 71 and duties of public bodies

The Race Relations (Amendment) Act 2000 ("RR(A)A") extended the scope of the RRA to forbid discrimination by the police and other public authorities in carrying out any of their functions. This is set out in an expanded section 19 of the RRA and is relevant to the non-employment parts of the RRA, which are beyond the scope of this book.

The RR(A)A also introduced a new section 71 into the RRA, which places a positive duty on a public authority "in carrying out its functions to have due regard to the need (a) to eliminate unlawful race discrimination; and (b) to promote equality of opportunity and good relations between persons of different racial groups". This would include the authority's employment functions.

Schedule 1A lists which authorities are subject to the section 71 duty: it includes central and local government, the NHS, water, fire and police authorities, and educational bodies. The full text of the RR(A)A is set out on the HMSO website (see p319).

Specific duties for public authorities have been set out in Regulations. Authorities were required to publish a Race Equality Scheme by 31st May 2002. Also, with a few listed exceptions, the authorities in their capacity as employers had to put monitoring in place by the same date. Authorities must monitor existing staff, job applicants, staff applications for training and promotion. Authorities with 150 or more full-time staff must also monitor disciplinaries, grievances, performance appraisals, training and leavers. Results must be published annually.

The public authorities are legally required to review their list of functions, policies and proposed policies, for relevance to the general statutory duty every 3 years. This is to ensure their Race Equality Scheme is kept up to date and there are effective arrangements for implementation. The review deadline for public authorities in England and Wales is 31st May 2005, and for most public authorities in Scotland, is 30th November 2005.

The CRE has enforcement powers if these duties are not carried out. It has produced a statutory code of practice and four non-statutory guides which give practical guidance to help authorities meet their duty. There is a separate Code and guidance for authorities in Scotland. The code and guides can be obtained from the Stationery Office (tel: 0870 240 3697) or via e-mail from cre@tso.co.uk or can be downloaded from the CRE website (see Bibliography). There is also detailed guidance on completing the statutory three-year review on the CRE's website.

The statutory Code of Practice on the Duty to Promote Race Equality is a useful negotiating tool, expanding on the basic obligations to monitor and publish results annually. The Code recommends:

– When a public authority publishes results, it should explain how it is dealing with trends or problems highlighted by its monitoring. (Clause 5.7)

– It may be useful to combine and analyse monitoring data with other data, eg on sex and disability. (Clause 5.7)

– If monitoring shows that current employment policies and practice are leading to unlawful discrimination, the authority should take steps to end the discrimination. As a first step, the authority should examine each of its procedures closely to find out how discrimination might be happening.

– Consulting people through various methods, especially those likely to be affected by a policy, and taking account of their views. (Clauses 4.20-4.22)

UNISON has produced a Guide to Branches on the Race Relations (Amendment) Act 2000 (stock no.2122). There are also two UNISON negotiating guides which may help in negotiating on race issues with the employers: "Local Bargaining – A guide for UNISON negotiators" (stock no.1801) and a guide on issues arising out of the Stephen Lawrence enquiry (stock no.1761). These are available through your branch from UNISON'S Communications Unit. There is further information on negotiating and equality issues on UNISON's website.

Checklist: possibly discriminatory requirements and conditions

Qualifications
- Formal qualifications.
- Qualifications only obtainable in GB.
- University degree.
- Qualifications from certain universities / organisations / Oxbridge.
- English language qualifications.

Language / Expression / Culture / Confidence
- English language fluency - written / verbal.
- Communication skills.
- Writing skills.
- Essay-based tests and application forms.
- Psychometric testing.
- Culturally-biased testing.
- Fluency in interview performance.
- Acquiring new technical skills / knowledge, within short time periods / without special training (difficult in an unfamiliar language / with foreign technology).

Experience / service / Paid employment
- Previous kinds of work experience.
- Previous management experience.
- Already being at a certain grade / holding a certain high level job.
- Previous (fast) promotions.
- Previous width / variation of experience.
- Length of previous experience or service in certain positions / with the present employers / in the industry / with past employers.
- Previous paid employment / paid relevant experience.
- Previous steady employment / no periods of unemployment.
- Having attended refresher / training courses (usually unavailable to night staff who tend to be black / women).
- Previous acting-up or substitution experience.
- Being on a permanent contract rather than temporary.

Dress
- Uniform / short dress / no turbans.
- Clean-shaven (eg affect Sikhs).

Attendance / Shifts
- Days / hours of work / shifts / flexibility (Sabbaths / religious holidays).
- Not taking holiday entitlement at one time (visits to family abroad).
- Limited unpaid / compassionate leave (need to visit ill family abroad).
- Good attendance record (extended holidays / unpaid leave to visit family abroad).
- Late travel home (danger of racial attacks).

Keeping it internal / References in and out / Being part of the club
- Nomination / recommendation by / reference from particular staff / management for recruitment / promotion.
- Word of mouth recruitment (knowing existing workers).
- Favouring children from existing staff.
- Jobs / vacancy lists only on enquiry.
- Internal applications only.
- Customer satisfaction (liability to racist complaints).
- Membership of certain organisations, professional bodies or trade unions / certain (culturally specific) leisure activities or interests.

A member may be dismissed (disciplined or harassed) because s/he is black. The question to ask is: "If the member was white (or of a different racial group), would the employers have disciplined or dismissed him/her and generally treated him/her in the same way?" If not, this is direct discrimination.

It may also be that the member is disciplined or dismissed, whatever her racial group, because s/he raised an issued of race discrimination. This is victimisation.

To prove that the real reason for the disciplinary action or dismissal is race discrimination, it is helpful to:

1 Discredit the employers' reasons for disciplining or dismissing the member.

→ Find out and pin down the employers' reasons. Is there a letter?

→ Get the member's comments on the reasons.

→ Show that the employers would not discipline or dismiss a white worker who committed the same or an equivalent offence:

– Find examples where white workers have received a lesser penalty or no penalty for the same or similar offence. This is extremely helpful. Consider whether the employers will be able to explain away the different treatment.

– Check whether the usual disciplinary procedure has been followed.

→ If no comparison can be found, try to discredit the employers' reason altogether, eg by showing that:

– there was nothing at all wrong with the member's work, or

– s/he did not commit the offence and the employers must have known that, or

– it was an extremely trivial offence which would not rationally lead to disciplinary action or dismissal.

→ Even if you have found a comparison, it is still important to discredit or weaken the employers' reasons for their action.

→ If the member was dismissed for redundancy, show that:

– The employers had no objective selection criteria and it was not obvious to select the member rather than white workers; or

– On the employers' objective criteria, the member should have been scored higher than white workers who were retained.

2 Find other evidence of racism in the workforce, particularly involving those who made the relevant decisions concerning the member.

→ Have there been any racist remarks or so-called "jokes"? Who made them and when? What exactly was said? Can they be proved? Note that it is not essential to prove discrimination that such remarks were ever made.

→ General patterns in the workforce:

– Look at the positions of black and white workers in the workplace as a whole; in the relevant department; according to status and type of job. Are black staff in lower grades or less visible jobs?

– Are black workers disproportionately disciplined and dismissed?

– Are black workers generally given lower appraisal ratings than white workers?

– Are white workers disproportionately recruited or promoted? (This is often relevant, but particularly so in a case involving recruitment or promotion.)

→ Check the "race" of the managers and personnel who have made decisions against the member. Are they of the same racial group as the member?

Note that:

– Tribunals can find it hard to believe that large numbers of people have discriminated against the member or acted in bad faith. Cases are usually stronger when there are only a few people who made or influenced key decisions adversely affecting the member. Try to identify who made the important decisions against the member and consider what evidence exists against each of them.

– It can be hard to convince a tribunal that a member has been discriminated against by someone of the same racial group as him/herself, although this can happen. If this seems to be the case, consider whether:

● There is strong evidence that the discriminator is acting on racial grounds (as opposed to personal dislike), and any convincing reason why they should be doing so; or

● The real decision-maker is someone else.

3 Check whether the member or other black workers have

complained of race discrimination in the past, particularly against the same managers.

→ Can the past complaint be proved?

→ What was the outcome? Was it properly investigated? Was the complaint upheld?

→ When was the complaint made and to whom?

→ If it was the member who complained, has s/he been victimised since?

– Did s/he get a hostile reaction to the fact s/he had complained?

– Did her managers generally start to treat him/her differently after that?

– Do the managers who have now disciplined or dismissed him/her know about the past complaint? Can that be proved? Is there any evidence that this is why they have now disciplined or dismissed him/her?

Checklist: race or sex discrimination in promotion: evidence

Direct discrimination

Warning signs (none of these in themselves necessarily indicate that direct discrimination in the promotion decision has occurred):

1 The worker is of a group statistically likely to be discriminated against, eg
→ A black or minority ethnic worker.
→ A pregnant worker.
→ A worker trying to get a supervisory position over workers primarily of another race/sex.

2 The worker has not been short-listed for a job when one would expect him/her to be short-listed, comparing his/her application with the advertisement and job specification.

3 Comments or questions at interview indicating hostility or stereotyping of the worker on racial grounds or questions regarding childcare.

4 Subjective promotion procedures, eg
→ Decision making by one individual or one individual with particular influence.
→ No pre-fixed selection criteria.
→ No objective marking or scoring system.
→ Pre-fixed criteria which are departed from by the decision-makers.
→ Breach of the employer's own recruitment or EOPs procedures.
→ Breach of relevant guidelines in the CRE or EOC's Code of Practice.

5 Unsatisfactory or vague reasons for rejection.

6 Few employees of the worker's race/sex at higher levels in the organisation including at the level to which the worker attempted to get promoted; general pattern of promoting more men/white workers than women/black workers.

7 Past failed promotion attempts.

8 The worker has successfully "acted-up" or "substituted" into the higher grade post in the past.

9 Other evidence of discriminatory tendencies by those making the decision, eg

→ Towards other black/female workers.

→ Towards the particular worker.

10 If someone else has been promoted, they are patently less suitable for the job and are of a different race or sex.

Indirect discrimination

To spot hidden indirect discrimination, watch out for:

1 Merit promotions, not in response to specific vacancies. What hidden criteria are in fact applied? Who makes the decision?

2 Does the promotion require nomination by a particular manager first?

3 Reliance on management assessment (past or present). On what criteria is the assessment based? Is this a discriminatory requirement in itself, if the manager making the assessments treats black/minority ethnic staff or women less favourably?

4 How is the promotion advertised? Is it at a time or in a place where certain staff may not see it?

5 Is the position only available by internal promotion rather than to external candidates? This would discriminate if the existing workforce is all white or of one sex. Black/female workers would only gain access to the lower levels of the organisation and it would take a long time for them to work up to the higher positions (especially if management controlling the promotions was all white/male.)

6 Method of selection: over-emphasis on interviews can disguise hidden requirements of fluency, confidence etc. and tends to benefit white male workers or workers with an academic background.

7 Requirements of the job: these should be kept to the minimum necessary and relevant to the job. Possibly discriminatory requirements could be:

→ Excessive qualifications.

→ Previous experience at certain levels, specific types of previous experience, good record of previous promotions, previous management experience, previous acting-up experience etc. This type of requirement is a key issue of indirect discrimination. For example, as black workers are often concentrated in the lower levels of the workforce, measuring potential only by what level they have already achieved puts them into a catch 22 situation.

→ Requirements as to how the job should be performed, eg dress and appearance, late night working, no provision for extended unpaid leave.

→ Full-time work requirements; shift-working; overtime requirements.

→ See fuller list of possibly discriminatory requirements on pages 179 (race) and 202 (sex).

Victimisation

The worker may not have been promoted because those making the decision know that s/he has previously alleged race or sex discrimination against the organisation.

Race discrimination: myths

- *Myth:*
If a black member is unfairly treated by the employers, that is race discrimination.
Truth:
Not necessarily. The employers may treat everyone unfairly. The important thing to look for is different treatment. (See p168 and checklists at pp181-185.)

- *Myth:*
You cannot prove direct race discrimination unless there is evidence of racist remarks.
Truth:
Racist remarks only occur in a minority of race discrimination cases and even then, are hard to prove without independent witnesses. Many other types of evidence can prove direct race discrimination. (See p168.)

- *Myth:*
Race discrimination is carried out by managers or work colleagues who secretly hold racist views.
Truth:
Not necessarily. The law recognises that all sorts of motives may lead to race discrimination and that some people may even unconsciously discriminate. (See p166-167.)

- *Myth:*
The member can safely complain about race discrimination to his/her employers, because it is unlawful to victimise him/her for doing so.
Truth:
In theory, the member does have this protection. However remember that victimisation needs to be proved. The employers will probably try to disguise it and allege they are disciplining or dismissing the member on unconnected grounds. (See p164.) Also, even if the member can prove victimisation, it will still be a traumatic experience which may lead to him/her losing his/her job.

Race Discrimination: Key points

- The law against race discrimination is contained in the Race Relations Act 1976.
- The RRA does not prohibit discrimination on grounds of religion as such, though certain religious practices are protected as indirect race discrimination.
- Discrimination on grounds of religion and belief is unlawful under the Employment Equality (Religion or Belief) Regulations
- As with the other discrimination legislation, the RRA is wider than unfair dismissal law and does not purely protect employees. No minimum service is necessary.
- Individuals can bring cases of direct discrimination, indirect discrimination, victimisation and harassment. There is no concept of institutional racism under the RRA.
- If the member wants to bring a tribunal case, s/he may have to follow the statutory disputes resolution procedures first.
- Section 71 of the RRA places a positive duty on local authorities, the NHS and other specified public bodies to elimination discrimination and promote equal opportunities. There are specific monitoring duties. Guides and Codes of Practice are available from the CRE.
- The CRE's website is a useful source of guidance booklets and research reports.
- See p300 for the important questionnaire procedure and special time-limits applicable to discrimination cases.
- See Chapter 12 for racial harassment, p74 for race discrimination in disciplinaries and grievances, p128 for redundancy.

Chapter 9:

Sex discrimination
Contents

Legal framework

The law against sex discrimination in employment and other areas is set out in the Sex Discrimination Act 1975 ("SDA"). Sex discrimination in pay and contract terms is dealt with by the Equal Pay Act 1970. In borderline cases, it may not be clear which Act applies.

A "Code of Practice for the elimination of discrimination on grounds of sex and marriage and the promotion of equality of opportunity in employment" came into effect in April 1985 under section 56A of the SDA. The Code lays down guidelines for good employment practice but it is not legally enforceable in itself. However, a tribunal must take into account any relevant provision of the Code in reaching its decision. The Code is also a useful tool for negotiating with employers.

European law also forbids sex discrimination. Article 141 of the Treaty of Rome and the Equal Pay Directive deal with equal pay and the Equal Treatment Directive ("ETD") provides for equal treatment between men and women at work in other respects.

With effect from October 2005, the Employment Equality (Sex Discrimination) Regulations 2005 will make several changes to the SDA, to bring into line with the Equal Treatment Amendment Directive. At the time of writing (April 2005), draft Regulations have been issued, which may not be passed in the same form. The anticipated changes will be indicated in the following text where they apply. In small but sometimes important respects, the ETD may give greater legal rights than the SDA. Where this happens, the legal position is very complicated. In summary, workers employed by an "emanation" of the state, eg local authority or NHS, may be able to claim directly under European law. Private sector workers will only have the unpractical option of suing the government, but privatised utilities have been ruled to be "emanations of the state". Wherever possible, the SDA should be interpreted consistently with European law. Some cases go to the European Court of Justice ("ECJ") for its rulings.

The Equal Opportunities Commission is the organisation set up under the SDA with overall responsibility for the workings of the SDA and the Equal Pay Act.

Which workers are covered

There is no minimum service requirement under the SDA. The SDA protects:

→ Job applicants.

→ Employees.

→ The self-employed working on a contract personally to execute any work.

→ Work-trainees.

→ Contract workers. (See p161 for meaning.)

Scope of SDA

The SDA forbids discrimination on grounds of sex or marital status (being married). It also prohibits discrimination against a worker on grounds that s/he intends to undergo, is undergoing, or has undergone gender reassignment. Gender reassignment means any process undertaken under medical supervision, but not necessarily surgery, for the reassignment of a person's sex by changing physiological or other characteristics. The DTI's Women and Equality Unit has a useful guide: "Gender Reassignment – A Guide for Employers", on its website at www.womenandequalityunit.gov.uk.

The SDA does not cover discrimination on grounds of sexual orientation, but this is covered by the Employment Equality (Sexual Orientation) Regulations (see Chapter 11).

Vicarious liability

The law on vicarious liability is the same as under the Race Relations Act (see p162 for details).

When may discrimination happen?

Unlike the law on unfair dismissal, the SDA does not only cover dismissal situations. In section 6 it forbids discrimination in a whole range of employment situations. In summary, employers discriminate against a worker:

→ When choosing whether to employ him/her.

→ When choosing whether to promote him/her.

→ In the terms and conditions offered to a worker.

→ In offering training opportunities.

→ In access to benefits and services generally.

→ By dismissing him/her.

➔ By subjecting him/her to any other detriment, eg disciplinary action or sexual harassment. (Chapter 12 expands on harassment.)

In some circumstances, it also covers discrimination against ex-employees, eg who are given a bad reference because they have brought a sex discrimination case.

Because discrimination (whether direct, indirect or victimisation) can occur at so many points, you need to be constantly alert to the possibility.

The definition of unlawful discrimination

Overview

There are four kinds of unlawful discrimination under the SDA: direct discrimination, indirect discrimination, victimisation and (from October 2005) harassment. Each of these words has a very precise legal meaning, which is different from its meaning in natural every-day language. You need to remember this. The definitions are set out in more detail later in this Chapter.

Summary of legal definitions

The following is a summary. For more detail, see later in the Chapter.

Direct discrimination: s1(1)(a)

This is where the member is treated differently because of his/her sex. For example, the employers fail to recruit the member because she is a woman. There is no defence to direct discrimination. You should always ask the "but for" question, ie

"But for the fact that the member is a woman (or a man), would the employers have treated her (him) the same way?"

Direct discrimination against a man or woman because s/he is married is also unlawful.

Indirect discrimination: s1(2)(b)

(From October 2005) this is where the member fails to get a job or is selected for redundancy or is otherwise disadvantaged:

➔ because of a provision, criterion or practice applied by the employers; and

➔ that particular provision, criterion or practice puts women at a particular disadvantage compared with men; and

→ the employers cannot justify applying the provision, criterion or practice, by showing it is a proportionate means of achieving a legitimate aim.

For example, the member is a woman who is unable to work full-time due to child-care obligations. Fewer women than men would be able to work full-time. Whether or not it is justifiable to require her to work full-time would depend on the nature of the job.

Indirect discrimination against married workers is also unlawful.

Victimisation: s2

This is where the member is punished or treated less favourably because s/he has complained about sex discrimination or equal pay in some way, eg in a tribunal, formally or informally, on his/her own behalf or on behalf of someone else.

For example, the member brings a grievance regarding sex discrimination by her manager. Shortly afterwards she is made redundant.

The employers can defend a case of victimisation if the member's complaint of sex discrimination was false and made in bad faith.

Harassment

At the time of writing (April 2005), there is no explicit definition of harassment in the SDA. Harassment cases are dealt with as acts of direct discrimination or victimisation. From October 2005, it is intended to include an explicit definition, to match and expand on the definitions in the other discrimination legislation. For more detail, see Chapter 12.

Several types of discrimination

More than one type of discrimination may have taken place. For example a woman may be refused promotion (direct discrimination); when she complains to management, she is sacked (direct discrimination or victimisation).

S/he could also be subjected to race and sex discrimination. For example, a black woman may not get promoted due to her race and sex.

A focused approach

Sometimes the member tells you a long and complicated story and it is hard to focus on the key legal issues. This can particularly happen on harassment cases. You can establish a useful framework if you work through the following stages:

→ What are the incidents of bad treatment about which the member is complaining? These are the potential "acts of discrimination". For example, unwanted remarks, physical assaults, disciplinary action.

→ On what date did each act of discrimination occur. (This is very important for time-limits. See p295.)

→ Who carried out the act of discrimination? (It may not always be possible to identify the decision-makers.)

→ What type of discrimination (direct, indirect or victimisation) does each act seem to be? It may be more than one type.

Direct discrimination

Direct discrimination is the most obvious form of discrimination. The formal definition is in SDA s1(1)(a):

"A person discriminates against a woman if on the ground of her sex he treats her less favourably than he treats or would treat a man."

Section 2 prohibits direct discrimination against men. Section 3 prohibits direct discrimination against a married person.

The real question is whether a person is treated differently as a result of their sex or marital status, eg "but for" the fact that the worker was a woman or married, the employers would have promoted her/him.

Direct discrimination cases are easiest to prove where the member can point to another worker of the opposite sex who has been treated differently or better in identical circumstances. For example:

→ A woman unsuccessfully applies for a job. She has better qualifications and experience than the successful male candidate.

→ A woman is dismissed for failure to meet performance targets. A man who does not meet the targets is offered training.

The comparison need not be identical. For example, a woman is dismissed for one form of gross misconduct but a man who commits another form of gross misconduct receives only a final written warning.

The case will lose if the employers can prove an "innocent" reason for treating the workers differently, eg that the woman had a worse disciplinary record than the man. It is always important to find out and pin down the employers' reasons for treating the member as they have.

Unlike the Equal Pay Act, it is not essential to have an actual comparator, if a woman can persuade the tribunal that a man would have been treated differently.

For example, a woman with good experience and relevant qualifications unsuccessfully applies for a job in a traditionally male industry. The employers fail to make any appointment. The woman may prove her sex discrimination case even though there is no successful male candidate to compare herself with, by pointing to the other evidence, eg her obvious ability to do the job, the lack of a good explanation by the employers for rejecting her and the fact that it is a traditionally male industry.

It is direct discrimination under the SDA to treat the member less favourably because she is pregnant or on maternity leave. (See p00).

The employers' motives

The employers' motives are irrelevant. What matters is what the employers do. It is not lawful to discriminate against a woman, eg to protect her from harassment by male colleagues or because customers would prefer to deal with a man.

There is no defence to direct discrimination. Different treatment, whatever the motive, is inexcusable. However there are some limited exceptions for genuine occupational qualifications and pregnancy (see p199).

Evidence of direct discrimination

The following types of evidence may help prove direct discrimination:

■ **Sexist or stereotyped remarks.** Remember these need to be proved.

■ **Comparators.** It is very helpful to find another worker of the opposite sex or who is unmarried, who has been treated differently or better in comparable circumstances. The employers will then need to explain their different treatment.

■ **Extremely unfair or irrational treatment of the member**, although this will not be enough on its own. The employers may simply dislike the member personally or they may be bad employers generally.

■ **Statistics and patterns**, eg a male dominated hierarchy would be relevant in a promotion case.

■ **Poor equal opportunities practices** or failure to follow any relevant provision of the EOC Code of Practice will be helpful, but you still need to prove the "but for" question, ie that on the particular occasion, the member would have been treated differently if s/he was of the opposite sex.

■ **Find out and discredit the employers' explanation** for their treatment of the member.

For sex discrimination in promotion, see checklist on p184.

Indirect discrimination

The definition of indirect discrimination is set out in section 1(2)(b). Indirect discrimination is when the employers apply a provision, criterion or practice which puts a woman at a disadvantage and which would put women at a particular disadvantage compared with men.

It is also unlawful to indirectly discrimination against a man or married worker.

Unlike direct discrimination, there is a defence to indirect discrimination if the employers can justify applying the provision, criterion or practice by showing it is a proportionate means of achieving a legitimate aim. (See p198.)

For example:

→ A woman is rejected from a job because she is not 6' tall. A requirement that job candidates be 6 foot tall or over would put women at a particular disadvantage when compared with men. The employers would then need to justify why they needed the worker to be 6 foot.

→ A woman or married man needs to work part-time to look after his/her child. The employers refuse. A requirement for full-time working could put women at a particular disadvantage compared with men due to childcare obligations. (It may have a similar effect on married workers, male or female.) The employers would need to justify why they needed a full-time worker.

It is important to identify indirectly discriminatory practices in the workplace, but individual cases can be hard to run due to the technicalities of the legal definition.

Note that the above definition is taken from the draft Regulations and is anticipated to be confirmed in October 2005, since it matches that in other discrimination legislation. Prior to October 2005, it is necessary to show that the provision, criterion or practice is to the detriment of a "considerably larger proportion" of women than men. Under this wording, a statistical approach is necessary when proving women are more disadvantaged.

Provisions, criteria and practices

There are countless everyday working practices which disadvantage certain groups of workers. These practices often create unnecessary barriers to true equal opportunities for getting jobs, promotion and improvement in pay and conditions. For women, the most problematic criteria and practices tend to interfere with childcare, eg requirements for full-time working, mobility, shift-working, overtime.

Some criteria or practices with adverse effects are unavoidable and it is not unlawful for employers to adopt a practice which they can objectively justify. However, many provisions, criteria and practices cannot be justified once challenged.

Discriminatory criteria and conditions are often hidden and members may not themselves notice them. You need to be alert to identify indirect discrimination when members present individual problems to you, and also when you look at the employers' policies and practices.

Discriminatory practices may occur in a whole range of working situations. On page 202 is a list of criteria which, unless justifiable, often have a discriminatory effect on women in particular. Page 128 give examples of criteria to be wary of in redundancy situations and page 184 in promotion situations.

Is the provision, criterion or practice to the member's detriment?

Indirect discrimination occurs where a worker is disadvantaged by a particular provision, criterion or practice at the time it is imposed. This should not be taken too literally and includes the following situations:

→ **The member physically cannot comply with a criterion.** For example: a criterion that workers be over 6 foot tall would disproportionately disadvantage women.

→ **The member cannot meet the criterion at the time it is imposed.** For example: a decision to make existing part-timers redundant, without offering them the chance to change to full-time working. It is irrelevant if they would have been able to move to full-time working.

→ **The work practice is to a member's detriment because of child-care obligations.** For example: a flexi-shift system which can change at short notice interferes with child-care arrangements.

Are others of the same sex (or married people) at a particular disadvantage?

It is not sufficient that the member is disadvantaged by the criterion or practice. The member needs to prove that many other workers of the same sex would have the same difficulty. It is not necessary to show that a criterion or practice excludes all men or women or married people. It need only be a particular disadvantage for those of the relevant group.

For example, if the employers require job candidates to be 6 foot tall, it does not matter that some women are 6 foot or that many men are not 6 foot. Statistically, far more women than men would be excluded and women would therefore be at a particular disadvantage.

Is the provision, criterion or practice justifiable?

If the employers can prove that it was "justifiable" to impose the provision, criterion or practice, then it will not be unlawful. The proposed Regulations state that the employers must prove the provision, criterion or practice was a proportionate means of achieving a legitimate aim.

Case-law has established that:

→ It is not enough for employers to say that they considered their reasons for imposing the provision, criterion or practice adequate. The provision, criterion or practice must be objectively justifiable regardless of sex, not simply justifiable in the personal opinion of the particular employers.

→ The provision, criterion or practice must serve a real business need of the employers, eg administrative efficiency, hygiene, safety or significant economic savings.

→ Whether there is sufficient justification will depend on the facts and circumstances of the particular case. The more people of a particular sex are adversely affected by a particular practice, the better justification the employers must provide.

Criteria and practices should be kept to the minimum necessary for the employers' needs. Where there is a fairer way of achieving the same end, the provision, criterion or practice is unlikely to be justifiable.

Action

Do not just wait for members to complain to you about indirect discrimination. You should be alert to policies and practices which ought to be challenged. See p172 for action checklist on indirect race discrimination.

Victimisation

Under the SDA "victimisation" has a specific meaning, which is different from the normal meaning of the word. Employers must not victimise a worker by punishing him/her for raising the issue of sex discrimination or equal pay. Section 4 states that a worker must not be less favourably treated because s/he has done a "protected act" or because the employers think s/he has done or may in the future do a protected act. The protected acts include:

→ Taking a tribunal case of sex discrimination or equal pay.

→ Bringing a formal grievance about sex discrimination or equal pay.

→ Making an informal allegation of sex discrimination or equal pay, verbally or in writing.

→ Giving evidence for a colleague who is bringing a sex discrimination or equal pay case or grievance.

→ Doing anything else by reference to the SDA, eg contacting the EOC.

Examples of victimisation:

→ A worker is sacked because s/he brings a grievance complaining about sex discrimination in a recent failed promotion attempt.

→ A worker is transferred and demoted because s/he complains of sexual harassment.

The employers' only defence is if the worker's allegation of sex discrimination was false and it was made in bad faith. As long as the worker genuinely believes s/he was discriminated against, it is unlawful to victimise him/her. Unfortunately in sexual harassment cases, employers often try to rely on this defence.

Evidence of victimisation

Victimisation is extremely common and you should be careful not to miss it. It provides important protection, but it is important to remember that it can be hard to prove. For guidance on what needs to be proved, see p173 on the equivalent part of the RRA.

Some permitted sex discrimination

Genuine occupational qualifications (GOQs)

It is permitted to discriminate against women where being a man is a GOQ for a job (or vice versa). Such discrimination may only occur in selecting who to offer a job, promote, transfer or train. It does not allow discrimination in the terms offered or in access to benefits, facilities or services, or in dismissal or any other detriment.

GOQs are set out specifically and interpreted in a restrictive way by the courts. The categories are set out below, although the exact wording of the SDA should be referred to in any case.

It is not necessary for all the job duties to fall within the GOQ categories; it is enough if only some of the duties are covered.

However, an employer may not use the GOQ defence if s/he already has employees of the relevant sex who could cover the relevant duties without undue inconvenience.

The categories

Being a man (or a woman) is a genuine occupational qualification for a job:

■ For reasons of authenticity as an actor or entertainer or for reasons of physiology (excluding physical strength or stamina).

■ To preserve decency or privacy because of likely physical contact or contact with persons in a state of undress or using sanitary facilities or, where work is in a private home, because of close physical or social contact with someone living in the home.

■ Because it is necessary to live on work premises and there are no separate sleeping and sanitary facilities and it is not reasonable to expect the employer to supply these.

■ Where the work is in a single–sex establishment or part of an establishment for persons requiring special care, supervision or attention, eg a hospital or prison.

■ Where the job is one of two to be held by a married couple.

■ To provide personal services promoting the welfare or education or similar services to persons of the same sex.

GOQs also apply to permit discrimination against transsexuals in certain circumstances.

Genuine occupational requirements (GORs)

Under the Regulations proposed for October 2005, the exceptions will not be limited to the categories specified above. The latest position should be checked if relevant, but any additional GOR exception is likely to be very limited in practice.

Positive action

Where within the previous 12 months, the number of women (or men) doing a particular kind of work was comparatively small, the employers *may:*

→ Offer training exclusively to women (or men).

→ Exclusively encourage women (or men) to apply for jobs.

Note that the employers are not obliged to undertake any positive action. They are also not allowed to discriminate at the point of selection for a job.

Pregnancy and childbirth

It is permitted to treat women more favourably than men in connection with pregnancy and childbirth.

Statutory disputes resolution procedures

If the member is an employee and wishes to bring a tribunal case against his/her employer for sex discrimination, the statutory disputes resolution procedures will apply. If s/he wishes to complain about dismissal, the statutory minimum disciplinary and dismissal procedure (DDP) will apply. If s/he wishes to complain about anything else, including constructive dismissal, s/he must bring an internal grievance before starting a tribunal claim. There are a few exceptions, for example, if s/he has been subjected to harassment and fears that going through a grievance would cause him/her to be subjected to further harassment. For full details of the rules, exceptions and effect on time-limits, see p57 onwards.

Duties of public bodies

At the time of writing (April 2005), it is proposed to bring in a new public duty to promote equality of opportunity, similar to the duty under section 71 of the Race Relations Act (see p177).

Checklist: possibly discriminatory provisions, criteria and practices

Many of the provisions, criteria and practices relevant to indirect race discrimination set out on p179 would also adversely affect women or married workers. Additional provisions, criteria and practices which would specifically affect women could be:

Attendance/shifts/flexibility/mobility

Requirements likely to cause difficulty for women – and sometimes for married men – usually due to child–care commitments.

Hours

→ Full–time work (refusal to allow job–share or part–time working).

→ Permitting part–time working, but requiring some hours to be worked each day.

→ Overtime or weekend working.

→ Shift–working, especially rotating shifts varying from day to day or week to week.

→ Requirements to work overtime or varying shifts imposed at very short notice.

→ Specified and inflexible start or finish times (interfering with times of taking or collecting children from school or child–minding).

→ All year round working (eg, as opposed to term–time only).

→ Requirements entailing certain (high) attendance levels/limited absences.

Mobility

→ Long journeys to and from work locations (necessitating earlier departures from and returns to home).

→ Work trips necessitating staying overnight away from home.

→ Relocation (may be unacceptable if woman is not the primary earner in the household)

Note that flexibility and mobility requirements often do cause women difficulties and should therefore be justified by the employers. However, it would be direct discrimination if the employers wrongly assumed a woman would be less flexible and treated her less favourably for that reason.

Miscellaneous

→ Age bars (women may be out of the job market during child–bearing age).

→ To have acquired a certain level of experience by a certain age.

→ Certain forms of dress or uniform (eg, may indirectly discriminate against Muslim women).

→ Late finishing hours (possibly dangerous travel home).

→ Home visits, eg to patients or tenants unaccompanied (in some circumstances may be dangerous).

Note that employers should provide a safe system of work for all workers, but should not directly discriminate against women unless allowed by statute (eg, in relation to pregnancy and childbirth).

Sex discrimination: Key points

● The law against sex discrimination is contained in the Sex Discrimination Act 1975. The Equal Pay Act covers sex discrimination in pay and contract terms.

● The SDA forbids discrimination on grounds of gender, marital status or gender reassignment. Discrimination on grounds of sexual orientation is covered by the Employment Equality (Sexual Orientation) Regulations.

● As with the RRA, DDA, religion and sexual orientation discrimination regulations, the SDA is wider than unfair dismissal law and does not purely protect employees. No minimum service is necessary.

● Individuals can bring cases of direct discrimination, indirect discrimination and victimisation. The concepts are very similar under the RRA.

● The most common form of indirect discrimination relates to requirements for full-time working, shift-working and flexibility.

● European law also applies to sex discrimination: the Equal Treatment Directive and in the pay field, Article 141 of the Treaty of Rome and the Equal Pay Directive.

● The Equal Treatment Amendment Directive must be implemented by 5th October 2005. Draft Employment Equality (Sex Discrimination) Regulations have been issued. Amongst other changes, they will bring the definition of indirect sex discrimination closer to that to be introduced into the RRA. They will also introduce a specific definition of harassment.

● The EOC's website is a useful source of guidance booklets and research reports.

● See p300 for the important questionnaire procedure and special time-limits applicable to discrimination cases.

● The statutory disputes resolution procedures may apply. See Chapter 3.

● For sex discrimination related to pregnancy and part-time working, see Chapter 13. For equal pay, see Chapter 2. For sexual harassment, see Chapter 12. For checklist on sex discrimination in promotion, see p184. For sex discrimination and redundancy see p128.

Chapter 10:

Disability discrimination

Contents

Introduction

The Disability Discrimination Act, despite its deficiencies, is a very useful piece of legislation. Far more workers may be able to usefully rely on the DDA than may seem obvious. Not only does it protect workers with a wide range of mental or physical disabilities, but in many cases it covers long-term sickness or injury. For example, if a member loses his/her job because of an accident at work, you should not only consider whether s/he has a personal injuries claim. You should also consider if s/he could keep his/her job if the employers made adjustments as required by the DDA.

According to a report published on 14th February 2003 by the Department for Work and Pensions, every quarter, 2.6% of workers (over 600,000 individuals) become sick or disabled using the definition of disability under the DDA. This compares with only 0.3% (73,000) who would qualify for statutory sick pay or incapacity benefit.

The DDA is similar to the RRA, SDA, Employment Equality (Sexual Orientation) Regulations and Employment Equality (Religion or Belief) Regulations in some respects, but different in others. You need to be careful not to get confused. Most importantly, the definition of "discrimination" under the DDA is not the same as under the other statutes. The DDA is also unique in that it places a very positive duty on employers to make reasonable adjustments to enable the member to get a job or continue working.

The downside of the DDA from a policy point of view is that it looks at a "medical model" of disability. In other words, it tends to focus rather negatively on what the member is unable to do due to his/her disability, rather than the "social model" which looks at disability more positively just as another difference between people.

The DDA has replaced the quota systems and the concept of "registered disabled" workers from the previous 1944 legislation.

Legal framework

The law is mainly set out in the Disability Discrimination Act 1995 ("DDA"), but unlike other discrimination law, it is clarified by various regulations. Important guidelines for advisers and tribunals are set out in the "Guidance on matters to be taken into account in determining questions related to the definition of disability" ("the Guidance") and the revised "Code of Practice on Employment and Occupation" ("the

Code"). You should obtain both these documents. They can be downloaded from the Disability Rights Commission's website. The Guidance provides helpful guidelines for deciding whether a worker has a disability covered by the DDA. The Code is useful in assessing what reasonable adjustments the employers should make. It is full of examples, but as it is over 200 pages long, it is easier to get a hard copy from TSO (The Stationery Office). The online website is at www.tso.co.uk/bookshop.

The European General Framework Directive 2000 introduced European-wide anti-discrimination law concerning religion, sexual orientation, disability and age. The DDA was already in force in the UK, but certain amendments were made to make it fully compliant with the Directive. In April 2005, the Disability Discrimination Act 2005 received Royal Assent, making certain changes to the Disability Discrimination Act 1995. The changes made by the 2005 Act will be signalled in the text as the date when it comes into force has not yet been announced – December 2005 is likely.

The Disability Rights Commission is the organisation equivalent to the CRE and the EOC in the disability field. For more details, you can look up its very useful website (see Bibliography, p314).

Which workers are covered

As with other discrimination legislation, there is no minimum service requirement, and the DDA does not purely protect employees. (See p161 for equivalent position under the RRA.) There is no longer any small employer exemption under the DDA.

Vicarious liability

As with race, religious, sex and sexual orientation discrimination, employers are vicariously liable for discrimination carried out by their own employees during the course of employment unless they took all reasonably practicable preventative steps. For more detail, see p162.

When may discrimination happen?

Again, as with other forms of discrimination law, the DDA forbids discrimination in the whole range of recruitment and employment situations and not simply in dismissal. Harassment of a worker on grounds of disability would fall within the DDA as a form of discrimination. See also Chapter 12 on harassment. Discrimination against former employees, provided it arises out of the former employment relationship, eg giving discriminatory references, is also covered.

The meaning of "disability"

The DDA prohibits unlawful discrimination against a "disabled person" in employment. Except in obvious cases, one of the most important and difficult issues is whether a worker has a "disability" as defined by the DDA. The DDA covers many workers with long-term ill-health which would not conventionally be seen as a "disability". On the other hand, some conditions you might expect to fall within the DDA, do not because they do not meet every stage of the definition. Section 1(1) says:

"A person has a disability for the purposes of this Act if he has a physical or mental impairment which has a substantial and long-term adverse effect on his ability to carry out normal day-to-day activities."

Many cases are won or lost on the issue whether the worker meets this definition. Except in very obvious cases, the member will need to prove each stage of the definition. You need to interview a member very sensitively and by reference to the Guidance, to find out the nature of his/her disability. Some members may not wish to be labeled "disabled". You could explain that the DDA does in fact cover temporary ill-health and injury as well as disability in the conventional sense.

The following are examples of conditions which tribunals have found to be covered by the definition in some cases. It is crucial to understand that it is the effects of the condition which bring it within the DDA. Each case depends on the severity and duration of the condition's effects on the particular worker. The examples are: agoraphobia, arthritis, back injury, bronchial asthma, bulimia nervosa, clinical depression, colitis, diabetes, epilepsy, ME (chronic fatigue syndrome), paranoid schizophrenia, post-traumatic stress disorder, reactive depression.

Mental or physical impairment

The member must have a mental or physical impairment. The DDA 2005 abolishes the need for proving that any mental illness is "clinically well-recognised". Schizophrenia, agoraphobia and depression can all be covered, provided they are sufficiently serious and long-term (see below).

The following conditions are specifically excluded: hay-fever, tattoos and body piercings, exhibitionism, voyeurism, tendency to physical or sexual abuse of others, tendency to set fires or steal, and addictions to substances such as alcohol, nicotine or drugs, except where the addiction is the result of medically prescribed drugs or treatment. Impairments caused by an addiction, eg liver damage caused by alcoholism, are covered.

Affecting normal day-to-day activities

The impairment must affect the member's ability to carry out one or more of the day-to-day activities listed in Schedule 1 paragraph 4 of the DDA. These are:

→ Mobility.
→ Manual dexterity.
→ Physical co-ordination.
→ Continence.
→ Ability to lift, carry or otherwise move every day objects.
→ Speech, hearing or eyesight.
→ Memory or ability to learn concentrate or understand.
→ Perception of the risk of physical danger.

The test is not whether the impairment affects the member's ability to do his/her particular job or hobby, but whether it affects normal activities which anyone might carry out.

For example, the member may work on a refuse collection van and have to carry heavy dustbins as part of his/her job. Due to a back impairment, s/he cannot lift such heavy loads. The member may be perfectly capable of lifting normal items such as kettles, loaded trays and shopping bags. In this example, s/he would not be "disabled" under the DDA, even though s/he could no longer do his/her job.

Substantial adverse effect

The effect of the impairment must be more than trivial. It is unnecessary that the member is completely unable to do the activity in question. It is usually enough if s/he can only do it slowly, or with pain or if it causes extreme tiredness. Part C of the Guidance provides extremely useful guidelines and illustrations as to what would be a substantial effect on each of the activities.

Note that:

■ When interviewing the member, it is useful to go through the activities listed in Schedule 1 paragraph 4 of the DDA and the illustrations in the Guidance.

■ Although one or more of the listed activities must be affected, within each activity, the Guidance is only giving examples as an indication of the sort of effects to watch out for.

■ Members may play down the adverse effects of their disability. Unfortunately this is counter-productive in a legal context.

■ It helps if you already know something about the likely effects of the member's disability, though you must be very careful to listen to the member and not make assumptions. There are many specialist websites providing more information. Many of these are linked to the Disability Rights Commission's website.

■ It is irrelevant whether the member can do many of the activities or even many of the Guidance examples within each activity. The definition of disability is measured by whether the worker is unable to do particular things, however many other things s/he is generally able to manage.

■ Where medical treatment, medication or counselling controls the effects of the impairment, the correct test is the member's abilities if s/he were not receiving such treatment. The exception is glasses, where the test is the worker's abilities when wearing glasses.

■ A worker with a progressive condition, eg rheumatoid arthritis, is covered as soon as the impairment has any effect on his/her day-to-day abilities, even though the effect is not yet substantial. The DDA 2005 amends the law so that HIV, multiple sclerosis and cancer (with some exceptions for milder forms) are deemed a "disability" on diagnosis.

■ Severe disfigurement is deemed to have substantial adverse effect.

■ Workers registered with a local authority or certified by a consultant ophthalmologist as blind or partially sighted are deemed disabled without the need to prove the stages of the definition.

Long-term effect

The DDA does not protect those with short-term disabilities. To fall within the definition, the effect of the impairment must have lasted or be likely to last 12 months or the rest of the member's life, if less. If an impairment ceases to have a substantial adverse effect but is likely to recur, it is treated as continuing, eg rheumatoid arthritis or multiple sclerosis. For more detail, see section B of the Guidance.

It is also unlawful to discriminate against a worker because s/he had a disability (as defined) in the past.

The definition of unlawful discrimination

There are five kinds of unlawful discrimination under the DDA:

1 Less favourable treatment on grounds of disability: "direct discrimination"

2 Less favourable treatment for a reason which relates to the worker's disability: "disability-related discrimination"

3 Failure to make reasonable adjustments

4 Victimisation

5 Harassment

Direct discrimination

Under s3A(5), it is direct discrimination for employers to treat the member, on the ground of his/her disability, less favourably than they would treat a person not having that particular disability. This concept is equivalent to that of direct sex discrimination under the Sex Discrimination Act. Unlike for disability-related discrimination (below), there is no justification defence.

It is important to focus on the idea of a comparator, who the employers have treated or would treat differently in similar circumstances. Ideally (although this is not essential), the member can find an actual comparator, eg a colleague without a disability or with a different disability.

For example, the member (who is disabled) is sacked because his/her total sickness absence amounts to 3 months, whereas a non-disabled worker who is off sick for 3 months is not sacked. This suggests the employers have treated the disabled worker less favourably purely because s/he is disabled, unless the employers can prove a credible reason for the different treatment, which is unrelated to disability.

Disability-related discrimination

Under s3A(5), employers must not treat the member less favourably for a reason related to his/her disability unless they can justify such treatment.

This concept is different to that of direct discrimination. In the example of direct discrimination above, it may be that the employers would dismiss any worker who is off sick for 3 months and are not treating the disabled worker any differently. This would therefore not be direct discrimination. However, if the reason for the member's absences were related to his/her disability, it would be "disability-related discrimination".

Other examples of less favourable treatment related to a worker's disability would be

→ failing to employ a wheelchair user because of access difficulties

→ selecting a worker for redundancy because – as a result of his/her disability, s/he is unable to be as flexible in tasks as other workers.

It is not always clear whether the discrimination is direct or disability-related. But the difference is crucial. This is because there is no defence to direct discrimination, but the employers are allowed to justify disability-related discrimination.

Some workers believe that once they are covered by the DDA, they have absolute protection against dismissal or less favourable treatment by the employers. This is not true. The employers can dismiss or discriminate against a disabled worker for disability-related reasons, if they can justify doing so. The justification must be relevant to the particular case and substantial, ie not trivial or minor. The interests of the member as well as the employers' interests should be taken into account. The employers must also comply with any duty to make reasonable adjustments (see below). Examples of what may and may not be justified treatment are given at section 6 of the revised Code.

Failure to make reasonable adjustments

Sections 4A and 18B are the most helpful part of the DDA as they place a very positive duty on employers to make adjustments where any provision, criterion or practice or physical features of the premises would put a disabled worker at a disadvantage. Many managers and personnel departments still do not realise how much the law can require them to do. The duty is owed to the particular worker who is disabled and not generally.

Section 18B sets out a number of suggestions as to possible adjustments. A tribunal may also expect other adjustments to have been made which are not in the list. You should discuss with the member and any relevant specialist organisation what adjustments may be helpful. It is useful to find out whether there are available subsidies, although employers can be expected to spend money on adjustments. The following suggestions are taken from section 18B. You should also read the revised Code at section 5.

- Adjusting premises. (For example, workers with multiple sclerosis can have difficulties with doors and stairs.)
- Acquiring or modifying equipment. (For example, specialist software can assist workers with a visual impairment or dyslexia.)
- Modifying instructions or reference manuals.
- Modifying testing or assessment procedures. (For example, a worker with dyslexia may need more time and fewer written tests.)
- Providing a reader or interpreter. (It is important that the interpreter is available for the member and not constantly called away by others.)
- Providing supervision or other support.
- Adjusting hours of work or training. (A worker may wish to work shorter hours through tiredness or to travel outside rush-hour.)
- Allowing time-off for rehabilitation, assessment or treatment.
- Training or mentoring.
- Reallocating some duties.
- Assigning the person to a different workplace or training location.
- Transferring to any suitable available alternative posts.

A tribunal would decide whether it was reasonable to expect the employers to make an adjustment. Legally relevant factors are:

- The extent to which the adjustment would prevent the disadvantage.
- The practicability of the employers making the adjustment.
- The financial and other (staff and resources) costs of the adjustment and the extent of any disruption caused.
- The extent of the employers' financial or other resources, eg size of workforce.
- The availability of financial or other assistance to make the adjustment.
- The size of the organisation and nature of its activities
- Where the step would be taken in relation to a private household, the extent to which it would disrupt the household or disturb anyone living there.

The Code says it is also relevant to take into account:

- The extent to which the worker is willing to co-operate

- The effect on other employees
- Adjustments made for other employees.

The following are examples taken from tribunal cases as to adjustments which the tribunals have considered would have been reasonable for the employers to make:

1 Buying a chair of a particular design which would have cost no more than £200 with grant aid for a worker with a club foot.

2 Providing one-to-one training for a hearing impaired employee and to acquire a portable text telephone or pager for him to use.

3 Reviewing an employee's attendance record and discount absences related to his disability for the purposes of the sickness dismissal procedure.

4 Where a worker with emphysema was unable to climb ladders as required 2-3 times/day, allocating those duties to another worker.

5 Where a worker was unable to climb stairs without difficulty due to a back injury, moving her office to the ground floor and to rearrange the lay-out to overcome her difficulty lifting and bending.

6 Providing a desk-top photocopier for a wheelchair user with heavy paperwork and filing as part of his job; to increase computerisation of his job or provide an unskilled assistant to help him move files.

7 Providing a classroom assistant for a visually impaired teacher and meanwhile to ask a parent to help out.

8 Paying the worker full pay while she was off sick due to a failure to make reasonable adjustments to enable her to return to work. (See Court of Appeal in *Nottinghamshire County Council v Meikle*.)

9 Where a disabled worker cannot continue in his/her post due to sickness, injury or redundancy, the DDA requires a more proactive approach from employers than ordinary unfair dismissal law. Many tribunals have expected personnel to identify suitable vacancies, arrange training and slot the worker in, as opposed to merely handing over vacancy lists and telling the member to apply. The House of Lords in the key case of *Archibald v Fife Council* said it is potentially a reasonable adjustment to transfer a worker to an alternative job, even one at a higher grade, without interview, where s/he is unable to do his/her previous job.

10 The following UNISON case established an important principle regarding finding alternative employment for disabled workers.

Kent County Council v Mingo [2000] IRLR 90; 89 EOR 55, EAT

Due to a back injury, Mr Mingo could not continue in his job. He was therefore classified as a Category B redeployee ie redeployment on grounds of ill-health. Category A redeployees (on grounds of redundancy) were given priority on vacancies. As a result, Mr Mingo was excluded from several possibilities and eventually dismissed.

The EAT confirmed the ET's decision that the employers had failed to meet their obligations of reasonable adjustment under the DDA 1995. It was wrong to give priority to a category of employees (eg those who were or may be redundant) over a worker with a disability.

11 In the following UNISON case, the EAT said that as part of their duty to make reasonable adjustments, employers should first obtain a proper assessment of the worker's condition and its effects.

Mid Staffordshire General Hospital NHS Trust v Cambridge [2003] IRLR 566, EAT

Mrs Cambridge was employed by the Trust as a team leader for reception services. In March 1999, her vocal chords were injured due to dust caused by workmen demolishing a wall close to her work station. Her voice was seriously affected, but she found it difficult to avoid using it at work. Scents like perfume and air freshener exacerbated her condition. She also found it difficult to use public transport.

Mrs Cambridge was certified unfit for work from March – August 1999. In October, her manager suggested a possible redeployment to a smaller department, but she did not want to do this. No thought was given to making any other reasonable adjustments. In December, management was told that it would be at least 12 months before she was likely to make a full recovery. They did not want to wait and eventually dismissed her.

The employment tribunal found her dismissal was unfair and unlawful discrimination under the DDA. The tribunal said the employers had failed to make reasonable adjustments because they had failed to obtain a proper assessment of her condition and prognosis, the effect of her disability, the effect of the physical features of her workplace, and steps which could be taken to reduce the difficulties. The employers appealed.

The Employment Appeal Tribunal said that a proper assessment of what is required to eliminate a disabled person's disadvantage is a necessary part of the duty to make reasonable adjustment, since that duty cannot be complied with unless the employer makes a proper assessment of what needs to be done.

Note that:
— In most of the above cases, the size of the employers was a relevant factor in the expected adjustments.
— Sometimes there is no adjustment which can realistically be asked of the employers and which would solve the difficulty.
— The fact that the employers have made some (inadequate) adjustments, does not mean they have satisfied their duty to make all reasonable adjustments.
— On the other hand, employers only need to do what a tribunal would consider "reasonable". If a member rejects reasonable adjustments which are offered, and nothing else is feasible, the tribunal will say the employers have satisfied their duty.
— Probably the most important case on disability discrimination is *Archibald v Fife Council* [2004] IRLR 651. The House of Lords stressed the central importance of the duty of reasonable adjustment. It said:

"The DDA does not regard the differences between disabled people and others as irrelevant. It does not expect each to be treated in the same way. The duty to make adjustments may require the employer to treat a disabled person more favourably to remove the disadvantage which is attributable to the disability. This necessarily entails a measure of positive discrimination."

Victimisation

It is unlawful to discriminate against a worker because s/he has raised an issue under the DDA in good faith. The concept is the same as that under the RRA (see p164) and other discrimination legislation.

Harassment

There is a myth that disabled workers do not particularly get subjected to harassment on grounds of disability. Unfortunately this happens all too often. It is a specific offence under the DDA to subject a disabled worker, on grounds of disability, to conduct with the purpose or effect of violating his/her dignity or creating an intimidating, hostile, degrading, humiliating or offensive environment. For more detail, see Chapter 12 on harassment.

Statutory disputes resolution procedures

If the member is an employee and wants to bring a tribunal case for disability discrimination, s/he will probably have to send his/her employer a step 1 grievance letter about the discrimination first. If s/he has been dismissed, s/he need not do this, but the statutory disciplinary procedure will apply. There is an exception to the rules if the member has been subjected to harassment and reasonably fears that following the procedure would cause further harassment. For the rules on the statutory procedures and the effect on time-limits, see pp57-72.

Disability discrimination: Myths

● *Myth:*
The Disability Discrimination Act will not apply to many of the members – it is rather a specialist bit of law.
Truth:
The DDA applies to a surprising number of members and is a very useful piece of law. Not only do many workers have hidden and non-visible disabilities, the DDA also covers certain injuries and ill-health

Disability discrimination: Key points

● The law against disability discrimination is contained in the Disability Discrimination Act 1995.

● As with other discrimination legislation, the DDA is wider than unfair dismissal law and does not protect only employees. No minimum service is necessary.

● The definitions of discrimination are different in important respects under the DDA, although the concept of victimisation is the same as under the RRA , SDA, religion and belief regulations and sexual orientation regulations..

Uniquely under the DDA, employers have a positive duty to make reasonable adjustments for any disabled worker who would otherwise be at a disadvantage.

● The Disability Rights Commission web-site is a useful source of information and links to other specialist sites. Specialist sites such as that of the RNIB, the RNID and the British Dyslexia Association give a great deal of information regarding (i) the range of effects of the disability and (ii) equipment and other sources of assistance (which is relevant to adjustments). A Guide to proving the member has a disability under the DDA and to reasonable adjustments is listed in the Bibliography (p315).

● See p300 for the important questionnaire procedure and special time-limits applicable to discrimination cases. A specialist Guide to writing DDA Questionnaires is listed in the Bibliography (p315).

● The statutory disputes resolution procedures will often apply and have to be followed before the member brings a tribunal case.

● See p131 for disability and redundancy and Chapter 12 for harassment.

Chapter 11:

Age, religion, sexual orientation discrimination

Contents

Overview of discrimination law

Over the last few years, discrimination law has undergone a huge expansion, largely driven by Europe. The UK has had law against race and sex discrimination since the '70s, in the form of the Sex Discrimination Act, the Equal Pay Act and the Race Relations Act. Since 1996, disability discrimination has been unlawful under the Disability Discrimination Act. In December 2003, law against discrimination on grounds of sexual orientation, religion and belief was introduced in Regulations, as a result of the European General Framework Directive. Also under the Directive, law against age discrimination must be introduced by December 2006. In Northern Ireland, discrimination on grounds of religious belief or political opinion is unlawful under the Fair Employment and Treatment (Northern Ireland) Order.

Under section 71 of the Race Relations Act, there is a duty on public authorities to promote equality of opportunity. Similar duties are shortly to be introduced under the Sex Discrimination Act and Disability Discrimination Act.

The body with the remit to oversee the operation of the Sex Discrimination Act and the Equal Pay Act is the Equal Opportunities Commission (EOC). The Commission for Racial Equality (CRE) has a similar remit under the Race Relations Act and the Disability Rights Commission (DRC) covers the Disability Discrimination Act. These bodies are to be merged from 2007-8 into a new Commission for Equality and Human Rights (CEHR), which will also have responsibility for religious, sexual orientation and age discrimination and, to a lesser extent, human rights law.

In Spring 2005, the government announced two separate reviews, an Equality Review and a Discrimination Law Review. The Equality Review, chaired by Trevor Phillips, is to investigate causes of persistent discrimination and inequality in British society. The parallel Discrimination Law Review is to assess how anti-discrimination legislation can be modernised.

Discrimination law is currently very confusing because of the slight differences in wording between the various statutes and regulations. In the longer term, it is planned to develop a Single Equality Act, which will cover all strands of discrimination in a new and effective way.

This Chapter deals with the most recent areas of discrimination law: age, religion and belief, and sexual orientation. Race discrimination is at chapter 8; sex discrimination at chapter 9; equal pay in chapter 2; disability discrimination at chapter 10; harassment at chapter 12.

Age discrimination

There is currently no law forbidding discrimination on grounds of age, although certain forms of age discrimination may amount to indirect sex or race discrimination. There is also a voluntary Code of Practice on Age Diversity at Work, published by the Department of Work and Pensions, which can be downloaded from the Age Positive website (www.agepositive.gov.uk).

Under the European General Framework Directive, law against age discrimination must be introduced by 2nd December 2006. The government intended to publish the law some time before that deadline, in order to give businesses plenty of notice. However, the publication date has been delayed due to the controversy over whether a compulsory retirement age would be retained and other difficulties. Draft legislation should be produced for consultation in mid to late 2005.

After initial promising signs that it would abolish compulsory retirement age, the government unfortunately bowed to business pressure and decided not to do so. Instead, it seems that the retirement age will be 65, unless employers can prove a lower retirement age is objectively justified. Employees will have the right to request to work beyond 65. This is rather an empty right since all it does is entitle employees to be given a reason when they are refused. The retirement age will be monitored to see whether it should be changed in 5 years time.

Religion and belief discrimination

Legal framework

The law against religious discrimination is set out in the Employment Equality (Religion or Belief) Regulations 2003. These were passed to implement the EU General Framework Directive.

Until these Regulations were passed, there was no direct law forbidding religious discrimination. However, the Race Relations Act does forbid discrimination against certain ethnic groups, eg Jews and Sikhs. Also, the concept of indirect race discrimination protects workers of certain racial groups against discriminatory practices which would be contrary to their religion and culture.

ACAS has issued a guide which can be downloaded from its website (see Bibliography, p318): "Religion or Belief and the Workplace: Putting the Employment Equality (Religion or Belief) Regulations 2003 into practice." This guide has no legal status, but it is recognised as a useful reference point. It also gives information on various religions.

There is currently no body analogous to the Commission for Racial Equality or Equal Opportunities Commission, which is specifically responsible for overseeing religious discrimination law. The proposed Commission for Equality and Human Rights ("CEHR") will in future include this role (see p221).

The structure of the Regulations mirrors that of the Employment Equality (Sexual Orientation) Regulations 2003 (see p234). It is also very similar to the Race Relations Act and the Sex Discrimination Act.

The Regulations came into force in December 2003. Statistics for the first 11 months show 230 tribunal claims were made, of which ten were decided at a tribunal hearing. Two were successful. At the time of writing (April 2005), no cases have reached the EAT, so the various difficult legal questions arising from the Regulations remain untested.

Which workers are covered

The Regulations do not purely cover employees. The scope of workers covered is the same as under the Race Relations Act ("RRA") (see p161).

Religion and belief

There is no definition of "religion or belief" in the Regulations, which simply say that it means any religion, religious belief or similar philosophical belief. The ACAS guide lists the following as some of the most commonly practised religions and beliefs in Britain: Baha'i, Buddhism, Christianity, Hinduism, Islam, Jainism, Judaism, Rastafarianism, Sikhism, Zoroastrianism, and other ancient religions eg Druidry, Paganism, and Wicca. There is no reason why fringe religions should not also be included within the definition.

It is uncertain what is covered by "similar philosophical belief". It is thought to include beliefs such as humanism or pacifism, but not support for a particular political party. It is unknown whether it could be stretched further, eg to cover vegans or animal rights activists.

At the time of writing, it is planned to amend the Regulations in the Equality Bill to confirm that they also prohibit discrimination on grounds of lack of religion. In the original Regulations, this is unclear. Strongly held views such as atheism or agnosticism should be covered as a "similar philosophical belief", but it is less clear if workers are protected when they are discriminated against simply because they are vague and unsure about religion. Or because they are not of a particular religion favoured by the employers, eg not Christian.

Vicarious liability

The concept of vicarious liability is the same as under the RRA (see p162).

When may discrimination happen

The stages at which discrimination may happen is the same as under the RRA (see p163).

The definition of unlawful discrimination

Overview

There are four kinds of unlawful discrimination under the Regulations: direct discrimination, indirect discrimination, victimisation and harassment. Each of these words has a very precise legal meaning, which is different from its meaning in natural every-day language. You need to remember this.

Direct discrimination

The formal definition is in reg 3(1)(a):

"A person ("A") discriminates against another person ("B") if, on grounds of religion or belief, A treats B less favourably than he treats or would treat other persons."

The definition mirrors that for direct race discrimination under the Race Relations Act.

Under the religion and belief Regulations, there are several possibilities for direct discrimination:

■ The member is treated differently because of his/her own religion or belief.

For example, the employers refuse to recruit a worker because s/he is Jewish.

■ The member is treated differently because of the employers' false perception of his/her religion or belief.

For example, the employers refuse to recruit an Egyptian man of Christian religion, because they (wrongly) assume him to be Muslim and they do not want to recruit a Muslim.

■ The member is treated differently on grounds of someone else's religion or belief.

For example, a Christian woman is not invited to a works outing, because she has a Rastafarian boyfriend.

There is often an overlap between race and religious discrimination. In fact, all three of these examples may also be an example of direct race discrimination. This is why:

→ example 1: Jewish people are considered an ethnic group under the Race Relations Act. Direct discrimination against someone because s/he is Jewish is therefore both race and religious discrimination.

→ example 2: The reason for the assumption that the job applicant is Muslim seems to be because he is Egyptian. This is therefore an assumption based on race.

→ example 3: Depending on the precise evidence, it is possible that the prejudice against the worker is also based on her boyfriend being black and not solely because he is Rastafarian.

Strangely, it is not unlawful for the discriminator to discriminate against someone because of the discriminator's own religion. For example, Hindu employers refuse to appoint the member because s/he is not Hindu. This exception is likely to cause difficulties in practice, but as yet it is legally untested.

There is no defence to direct discrimination. There are some very limited Genuine Occupational Requirement and positive action exceptions (see p233).

You should always ask the "but for" question:

"If the member was of a different religion or of no religion (ie but for the member's religion), would the employers have treated him/her the same way?"

The kind of evidence necessary to prove direct religious discrimination is similar to that needed to prove direct discrimination under the Race Relations Act (see p168).

Indirect discrimination

The definition of indirect discrimination is at regulation 3(1)(b). There are four stages to the definition:

1 The member fails to get a job or is selected for redundancy or is otherwise disadvantaged.

2 This is because of a provision, criterion or practice applied by the employers.

3 That provision, criterion or practice puts those of the member's religion or belief at a particular disadvantage compared with others.

4 The employers cannot justify applying the provision, criterion or practice by showing it is a proportionate means of achieving a legitimate aim.

For example, a hospital puts all staff on rotating shifts, so that their days off change from week to week. An observant Jewish employee asks not to be rostered on Friday afternoons through the Winter, because he needs to get home before nightfall, when the Sabbath comes in. The employers refuse, stating that no one can have fixed days off.

In this example, the member is disadvantaged because of the general rule imposed by the employers that no one has any fixed days off. This would also put other observant Jewish workers at a particular disadvantage. The final question is whether the employers can justify their position. If there are other staff who could cover Friday afternoons, the answer is probably not.

There are many practices which may disadvantage workers because of their religion. Very often the key issue is whether the employers can justify the practice. It does not matter that some less observant workers of the same religion would not be particularly disadvantaged.

For further examples of potential indirect religious discrimination, see pp228-233.

Victimisation

The definition of victimisation is the same under each piece of discrimination legislation. Under reg 4 of the Employment Equality (Religion and Belief) Regulations, it is where the member is punished or treated less favourably because s/he has complained about religious discrimination in some way, eg verbally, in a letter, in a formal grievance or in a tribunal, on his/her own behalf or on behalf of someone else. For example, the member brings a grievance regarding religious discrimination by her manager. Shortly afterwards she is made redundant in suspicious circumstances.

The employers can defend a case of victimisation if the member's complaint of religious discrimination was false and made in bad faith. For more detail on victimisation and the kind of evidence necessary to prove a case, see the section on victimisation under the RRA (p164).

Harassment

Under reg 5(1), it is unlawful, on grounds of religion or belief, to engage in unwanted conduct which has the purpose or effect of violating the member's dignity or creating an intimidating, hostile, degrading, humiliating or offensive environment for the member. The test is whether, having regard to all the circumstances and particularly the member's perception, the conduct should reasonably be considered as having such an effect.

As with direct discrimination, the harassment may be on grounds of the member's own religion or belief, or that of someone else, or due to a false perception of his/her religion or belief.

However, unlike direct discrimination, it is also unlawful to harass someone because of your own religion or belief, eg because they do not share your religion.

The ACAS guide says harassment may be intentional and obvious bullying, or unintentional or subtle behaviour. It may involve nicknames, teasing, name calling or other behaviour which is not intended to be malicious, but nevertheless is upsetting. It may not be targeted at the individual but may consist of a general culture, eg which tolerates the telling of religious jokes.

Examples of harassment, deliberate or unintentional, could be:

→ Anti-Muslim remarks or so-called "jokes" and "banter" referring to terrorist attacks, or demonstrating general prejudice towards Muslims as a group (Islamophobia).

→ Allowing excessive expression of overt football allegiances where these are a proxy for sectarian rivalry, eg as may happen in Glasgow as between Celtic and Rangers fans.

→ Harassing Jewish workers because of their (perceived) support for Israel. Allowing hostility towards the State of Israel to develop into an atmosphere of anti-Semitism.

→ A devout Christian haranguing colleagues for being insufficiently religious.

The ACAS guide notes that although some religions have strong views about sexual orientation, most do not advocate persecution of people because of their sexual orientation. Everyone has the right to be treated with dignity and respect in the workplace, whatever his/her race, sex, age, disability, religion or sexual orientation. Workers need not be friends, but they should treat each other professionally.

Indeed, harassment of a worker because s/he is gay or lesbian would be contrary to the Employment Equality (Sexual Orientation) Regulations 2003 (see p238).

Several types of discrimination
More than one type of discrimination may have taken place. For example, a member complains about his/her employers' failure to let him/her pray at work. Shortly afterwards, s/he fails to gain promotion. This may be:

1 Direct discrimination in the original refusal to let the member pray at work.

2 Direct discrimination or victimisation in the failure to get promotion.

The member may also have suffered discrimination on more than one ground. For example a Muslim of Algerian background may be subjected to racial and religious harassment at the same time. A Hindu woman may have failed to gain promotion because she is a woman and because she is Hindu. You need to consider the facts to see whether they clearly indicate one ground is dominant or whether they are consistent with both grounds being present.

Common issues

Policy and preventative action

It is useful to know more about the most commonly practised religions in your workplace, as you may be able to identify in advance certain problem areas and prevent them happening. For example:

→ Training days or works outings should not be fixed on important religious holidays.

→ Work-related social or client outings should be at acceptable locations and provide appropriate food and drink.

→ When negotiating dress codes, exceptions should be made for religious dress and jewellery.

→ Recruitment interviews on Fridays should be avoided.

→ Arrangements for shower and changing room facilities should ensure privacy.

→ The length of compassionate leave should take account of periods of formal mourning required by certain religions.

Further information about the requirements and obligations of different religions can be obtained from a variety of sources, including the individual members. Remember that in each religion there is usually a large range of observance, from very strict to largely social. However, individuals are likely to feel very strongly about their particular level of observance, however small or great.

Amongst others sources, information can be obtained from:

→ The ACAS guide, regarding the religions listed there (see above).

→ The Muslim Council of Britain has useful information on its

website at www.mcb.org.uk and has produced a Good Practice
Guide: "Religious Discrimination at the Workplace" - telephone:
0208 432 0585.
→ The Board of Deputies has published "Employment. A Practical
Guide for Employers and Jewish Employees". This can be
downloaded from www.bod.org.uk or telephone 020 7543 5400.

Dress codes and appearance

Many religions have obligations in terms of dress and appearance.
How people dress will depend on their level of observance. Example
of religious dress are:
→ As part of the 5 Ks of their faith, strictly practising male Sikhs do
not shave or cut their hair, which is covered with a turban. They wear
a "Kara" (metal bracelet) and a "Kirpan" (short ceremonial sword
under clothing).
→ Many Sikh women cover their hair with a scarf ("dupattah" or
"chooni").
Rastafarians wear uncut hair, plaited into dreadlocks. They often wear
a hat (usually, red, green and gold).
→ Muslim men usually wear Western shirts and trousers (not shorts),
though a few may wear traditional dress. Some men will keep their
heads covered at all times. Many Muslim men also grow a beard,
which is considered obligatory within some schools of thought.
→ Muslim women may dress modestly, covering arms and legs. Some
may wear a "hijab" (headscarf). More unusually, in some
communities, women may wear a "burqa" or "chador", which covers
them from head to ankle and conceals the shape of their body.
Muslims may wear jewellery signifying marriage or religious devotion.
→ Many Hindu women wear modest dress, covering their legs, eg a
sari or top over loose trousers. They often wear a "bindi" (a red dot
on the forehead). Many married women wear a necklace ("mangal
sutra") or other wedding jewellery, eg bangles or nose rings, as well as
a wedding ring.
→ A few Hindu men wear a small tuft of hair ("shikha") similar to a
ponytail, although this is often hidden under the remaining hair.
→ Orthodox Jewish men keep their head covered at all times, usually
wearing a skullcap ("kappel", "kippah" or "yarmulke"). Orthodox
women will dress modestly, avoiding trousers or short sleeves and
skirts. They may cover their heads with a scarf.

Employers imposing rigid dress codes forbidding jewellery, headwear, beards or long hair for men, or who impose uniforms with short sleeves or skirts, may indirectly discriminate against members of certain religious groups. Whether or not it is unlawful indirect discrimination, will usually depend on the employers' reason for imposing the rule. Reasons such as safety or hygiene are the most likely justification, but there are ways around most difficulties.

Differential rules may also amount to direct discrimination, eg if the employers allow Sikh men to wear turbans but do not allow Muslim women to wear hijabs.

Prayer breaks

Observant Muslims need to pray five times/day at fixed times. The times are: dawn, just after midday, mid afternoon, immediately after sunset and at night, just before going to bed. The number of occasions which fall at work therefore depends on the member's shifts and the season. The prayer breaks take about 10 minutes on each occasion, the same time it may take any worker to make coffee, have a chat or go to the toilet. Devout Hindus may also pray three times / day, at sunrise, noon and sunset.

Unjustified refusal to allow time off to pray will be indirect discrimination. Moreover, if the employers allow other workers to take breaks for different reasons, eg cigarette breaks, refusal of a prayer break could also be direct discrimination.

It is difficult to see how such a refusal could be justified, although if the employers refuse to allow any workers to take breaks of any kind, the member may have to offer to make up the time. It is helpful that a worker is entitled to at least one 20 minute break away from the work station every six hours under the Working Time Regulations (see p30). Employers are probably not required to provide a prayer room, but if there is an available quiet space, it would almost certainly be discriminatory not to allow the member to use it.

Sabbath working

Members may need certain days off for religious holidays (below) or because of the Sabbath. The Muslim holy day is Friday and many Muslim men try to attend mid-day prayer at a mosque every Friday. For Jewish people, the Sabbath ("Shabbat") is Saturday, but it starts at sundown on Friday. Observant Jews must arrive at home before Sabbath begins, which means leaving work in early afternoon during Winter.

A requirement to work Friday, Saturday or Sunday may therefore indirectly discriminate against certain members. Whether or not such a requirement is justifiable depends on the nature of the job and whether other arrangements can be made.

There are also long-standing rules under the Employment Rights Act 1996, allowing shop and betting workers to refuse to work on Sundays.

Religious holidays

Every religion has a range of holidays of varying importance. Each individual will have his/her own feelings as to which holidays s/he feels obliged to observe. Very often the holidays are part of a cultural as well as a religious tradition and there are social and family pressures to observe the day, even if the individual is not particularly religious.

The dates of the holidays can be hard to ascertain in advance, as many follow the lunar year. Jewish holidays start at sundown the previous evening. Advance dates of Jewish holidays can be found on the following website: www.jewishgen.org/jos/josfest.

Some well-known holidays

The two most important festivals for Muslims are Eid-al-Fitr, which marks the end of Ramadan, and Eid-al-Adha. The exact date depends on a sighting of the new moon and is not known far in advance. "Eid" means festival. Muslim workers would need at least one day off on each occasion to celebrate appropriately.

Major Hindu festivals include Divali (or Deepavali) in October/November, which marks the end of the Hindu year, Holi (in February/March), Raksha bandhan (in August) and Navratri (in September/October).

The main Sikh festivals include the Birthday of Guru Nanak (in October/November), Vaisakhi, the New Year festival, normally on 13th April, and Bandhi Chhord (October/November), at the same time as Divali – many Sikhs celebrate both.

There are 13 key days which a minority of observant Jews would follow. The most important and universally observed dates requiring time off work are Yom Kippur (the Day of Atonement) and Rosh Hashannah (the New Year). These fall in September/October. Pesach (or Passover), near Easter, and Chanukah, near Christmas, are also commonly celebrated. Other holidays include Sukkot, Shavuot and Tish'ah B'av.

Time off

Not all religious holidays require time off work, but most do. Difficulties arise when employers object to granting time off, saying that the member has benefited from time off over Christmas and Easter.

In most circumstances, refusal to allow the member time off for a religious holiday would be discriminatory. It should not be underestimated how important many of these religious holidays are to the individual and his/her family. The question is whether the time should be paid or unpaid, or whether it should come out of the member's annual holiday entitlement. Legally, this is difficult to answer. Requiring the time to come out of existing holiday entitlement is arguably indirect discrimination, because the member is disadvantaged by using up one of his/her holiday days to meet religious obligations, which may not even be of a festive nature (eg a fast day). The best solution would appear to be paid leave. Arguably this directly discriminates against those who are not of a religion requiring additional holidays, but it is doubtful this is a comparable situation.

Fixing training and outings on religious holidays

It is thoughtless, unfair and possibly discriminatory to fix social events or one-off training on important religious holidays. Dates should routinely be checked in advance.

Food and drink

Muslims and orthodox people of certain other religions do not drink alcohol. Many religions also have dietary restrictions, either avoiding certain animals or complete vegetarianism. This means that:

➔ Vegetarian food and non-alcoholic drinks should be available in works canteens and at out-of-work outings.

➔ Out-of-work events should not be located in pubs or wine-bars.

➔ Separate storage space for food should be available.

During the holy month of Ramadan, it is particularly important that any Muslim workers who must start or end their daily fast at work have access to a fridge and food storage space. Muslims fast during Ramadan, taking no food or drink between dawn and darkness. Most people get up one or two hours before dawn to eat before the fast begins. Workers may feel faint and irritable with headaches in the first week. By the fourth week, they may have little energy. They may find it difficult to be in the presence of others who are eating or cooking at this time. The dates of Ramadan change each year. When it falls in the Summer, the fast days are particularly long.

Some permitted religion or belief discrimination

Genuine occupational requirements

It is permitted to discriminate in very limited circumstances under regulation 7 of the Regulations, where being of a particular religion or belief is a genuine occupational requirement ("GOR"). This exception should be applied only rarely.

There are two types of GOR:

1 The general requirement.

2 A requirement based on the employers' religious ethos. This is where the employers have an ethos based on religion or belief, eg a religious organisation, school or care-home.

The employers must prove that:

■ There is a genuine requirement for the member to be of a particular religion or belief. It is not just an excuse to discriminate.

■ For the general GOR, the requirement must also be "determining" ie being of the particular religion or belief is decisive and crucial to the post, not just one of several factors.

■ It is proportionate to apply the requirement in the particular case. In other words, it is an appropriate and necessary means of achieving the employers' aim and not just a matter of convenience. The aim cannot be achieved in another less discriminatory way.

■ This is measured in view of the nature of the employment or the context in which it is carried out.

■ For the religious ethos type of GOR, it is also measured in the light of that ethos.

For both types of GOR, it is the particular job which must be considered. It is unlikely to be a GOR for a caretaker of a religious care-home to be of the same religion. (There is separate legislation which already covers faith-based schools.)

Positive action

Limited positive action is permitted under the Regulations. Where it compensates for disadvantages linked to religion or belief suffered by workers of that religion or belief generally, the employers may:

→ offer exclusive training courses to fit workers for particular work

→ encourage those of a particular religion or belief to take advantages of job opportunities – eg they can target their recruitment advertising (although they may not discriminate at the point of deciding who to take on).

Sexual orientation discrimination

Legal framework

There are estimated to be between 1.3 and 1.9 million lesbians, gay men and bisexual people in employment. In a survey carried out for UNISON in early 2003, 52% of members responding said they had experienced harassment because they are lesbian or gay.

In December 2003, law against discrimination on grounds of sexual orientation came into effect. The law is set out in the Employment Equality (Sexual Orientation) Regulations 2003. These were passed to implement the EU General Framework Directive.

Until these Regulations were passed, there was no direct law forbidding discrimination against workers because they are lesbian or gay. There were various unsuccessful attempts to make sexual orientation discrimination fit within the Sex Discrimination Act. However, discrimination against gay workers can be a breach of the Human Rights Act, violating article 8 (the right to privacy) taken with article 14 (non-discrimination) of the European Convention of Human Rights.

ACAS has issued a guide which can be downloaded from its website (see Bibliography, p314): "Sexual Orientation and the Workplace: Putting the Employment Equality (Sexual Orientation) Regulations 2003 into practice." This guide has no legal status, but it is recognised as a useful reference point.

There is currently no body analogous to the Commission for Racial Equality or Equal Opportunities Commission, which is specifically responsible for overseeing sexual orientation law. The proposed Commission for Equality and Human Rights ("CEHR") will in future include this role (see p221).

The structure of the Regulations mirrors that of the Employment Equality (Religion and Belief) Regulations 2003 (see p222). It is also very similar to the Race Relations Act and the Sex Discrimination Act. UNISON has issued a bargaining support guide: "Negotiating Equality for Lesbian, Gay and Bisexual Workers". This is available on the website under Resources / Online Catalogue / Equalities.

Which workers are covered

The Regulations do not purely cover employees. The scope of workers covered is the same as under the Race Relations Act ("RRA") (see p161).

Sexual orientation

The Regulations cover sexual orientation towards persons of the same sex or of the opposite sex or both. In other words, workers must not be discriminated against because they are lesbian, gay, bisexual or heterosexual.

The definition of sexual orientation does not extend to sexual practices, eg sado-masochism or paedophilia.

Vicarious liability

The concept of vicarious liability is the same as under the RRA (see p162).

When may discrimination happen

The stages at which discrimination may happen is the same as under 163).

The definition of unlawful discrimination

Overview

There are four kinds of unlawful discrimination under the Regulations: direct discrimination, indirect discrimination, victimisation and harassment. Each of these words has a very precise legal meaning, which is different from its meaning in natural every-day language. You need to remember this.

Direct discrimination

The formal definition is in reg 3(1)(a):

"A person ("A") discriminates against another person ("B") if, on grounds of sexual orientation, A treats B less favourably than he treats or would treat other persons."

The definition mirrors that for direct race discrimination under the Race Relations Act.

Under the sexual orientation Regulations, there are several possibilities for direct discrimination:

■ The member is treated differently because of his/her own sexual orientation.

For example, the employers refuse to recruit a worker because she is a lesbian.

■ The member is treated differently because of the employers' false perception of his/her sexual orientation.

For example, the employers refuse to recruit a man, because they (wrongly) assume he is gay and they do not want to recruit a gay worker.

■ The member is treated differently on grounds of someone else's sexual orientation.

For example, a woman is made redundant because the employers do not like it that she has gay friends.

There is no defence to direct discrimination. There are some very limited Genuine Occupational Requirement and positive action exceptions (see p240).

You should always ask the "but for" question:

"If the member was of a different sexual orientation (ie but for the member's sexual orientation), would the employers have treated him/her the same way?"

Other examples of direct discrimination could be:

➔ Discouraging lesbian and gay workers from bringing their partner to a works outing, when their heterosexual colleagues are allowed to bring along their partners.

➔ Dismissing a lesbian or gay worker for having a relationship with a work colleague of the same sex, when a worker involved in a heterosexual relationship with a colleague would not be dismissed.

➔ Instructing lesbian and gay workers (but not heterosexual workers) to conceal their sexual orientation to avoid homophobia from service users and members of the public.

The kind of evidence necessary to prove direct sexual orientation discrimination is similar to that needed to prove direct discrimination under other discrimination legislation (eg see p168 under the RRA).

Indirect discrimination

The definition of indirect discrimination is at regulation 3(1)(b). There are four stages to the definition:

1 The member fails to get a job or is selected for redundancy or is otherwise disadvantaged.

2 This is because of a provision, criterion or practice applied by the employers.

3 That provision, criterion or practice puts those of the member's sexual orientation at a particular disadvantage compared with others.

4 The employers cannot justify applying the provision, criterion or practice by showing it is a proportionate means of achieving a legitimate aim.

For example, the employers allow first choice of time off at Christmas to staff with children. Although this is a general rule, which would also affect heterosexual workers without children, it is a rule which would be likely to affect lesbian and gay workers more than others. However, the rule will not be unlawful if the employers can show it meets a legitimate aim and is proportionate.

The Regulations make it unlawful for employers to provide survivors' pension benefits or other perks, eg private health insurance, to opposite-sex partners only. Unfortunately it is explicitly permitted to confine access to such benefits to married partners. In a test case, UNISON and other trade unions unsuccessfully challenged this exception.

Victimisation

The definition of victimisation is the same under each piece of discrimination legislation. Under reg 4 of the Employment Equality (Sexual Orientation) Regulations, it is where the member is punished or treated less favourably because s/he has complained about sexual orientation discrimination in some way, eg verbally, in a letter, in a formal grievance or in a tribunal, on his/her own behalf or on behalf of someone else.

For example, the member brings a grievance regarding sexual orientation discrimination by her manager. Shortly afterwards she is made redundant in suspicious circumstances.

The employers can defend a case of victimisation if the member's complaint of sexual orientation discrimination was false and made in bad faith.

For more detail on victimisation and the kind of evidence necessary to prove a case, see the section on victimisation under the RRA (p164).

Harassment

Under reg 5(1), it is unlawful, on grounds of sexual orientation, to engage in unwanted conduct which has the purpose or effect of violating the member's dignity or creating an intimidating, hostile, degrading, humiliating or offensive environment for the member. The test is whether, having regard to all the circumstances and particularly the member's perception, the conduct should reasonably be considered as having such an effect.

As with direct discrimination, the harassment may be on grounds of the member's own sexual orientation, or that of someone else, or due to a false perception of his/her sexual orientation.

The TUC says the most common form of discrimination faced by lesbian and gay workers is harassment. The ACAS guide states that harassment may be intentional and obvious bullying, or unintentional or subtle behaviour. It may involve nicknames, teasing, name calling or other behaviour which is not intended to be malicious, but nevertheless is upsetting. It may not be targeted at the individual but may consist of a general culture, eg which tolerates the telling of homophobic jokes. Examples of harassment, deliberate or unintentional, could be:

→ "Outing" a lesbian, gay or bisexual worker for malicious reasons or against his/her wishes.

→ Spreading rumours that a gay man has HIV just because he takes sick leave or loses weight.

→ Where lesbian, gay or bisexual workers complain of harassment, accusing them of being over-sensitive, having no sense of humour or bringing it on themselves by hiding (or revealing) their sexual orientation.

Much has been made of the possible conflict with the law against religious discrimination, ie can a worker be prevented from making homophobic observations if these are an expression of his/her religious views? Hopefully this will rarely occur in practice. The ACAS guide notes that although some religions have strong views about sexual orientation, most do not advocate persecution of people because of their sexual orientation. Everyone has the right to be treated with dignity and respect in the workplace, whatever his/her race, sex, age, disability, religion or sexual orientation. Workers need not be friends, but they should treat each other professionally.

Several types of discrimination

More than one type of discrimination may have taken place. For example, a member complains about homophobic remarks. Shortly afterwards, s/he fails to gain promotion. This may be:

1 The harassment in respect of the remarks.

2 Direct discrimination or victimisation in respect of the failure to get promotion.

The member may also have suffered discrimination on more than one ground. For example a gay man who is black, may be subjected to racial and sexual orientation harassment at the same time.

Common issues

Visibility and confidentiality

A survey in 2003 showed that nearly 40% of UNISON's lesbian and gay members were not out to all their managers, and over 80% were not out to their client group. Men were twice as likely to be out at work as women. This has implications for the nature of workplace policies, the purpose of monitoring, and the willingness of individuals to complain about discrimination or harassment. It is also very important that UNISON reps ensure confidentiality when advising members.

Monitoring

The Regulations do not require employers to monitor sexual orientation. Whether or not they should monitor this and what its purpose would be, are difficult questions given that, unlike with race and gender, workers may choose to hide their sexual orientation at work. The TUC has produced a useful guide, which also covers trans-sexual workers: "Monitoring LGBT workers", available on its website (see p00). The UNISON Bargaining Guide mentioned above also discusses this issue.

General policy

In general, do not assume and act on the basis that everyone is heterosexual. Care should be taken over interview questions, even those designed to put the candidate at ease, concerning family or social matters, which would force someone to out him/herself. On social and works outings, take care with the wording of invitations to ensure it includes same-sex partners.

Policies should state that the following are equally available to same-sex partners: compassionate and bereavement leave; parental and adoption leave; carers' leave; perks such as private healthcare insurance, free travel and discounts on company goods. The statutory entitlements to dependant, parental, adoption and "paternity" leave are all available to same sex partners.

Criminal convictions

Historically, gay men have been vulnerable to criminal convictions in respect of offences which are no longer unlawful or have no heterosexual equivalent. Employers who refuse to recruit anyone with any kind of criminal conviction or arrest record may therefore indirectly discriminate against gay men, unless the particular job justifies their policy. The ACAS Code suggests that employers take into account the fact that laws relating to gay men have changed significantly over time and many convictions are unlikely to have any bearing on the individual's skills and suitability for the job. For more detail, see the section on unrelated criminal convictions in the UNISON Bargaining Guide mentioned above.

Some permitted sexual orientation discrimination

Genuine occupational requirements

It is permitted to discriminate in very limited circumstances under regulation 7 of the Regulations, where being of a particular sexual orientation is a genuine occupational requirement ("GOR"). This exception should be applied very rarely.

There are two types of GOR:

1 The general requirement.

2 A requirement where employment is for the purpose of an organised religion.

If a GOR applies, it is permitted to discriminate against the member either because s/he is in fact not of the required sexual orientation, or because the employers reasonably don't think s/he is of the required orientation.

For the general GOR, the employers must prove that, having regard to the nature of the employment or the context in which it is carried out:

■ There is a genuine requirement to be of a particular sexual orientation. It is not just an excuse to discriminate.

■ For the general GOR, the requirement must also be "determining" ie decisive and crucial to the post, not just one of several factors.

■ It is proportionate to apply the requirement in the particular case. In other words, it is an appropriate and necessary means of achieving the employers' aim and not just a matter of convenience. The aim cannot be achieved in another less discriminatory way.

■ This is measured in view of the nature of the employment or the context in which it is carried out.

The scope of this GOR is untested, but it is unlikely to apply very often. An example may be a position of leadership, representing the public face of an organisation which promotes the rights of lesbian and gay people, where it is necessary for the credibility of the organisation that this person is lesbian or gay.

Another example may be where it is necessary to recruit lesbian or gay counsellors to provide very sensitive psychiatric counselling to lesbian or gay clients. On the other hand, it is unlikely to be a GOR to be lesbian or gay in order to give advice to lesbian and gay workers on their legal rights under the new Regulations.

For the organised religion GOR, the employers must prove:

→ the employment is for the purpose of an organised religion.

→ the requirement is applied so as to comply with the doctrines of this religion, or

→ it is applied because of the nature of the employment and the context in which it is carried out, so as to avoid conflicting with the strongly held religious convictions of a significant number of the religion's followers.

This GOR has been very controversial because of the fear that it could be an excuse to exclude lesbian, gay or bisexual workers from a wide range of jobs. The government said it intended the exception mainly to cover ministers of religion or a small number of other posts outside the clergy, including those which exist to promote and represent a religion. In a test case brought by a number of trade unions, including UNISON, the High Court confirmed this exception must be interpreted in a very limited way.

> **R (on the application of Amicus - MSF section and others) v Secretary of State for Trade and Industry and Christian Action Research Education and others** [2004] IRLR 430, HC
>
> The trade unions argued that the organised religion GOR under reg 7(3) was too wide and outside the Directive. The High Court judge disagreed.
>
> However, he did say the reg 7(3) exception must be construed strictly and purposively, to ensure compatability with the Directive. The term "for the purposes of an organised religion" does not mean "for the purposes of a religious organisation". In particular, employment in a faith school is not likely to be for the purposes of an organised religion.
>
> The trade unions also unsuccessfully challenged the exception for benefits confined to married couples (see above).

Positive action

Limited positive action is permitted under the Regulations. Where it compensates for disadvantages linked to sexual orientation suffered by workers of that orientation generally, the employers may:
offer exclusive training courses to fit workers for particular work
encourage those of a particular sexual orientation to take advantages of job opportunities – eg they can target their recruitment advertising (although they may not discriminate at the point of deciding who to take on).

Age, religion, sexual orientation discrimination: key points

● Law against age discrimination must come into force by 2nd December 2006.

● The law against religion and belief discrimination is contained in the Employment Equality (Religion and Belief) Regulations 2003

● The law against sexual orientation discrimination is contained in the Employment Equality (Sexual Orientation) Regulations 2003

● As with other discrimination legislation, the law against religion, belief or sexual orientation discrimination is wider than unfair dismissal law and does not purely protect employees. No minimum service is necessary.

● Individuals can bring cases of direct discrimination, indirect discrimination, victimisation or harassment.

● There is currently no equality body with a remit to oversee age, religion, sexual orientation discrimination law. From 2007, a new Commission for Equality and Human Rights will have responsibility to oversee all areas of discrimination law and human rights.

● See p300 for the important questionnaire procedure and special time-limits applicable to all discrimination cases.

● See Chapter 12 for harassment, Chapter 3 for the statutory disciplinary and grievance procedures and for discrimination in disciplinaries and grievances, Chapter 6 for discrimination and redundancy.

Chapter 12:

Harassment and stress

Contents

Introduction

Bullying or harassment in the workplace can be a big problem, but the law is not always adequate to deal with it. Effective preventative policies are extremely important in this area.

Harassment on grounds of race, religion or belief, sex, sexual orientation or disability can be challenged in an employment tribunal under the Race Relations Act, Employment Equality (Religion or Belief) Regulations, Sex Discrimination Act, Employment Equality (Sexual Orientation) Regulations, or Disability Discrimination Act.

Harassment which is not on one of these specifically unlawful grounds is far harder to challenge legally. If the employers carry out the harassment or fail to deal adequately with a complaint, the member may be able to resign and claim constructive dismissal. However, constructive dismissal cases are hard to prove (see p118) and the member will also find him/herself out of a job.

If the harassment is sufficiently serious and particularly if there is any physical element, the member may be able to bring a civil or criminal claim in the high court or county court, including a claim under the Protection from Harassment Act 1997 (see below). Unfortunately this is not a very practical option as the proper courts involve more expense, technical procedures and costs against the member if s/he loses. If the harassment is serious and the evidence is strong, but the case cannot be brought under one of the discrimination statutes, it is important that the Employment Rights Unit is contacted as soon as possible through the correct union channels.

Harassment cases are difficult legally and usually involve detailed factual situations, difficulties of proof and considerable distress on the part of the member. Sexual harassment is particularly sensitive. See p252 for a checklist on interviewing in potential sexual harassment cases. You should also obtain "Harassment: a UNISON guide to policy and representation" (see Bibliography p314).

Harassment under discrimination legislation

The legal definition of harassment

Historically, there was no express prohibition in the Race Relations Act or Sex Discrimination Act against harassment or abuse. The law developed so that harassment was treated as direct race discrimination or direct sex discrimination. It covered detriments such as abuse, unwanted physical contact, assault and disciplinary action.

If the harasser's behaviour got worse after the member asked him/her to stop, this could be victimisation.

As a result of EU directives, there is now a specific definition of harassment under the RRA (on grounds of race, ethnic or national origin), DDA, sexual orientation regulations and religion and belief regulations. From October 2005, there will be a similar but wider definition in the SDA.

The specific definition of harassment has the following elements:

- on grounds of race, ethnic or national origin, religion or belief, sexual orientation, disability and, from October 2005, sex and gender reassignment, or conduct of a sexual nature
- the harasser engages in unwanted conduct
- which has the purpose of
    (a)   violating the member's dignity, or
    (b)   creating an intimidating, hostile, degrading, humiliating or offensive environment for the member.
- Or, even if it is not intended, it can reasonably be regarded as having that effect, taking account of all the circumstances, particularly the perception of the harassed member.

Sexual harassment

In 1991 the European Commission issued a Code of Practice on measures to combat sexual harassment. Tribunals must take the Code into account when deciding cases of sexual harassment. The Code contains useful guidelines for preventative steps and handling grievances. It is reproduced in UNISON's guide on Harassment (Bibliography p314.)

The Code provides the following definition of sexual harassment:
"Sexual harassment means unwanted conduct of a sexual nature, or other conduct based on sex affecting the dignity of women and men at work. This can include unwelcome physical, verbal or non-verbal conduct.

Thus, a range of behaviour may be considered to constitute sexual harassment. It is unacceptable if such conduct is unwanted, unreasonable and offensive to the recipient; a person's rejection of or submission to such conduct .. is used explicitly as a basis for a decision which affects that person's access to vocational training or employment, continued employment, promotion, salary or any other employment decisions; and/or such conduct creates an intimidating, hostile or humiliating working environment for the recipient.

The essential characteristics of sexual harassment is that it is unwanted by the recipient, that it is for each individual to determine what behaviour is acceptable to them and what they regard as offensive."

The Employment Appeal Tribunal has given very useful guidelines in the case of *Reed and another v Stedman* ((1999) 86 EOR 46.) The EAT confirms that it is for the individual to decide what s/he finds unwelcome or offensive. Some conduct would obviously be unwelcome and the woman does not need to say so. At the other end of the scale, where the conduct is unexceptional, a woman may need to indicate that she finds it unacceptable, though she does not have to make a public fuss about it. Any continuation of the behaviour after that would be harassment. A tribunal should not look at each incident separately to measure its harm. It should look at the totality of the circumstances.

Employers' liability for the harassment

The employers will be liable for harassment carried out by a manager or colleague against the member, provided it was in the course of employment. This usually means on the work premises or at a work-related event. Incidents occurring during group outings, eg to the pub straight after work, will usually also be covered. You need to be careful here, as there are some borderline situations. (See also p162 on vicarious liability.)

The employers cannot be "vicariously" liable for harassment or discrimination carried out by members of the public. However, they may be responsible for discrimination in the way they handle the member's complaint about such harassment (see below).

The employers' reaction to a complaint

As well as being responsible for the harassment itself, the employers may discriminate in their response to any complaint or grievance. This could be direct discrimination or victimisation. Failure to take a complaint seriously could also amount to fundamental breach of the member's contract, entitling him/her to resign and claim constructive dismissal (see p118).

Examples of direct discrimination:

– Personnel / H.R. fail properly to investigate a black worker's complaint of racial harassment, but they would properly investigate a complaint of equal seriousness by a white worker. Watch out for:
– Taking an unnecessarily long time over the investigation.
– Not using the correct procedure.
– Any other indication that the employers are not taking the

complaint seriously, eg casual dismissive remarks.

— In a sexual harassment case, management suspend the woman but not the man while investigating the complaint.

— Management take out an injunction against a tenant who assaults a male rent collection officer but take no action against a tenant who sexually assaults a female officer.

The above may also be examples of victimisation, eg the reason the member is suspended is because she made a complaint of race or sex discrimination. See p199 for the definition of victimisation.

Remember that the employers can defend a victimisation claim if they prove the member's allegation was untrue and made in bad faith. In sexual harassment cases in particular, employers often allege that the member has maliciously fabricated the allegation.

Evidence of sexual harassment

Harassment can be hard to prove as the harasser invariably denies or twists the allegations. You should consider the following possible evidence:

→ Direct witnesses, who saw or heard an incident.

→ Indirect witnesses, ie anyone the member told at the time. This may be another work colleague, job agency or doctor.

→ Anyone else who has been harassed by the same person.

→ If the harasser has criticised the member's work, as often happens, consider whether you can disprove the work-related allegations. This would generally discredit the harasser.

Time-limits

Tribunal time-limits are very often missed on sexual harassment cases. Partly this is inevitable, because women often put up with harassment for a long time before speaking out. The European Code recognises this:

"It should be emphasised that a distinguishing characteristic of sexual harassment is that employees subjected to it often will be reluctant to complain. An absence of complaints about sexual harassment in a particular organisation, therefore, does not necessarily mean an absence of sexual harassment."

Discrimination time-limits are set out at p295. In harassment cases, this means that:

■ Time runs from each act of harassment, not just the most recent. Even if some incidents are out of time, it is important to keep as many as possible of the more serious or more easily proved incidents in time. In some circumstances the tribunal may accept that the member has been subjected to continuing discrimination, so his/her claim is not out of time. However, you must not rely on this exception, except for incidents which are already out of time when the member first seeks your advice.

■ If the member is off sick for a period, it is unlikely she has been subjected to any discrimination during that time. Therefore be careful that the entire claim does not drift out of time.

■ Time runs from the harassment, not from the outcome of the grievance. The member may have to lodge her tribunal claim before the grievance is completed. Note that the European Code says "grievances should be handled promptly and the procedure should set a time-limit within which complaints will be processed, with due regard for any time-limits set by national legislation for initiating a complaint through the legal system".

■ Where the statutory disputes resolution procedures apply, the member may have to send a step 1 grievance letter before starting a tribunal claim. S/he does not need to take a grievance if s/he has reasonable grounds to believe that it will cause further harassment. Note that where the procedures apply, time-limits are extended in some circumstances. See pp57-72 for more detail on the procedures and time-limits.

Questionnaires

In harassment cases where there has been an investigation, discrimination questionnaires (see p300) are extremely important. If the member intends to bring a legal case, s/he should send the employers a questionnaire as early as possible. The questionnaire will enable the member to get information about the nature and content of the investigation and the record of the harasser. For sample questionnaires, see the various Questionnaire Guides referred to in the Bibliography (p314).

Protection from Harassment Act 1997 (PHA)

The PHA was not designed for employment situations, but it can apply. It defines harassment as conduct which occurs on two or more occasions, which a reasonable person would realise could cause distress. This could include verbal or physical conduct. The conduct is not unlawful if it is reasonable, eg legitimate disciplinary action. It is also unlawful to cause someone to fear violence will be used against him/her.

A claim can be made under the PHA for financial loss and anxiety and/or an injunction (non-harassment order) to restrain the harasser. The claim can be made against the harasser as an individual or against the employers as vicariously liable for the harassment, provided there was a sufficiently close connection with the employment. As with all claims in the High Court or County Court, the huge disadvantage is the more formal procedure and the risk of costs if the member loses. The advantage of the PHA is that longer time-limits apply; it is unnecessary to prove the harassment is on grounds of race, sex or disability etc; there is no problem regarding whether the harassment was carried out in the course of employment or even by a member of the public; and in extreme cases, an injunction can be obtained.

As a general rule, therefore, if the case fits within the RRA, SDA, DDA, sexual orientation or religion regulations, that is usually the correct cause of action. But if there is a technical difficulty with using one of those statutes and if the harassment is very serious with a good level of proof, the PHA should be considered. However, a potential PHA case would have to be referred to the Employment Rights Unit through the correct channels.

Protection against dismissal and detriment for challenging harassment

The member may be afraid, particularly if the harassment does not fall under the discrimination legislation, that s/he will not have any legal protection against dismissal if s/he makes a complaint. However, dismissing a member for complaining about bullying, assault or the risk of future assault, may amount to automatic unfair dismissal for taking up health and safety issues or for whistleblowing. No minimum service is required, and both workers and employees are also protected from action short of dismissal. For more detail, see p101-103.

Whistleblowing law allows members to raise concerns about various matters, including

→ an actual or threatened criminal offence.

→ a failure to comply with a legal obligation (including a statutory or contractual duty).

→ a risk to health and safety.

This means there is potentially protection for members complaining about harassment either on their own behalf or on behalf of colleagues. To gain the protection, it is crucial any complaint is made in good faith and done in the correct way. See p102 for more details.

Checklist: questions when interviewing a member who has raised an issue of sexual harassment

This is a sensitive area, with difficulties of law, evidence and the member's feelings. The checklist below suggests the information which needs to be obtained from the member to make an informed judgement about whether she can bring a legal case (or even risk speaking out). It may be best not to ask all the questions in the first interview, but to fix another meeting the next day or very soon after, to speak in more detail. If the member gives permission, it would be best to involve a Regional Officer/Organiser or Regional Women's Officer immediately.

The last part of the checklist suggests how such an interview should be conducted. The same questions will not always be appropriate. When interviewing the member you have to be thorough in your questioning and to listen carefully to the answers. This is why it may take two or more sessions. This is to ensure that the member is consistent in her allegations and the facts surrounding her case, throughout the grievance and the employment tribunal, if these courses of action are taken.

1 Questions to find out background information:

→ The harasser's job title and working relationship with the member.

→ The nature of the working day. How often the member has contact with the harasser.

→ The general office situation, lay-out and presence of other workers.

→ The member's start date and disciplinary record. (This is sensitive: explain that you are asking about her record only to see how vulnerable she is if management raise the issue.)

2 Questions about the harassment:
→ When the harassment started.
→ Details and dates of the harassment (verbal and physical). (This requires a sensitive approach as a woman may be embarrassed, particularly with a male representative.)

● Establish what is normal acceptable office behaviour and where the line is drawn.

● Witnesses? Has the member kept a diary? Has she seen / told her GP?

● Has the harasser done the same thing to other workers? Have others complained to management?

● Has the member said explicitly to the harasser or made it clear in any other way that she does not welcome his behaviour?

Note that many kinds of behaviour are obviously unwelcome and it is not essential that the member has said as much to the harasser, but it is helpful if she has. Note too that although this is important information to know, it is extremely sensitive as the member may feel she is to blame if she has not said anything to the harasser. Therefore do not ask this question until late in the interview when confidence is built. This also gives the member time to raise it herself, which is preferable. If you have to raise the issue first, be sure to give prior reassurance that it would be understandable if she had not felt able to say anything.

● If the member did tell the harasser, how and when did she do so and what was his reaction?

● Has the member raised the matter with anyone in management or told anyone else before? (This question also needs prior reassurance.)

3 Action:
● What does the member want to do? (This is the most important question of all, and however bad the situation is it is not up to the union representative to impose a solution.)

● Discussion of options including taking a grievance, going to the employment tribunal and time-limits, informal approach to the harasser, doing nothing but keeping a diary.

→ As this is a difficult area, it is wise to seek the assistance of a regional officer/organiser or regional women's officer immediately provided the member gives permission.

4 A sensitive approach by the rep.
A sensitive approach to interviewing the member is crucial. Remember she has been through a traumatic experience. The following would normally be helpful:

→ Take the matter seriously and give it the necessary time.

→ Be friendly and supportive but formal. Do not be authoritarian or too informal. Either could replicate the harasser's behaviour.

● Take a clear role and explain why sensitive questions are asked before asking them.

● In the first interview, allow the member to give you a broad picture before going back (in this interview or a subsequent interview) to ask for more detail.

● Do not try to get all the information in the first interview - focus on building confidence (although you must find out enough to ensure you do not miss a legal time-limit).

● A staged approach is recommended, leaving more sensitive questions to later interviews, so that confidence is built first.

● To maintain confidence, arrange swift follow-up interviews at the first interview. This is also essential before memories fade and witnesses lose interest.

● In case the member is embarrassed, offer her the opportunity to write down what has happened before discussing it. Note that this is not a substitute for spending time talking to the member.

● Where the UNISON rep is male, offer the member the chance to talk to a woman officer. Note that this must not be done in a way that suggests the representative is not interested or concerned about the matter.

● Provide reassurance that the member is entitled to feel upset and that the harasser has behaved unacceptably.

● Reassure the member that she has done nothing wrong.

● Acknowledge the member's feelings as genuine.

● Reassure the member on confidentiality, and that you will do nothing without her permission. It is important to take notes, but ask the member's permission first so you can reassure her.

● Discuss various options, taking account of what the member wants, offering appropriate UNISON support whatever she decides. However, do not mislead the member and make promises regarding legal support for tribunal cases without going through the correct UNISON channels. Your approach should be participative and consultative. Address any fear of reprisals.

→ Raise with the member her feelings and health and direct her to sources of support. **Do not:**

– Act as an amateur Counsellor yourself.

– Suggest she needs counselling / psychiatric help in a way which could be understood as meaning you think there is something wrong with her.

– Use this as an alternative to concrete remedial action.

5 In general, do not:

→ Make assumptions.

→ Suggest the member could be to blame in inviting the harassment.

→ Blame the member for not confronting the harasser or telling UNISON or management earlier.

→ Suggest the member may be misinterpreting events or being over-sensitive.

→ Say you know the harasser and are surprised he has acted in that way.

→ Express concern that the harasser is a member of UNISON.

→ Express any view as to the effect on the harasser or the harasser's wife / partner if the member makes an allegation.

→ Pressurise the member into taking any form of action.

6. Note that:

→ At the first interview, focus on the harasser's treatment of the member. Subsequent interviews will need to deal with likely counter-allegations, but this is extremely sensitive.

→ In general and especially if running a tribunal case, do not take information and detail for granted. The necessary time must be spent by UNISON as the employers will spend a great deal of time defending a case.

Stress

The Health and Safety Executive ("HSE") defines stress as "the adverse reaction people have to excessive pressure or other types of demand placed on them". Stress is different from pressure. Everyone experiences pressure in their daily work. It is when pressure becomes too much, without the chance to recover, that it becomes stress. Research commissioned by the HSE indicates that up to five million people in the UK feel very or extremely stressed by their work. Of those, about half a million believe it is making them ill.

The HSE says stress is a serious problem. There are practical steps which organisations can take to prevent and control work-related stress. Employers should carry out risk-assessments with stress in mind. The HSE has published Management Standards, which are a useful measure for assessment, including demands (workload, work patterns, work environment), control, support, relationships, under-standing roles and managing organisational change. Details of the HSE's research on stress, the Management Standards and other guide-lines are available on its site at www.hse.gov.uk/stress/index.htm.

In extreme cases, employers can be legally responsible for psychiatric injury to workers caused by stress at work, in the same way as they can be liable for physical injury. There have been several test cases over the last few years. These cases are hard to prove and each case depends very much on its particular facts. It is not enough that the employers caused the injury . There must be a real risk of psychiatric breakdown, which the employers ought reasonably to have forseen, and ought properly to have averted. Two useful cases to read are: *Sutherland v. Hatton* [2002] IRLR 263, CA and *Hartman v. South Essex Mental Health and Community Care NHS Trust and others* [2005] IRLR 293, CA.

Harassment: myths

● *Myth:*

It is impossible to prove sexual harassment unless there is a witness who saw it happen.

Truth:

It is hard, but not impossible, to prove sexual harassment without direct witnesses. See p249 for other kinds of evidence.

● *Myth:*

If the member did not tell the harasser that his/her conduct was unwanted, it is not unlawful.

Truth:

The law recognises that in most cases it is obvious that the conduct would be unwanted and it is unnecessary for the member to say so. However with totally unexceptional behaviour, the member may be expected to have a quiet word. (See p248.)

Harassment and stress: key points

● Harassment at work which is on grounds of race, sex, disability, religion or belief, sexual orientation can be challenged under the discrimination legislation, ie RRA, SDA, DDA, religion and belief regulations, sexual orientation regulations.

● The European Commission issued a useful Code of Practice to combat sexual harassment in 1991.

● Employers are legally responsible for harassment carried out by managers or colleagues of the member at work.

● Be careful not to miss time-limits in harassment cases.

● If the member is thinking of running a tribunal case, it is important to send the employers a Questionnaire at an early date.

● If the member is an employee, the statutory disputes resolution procedures will probably apply. If so, s/he will need to send a step 1 grievance letter before starting a tribunal case unless the harassment exception (or one of the other exceptions) applies.

● Where harassment is not on a discriminatory ground or where it occurs outside work or is done by a member of the public, the Protection from Harassment Act 1997 may be helpful.

● If the member suffers psychiatric damage due to the employers' unlawful conduct, including harassment, s/he may be able to bring a personal injury claim in the High Court or County Court. Such claims are very hard to prove and few succeed.

● The Health and Safety Executive recognises stress caused by work pressures, heavy workload and harassment as a serious problem. Guidelines for preventative action are on its website.

Work and family life

Contents

Pregnancy

In September 2003, the EOC launched a formal investigation into pregnancy discrimination, including discrimination while on maternity leave and on return to work. A very interesting interim report, the "Tip of the Iceberg", was published in September 2004 and can be downloaded from www.eoc.org.uk/cseng/policyandcampaigns/f_interim-report.pdf. Over 1000 women in England and Wales make a tribunal claim each year related to pregnancy discrimination. Nearly one quarter of those were dismissed within hours or days of telling their employers that they were pregnant. The report says that employers are more likely to have positive views of managing pregnancy if the workforce is large, predominantly female, or public sector.

What the member needs to know if she is pregnant

A member who is pregnant may seek your advice on any of a number of issues. Whatever she asks you, you need to make sure she knows she may have rights on all the matters set out below:

■ The member must find out her rights to maternity leave (whether statutory or contractual) and must understand the importance of strictly following the rules, both before she goes on to leave and again when she is wishing to return.

These rules are complex and are summarised below. You should seek up-to-date advice via your branch or regional office. Other sources of further information are:

– "Maternity rights: a guide for employers and employees (PL958 Rev 8)" available on the DTI website at http://www.dti.gov.uk/er/maternity.htm

– The Maternity Alliance has specialist leaflets available for a small fee (see their website on http://www.maternity alliance.org.uk).

■ The member should check her entitlement to statutory and contractual maternity pay.

■ Ask whether the member knows if she will wish to return to work part-time. If so, see legal position and time-limits issues set out at p270.

■ The member is entitled to reasonable time off on a paid basis for ante-natal care. This seems to include relaxation classes. There is no equivalent entitlement for the member's partner, but the government is keen to encourage employers to adopt a flexible approach. The DTI's "Fathers-to-be and antenatal appointments: a good practice guide" can be downloaded from the DTI website at www.dti.gov.uk/er/individual/fathers_to_be.pdf.

■ It is unlawful sex discrimination to treat a woman less favourably for a reason related to pregnancy including pregnancy-related illness. It is also unlawful under the Employment Rights Act 1996 and it is automatic unfair dismissal under section 99 of the ERA to dismiss her for this reason.

■ Check whether the member is being harassed, discriminated against or dismissed because she is pregnant. If she is, she may be able to claim sex discrimination and/or automatic unfair dismissal. (See p102.) Ensure the member is aware of the time-limits. (See p295.)

■ If the member is unable to do some of her duties or is sick due to pregnancy, it is unlawful to dismiss her or subject her to a detriment.

■ The member may be entitled to a paid health and safety suspension or modification of her duties (see below).

■ If the member is off sick for a pregnancy-related reason, she is entitled, as a minimum, to receive the same pay she would receive if she were off sick for any other reason. Watch out for the outcome of the test-case before the ECJ: *North-Western Health Board v McKenna*. It is possible the European Court of Justice will say that women who are off sick for pregnancy-related reasons during their pregnancy are entitled to full pay, regardless of whether the normal sick pay scheme provides full pay for sickness.

■ An employee who is dismissed while she is pregnant is entitled to written reasons for her dismissal, regardless of her length of service.

Health and safety protection

The rules regarding the health and safety protection of pregnant women are set out in sections 66-70 of the Employment Rights Act 1996 and the Management of Health and Safety at Work Regulations 1999. Women who have given birth in the previous six months or who are breastfeeding are also protected. The rules are as follows:

→ Where the employers employ women of child-bearing age and the work is of a kind which could involve risk to the health and safety of a new or expectant mother, the employers must include the assessment of such risk in their general health and safety assessment. Generally employers should take all reasonable steps to remove or avoid any identified risks. The EOC's interim report (above) says less than one in three pregnant women receive a health and safety risk assessment from their employers.

→ A woman who is pregnant, has recently given birth or who is breastfeeding may be entitled to a paid health and safety suspension if she is exposed to one of the listed biological, chemical or physical risks. This can entitle her to a modification of her duties, a reduction in hours or a fully paid suspension.

→ Quite apart from these health and safety rules, if the member is unable to do some of her duties or is sick due to pregnancy, it is unlawful to dismiss her or subject her to a detriment.

The risks

■ The risks covered are those set out in Annexes 1 and 2 of the European Directive No. 92/131/EEC.

■ The most commonly encountered risks are:

– Shocks, vibration or movement, eg driving or riding in off-road vehicles.

– Handling of loads. This is because hormonal and postural changes can make women vulnerable to injury.

– Prolonged exposure to loud noise, which can increase blood pressure and tiredness.

– Extremes of heat can cause stress, eg working in hot kitchens or laundry rooms.

- Movements and postures, eg fatigue from standing; working in tightly fitting workspaces; using step-ladders to retrieve heavy books or files; lifting patients.
- Travelling inside or outside the workplace.
- Mental and physical fatigue. Hours, volume and pacing of work should not be excessive. Seating should be available with longer rest breaks.
- Various chemical and biological agents, eg laboratory or healthcare workers exposed to a higher risk of infection from German Measles or Hepatitis B.

■ Where a registered medical practitioner or midwife certifies that it is necessary for a woman's health and safety that she does not work at night, the woman is entitled to a transfer to suitable day time work or if that is not reasonable, a paid suspension.

The rules:

■ To trigger her individual rights, the member should tell her employers in writing that she is pregnant, has given birth in the previous six months or is breastfeeding. It is useful to request a health and safety assessment and any modification which she has identified. It is helpful to check with her GP first that the GP will confirm there is a potential risk.

■ The employers must remove any risk. If that is not possible, they must temporarily modify her duties or, if that is still unsatisfactory, must offer any suitable available alternative employment. They cannot simply send the member home.

■ The alternative work must be:
- Of a kind which is suitable in relation to her and appropriate for her to do in the circumstances.
- On terms and conditions that are not substantially less favourable than her normal terms and conditions.

■ If the member unreasonably refuses suitable alternative work, she will lose her entitlement to a paid suspension.

■ If there is no possible modification or alternative, the member must be given a paid suspension.

Pregnancy dismissals or discrimination: evidence

A member who is dismissed (disciplined or harassed) because she is pregnant or for a related reason may be able to claim sex discrimination. She may also be able to claim automatic unfair dismissal or unlawful detriment (see p102). Her employers are unlikely to admit they are dismissing her because she is pregnant. The following evidence will help the member prove that the real reason is due to her pregnancy.

1 Evidence proving that at the time they dismissed (or discriminated against) her, the employers knew the member was pregnant. Check:

→ When did the member tell her employers that she was pregnant?

→ Did she tell them in writing? If verbally, who did she tell, what was the response and were there witnesses?

→ Is there other proof that they knew? Has she requested time off or been sick?

→ Did the particular manager who took the decision to dismiss know she was pregnant?

2 Evidence showing that the employers (or relevant manager) were unhappy that the member was pregnant. Check:

→ Their reaction and comments when she first told them.

→ Their attitude towards any time off for ante-natal care or due to sickness.

→ Their attitude towards any discussions about returning after maternity leave.

→ Any lack of sympathy towards any tiredness; unwillingness to modify or reduce any duties if necessary.

→ Any adverse comments generally, eg about the member's appearance or about whether she should be returning to work or stereotyped comments about women's roles.

3 Evidence showing that the employers changed their attitude towards the member after she became pregnant, eg

→ They became less friendly or helpful towards her.

→ They started to make criticisms of her work which they had not made before.

4 Evidence showing the employers (or particular manager) were generally unsympathetic towards pregnant workers, eg check:

→ How are other pregnant workers normally treated?

→ Do women often return after having babies?

→ What does the employers' pregnancy and maternity policy say?

ʃ The employers' reason for dismissing the member must be discredited.

→ Find out and pin down the employers' reasons for dismissing (disciplining or otherwise mistreating) the member. Obtain any letters.

→ Ask the member's comments. Can she answer the case against her? Does she believe the true reason was her pregnancy?

→ Ask yourself and the member, if a non-pregnant worker had behaved in the same way as the member, is it likely the employers would have sacked her?

→ Compare with non-pregnant workers who behaved in a similar way, eg:

– If the member was dismissed for misconduct: Have any non-pregnant workers committed the same or equivalent offences and received lesser penalties? Is there any innocent reason for greater leniency to the non-pregnant worker?

– If the member was dismissed for poor work: was this an issue before she became pregnant? Has she had warnings? How are other comparable workers treated? Note that an opposite - and possibly risky - argument is that her work has indeed suffered due to her pregnancy and it is unfair and discriminatory to penalise her for this.

– If the member was made redundant: Was it logical to select her rather than other workers who have been retained? How does the member measure on any criteria used as against retained workers? It is not essential to be able to make such a comparison, but it is very helpful when trying to prove the member's treatment was due to pregnancy.

→ Disproving the employers' reason altogether:

– Can the employers' reason be completely disproved, eg that there was nothing at all wrong with the member's work, or that she did not commit the offence and the employers must have known that, or that it was an extremely trivial offence which would not rationally lead to dismissal.

Maternity leave

The member may have rights to maternity leave and pay set out in her contract of employment. There are some minimum statutory rights which all employees must have, but you should check whether the member has better rights under her contract.

The rules on statutory maternity leave are set out in the Maternity and Parental Leave etc. Regulations 1999 (SI 1999/3312) as amended by the Maternity and Paternity (Amendment) Regulations 2002 (SI 2002/2789). The law is now simpler than it has been in the past, but it is still complicated and difficult to apply. This book outlines the general rules, but the member must be very careful to get accurate legal advice and follow the statutory procedures. There is an extremely useful guidance booklet available on the DTI website at http://www.dti.gov.uk/er/maternity.htm - click on "Maternity rights: a guide for employers and employees (PL958 Rev 8)". The Regulations are available on the HMSO website at http://www.hmso.gov.uk/legis.htm

The length of the statutory leave

All female employees, regardless of length of service, are entitled to ordinary maternity leave ("OML"). OML is 26 weeks statutory maternity leave in total, from going on leave to the date of return.

The 26 weeks will be extended if necessary to ensure the woman is on leave for at least two weeks following childbirth. This is called compulsory maternity leave.

Women who have been employed for at least 26 weeks at the start of the 14th week before the expected week of childbirth are entitled to additional maternity leave ("AML"). AML runs on from the end of OML for another 26 weeks, making 52 weeks in total.

Ordinary maternity leave starts on the date which the woman chooses, but it cannot start earlier than 11 weeks before the expected week of childbirth ("EWC"), even if the woman is on related sick leave. The member may want to delay starting her ordinary maternity leave so as to have as much time as possible after the birth. However the OML starts automatically (unless the employers agree otherwise) the first time the member is absent for a pregnancy-related reason in the four weeks prior to the EWC.

The required notifications

■ The member must give notice no later than the end of the 15th week before her EWC of her pregnancy, the EWC and (in writing if the employers so request) the date on which she intends her ordinary maternity leave to start. If her leave is triggered unexpectedly, she must give notice as soon as reasonably practicable afterwards. In all cases, it is safer to put everything in writing.

■ The member can change her mind about the date she wants her leave to start as long as she gives her employers at least 28 days notice before the date varied or the new date (whichever is earlier), or if that is not reasonably practicable, then as soon as is reasonably practicable. If the employers request, the member must produce a medical certificate stating the expected week of childbirth.

■ Within 28 days of receiving the member's notification of her leave date, the employers must notify her of the date when her OML or (if applicable) AML will end.

■ The member need not state her date of return. It is assumed she will return at the end of her OML or, if entitled, her AML. If she wishes to return earlier, she must give at least 28 days' notice.

■ If the member is unable to return at the end of her maternity leave due to sickness, she is regarded as absent from work on sick leave in the normal way and she should notify her employers accordingly, providing any necessary medical certificate. If she is dismissed as a result, she may be able to claim unfair dismissal or sex discrimination. The test for sex discrimination will be whether a man with a level of sickness equivalent to the time she has been sick since the end of her maternity leave would have been dismissed.

Rights during leave

A woman's rights while on leave and when trying to return are the most complicated area to apply in practice. This book sets out the main legal rules, but practical situations may be more complex.

■ The member's contract of employment runs throughout her ordinary and additional maternity leave unless either side expressly terminates it. The time also counts towards continuous service for the purpose of qualifying for various statutory rights such as unfair dismissal protection.

■ The member has no right to full pay during her maternity leave, although Statutory Maternity Pay or Maternity Allowance may be available for some of that period (see below).

■ During ordinary maternity leave, the member is entitled to the benefit of all terms and conditions (except pay) as if she was still at work, eg:

– Contractual non-cash benefits, eg health insurance or mobile telephone, unless it was for work use only.

– The ordinary maternity leave period counts for the purpose of accruing service-related contractual benefits, eg pay increments and holiday entitlement.

– Non contractual or discretionary payments which she would have received if at work.

■ During the additional maternity leave period, only minimal terms and conditions apply, eg the mutual obligation of trust and confidence and if the member is dismissed, notice entitlement.

■ The woman's statutory holiday entitlement under the Working Time Regulations (p32) continues to accrue through ordinary and additional maternity leave. She is entitled to take this leave at a time other than when she is on maternity leave. Any greater contractual holiday entitlement will only accrue through OML, unless the contract says otherwise.

■ A woman's pension position is generally protected during OML and any other periods of paid maternity leave, but the position is not entirely straightforward and you should take advice.

■ Remember that the member may have greater rights to pay and other benefits under her own contract.

Rights on return

The EOC's interim report into pregnancy discrimination found one in five women who returned to work for the same employer after maternity leave returned to a lower grade or level of job. Where a difficulty arises when a woman is trying to return to work, you should obtain expert advice via the regional office. Broadly speaking, the woman's statutory rights are as follows:

■ To return after maternity leave to the job on which she was previously employed on no less favourable terms and conditions than had she not been absent. She should get any pay-rise awarded while she was on leave.

■ If she took additional maternity leave (as opposed to purely ordinary maternity leave) and it is not reasonably practicable for the employers to let her return to the same job, the member's right is to return to another job which is suitable and appropriate for her in the circumstances.

■ If her position becomes redundant while she is on maternity leave, she must be offered any suitable available vacancy on no less favourable terms and conditions. (See p102.)

■ If the woman is not allowed to return to her previous job, she may be able to claim automatic or ordinary unfair dismissal and sex discrimination, depending on the reasons for the refusal.

■ A woman needs to be careful before turning down a suitable alternative offer where her original job has gone. If a tribunal thinks she unreasonably rejected a suitable alternative offer, she may lose her unfair dismissal case. Factors which may make a job unsuitable for the woman could be

– Increased travel time or different hours leading to additional childcare costs

– An unpleasant work environment, eg relocation in an unlit basement.

■ The rules for small employers (under five employees) are likely to be abolished from October 2005.

Contractual maternity leave

The employers may well have set out their maternity scheme in the member's contract. This may either mirror the statutory scheme precisely or be more favourable in some respects, eg by granting a right to fully paid leave, giving a longer period of leave and extending the leave entitlement to all female workers. You need to be very careful where a woman qualifies for statutory rights but has more favourable contractual rights in some respects. The procedures to be followed usually need to be read together. This requires expert advice via your branch or regional office.

Statutory maternity pay and maternity allowance

Women with sufficient service and earnings are entitled to receive statutory maternity pay ("SMP") from their employers for the 26 week OML period. This is calculated at 90% of normal pay subject to a weekly maximum of £106 from April 2005 (it is revised annually). The correct notifications need to be made to the employers. If the woman is not eligible for SMP, she may be eligible for a lesser amount of Maternity Allowance from the Benefits Agency. It is irrelevant whether the woman returns to work after her leave. The detailed rules are set out in the DTI guidance referred to above, but you should also check the latest position with the Maternity Alliance or a Citizens Advice Bureau.

The government is consulting on plans to extend SMP to nine months by April 2007 and eventually to twelve months. There is also a proposal that mothers can choose to transfer a proportion of their SMP and maternity leave to the fathers.

Returning to work part-time

A woman has no absolute right to return to work part-time or with modified hours, unless she has that entitlement under her contract. Even if she has no contractual entitlement, you may be able to negotiate with the employers to agree to the member's request, especially if they have a policy promoting part-time and flexi-working. The Best Practice Guidelines issued under the Part-Time Workers' Regulations (see p282 below) may also help.

If the employers refuse to allow the member to modify her hours to meet her child-care needs, this may amount to indirect sex discrimination. For more detail on sex discrimination and part-time working, see p283. In many cases, the key issue will be whether the employers can objectively justify the refusal.

If a woman wishes to return to work part-time, it may be useful to follow the following steps:

■ If eligible, make a statutory request for flexible working (see p278 below).

■ If not eligible, she can follow similar steps, eg:

– Inform her employers in writing as soon as possible that she will wish to return to work part-time or job share.

– Explain that the reason for her request is because of childcare obligations.

– If the employers refuse, request written reasons for the refusal.

– Consider any appropriate grievance or appeal.

■ If the employers refuse to agree to part-time working, consider taking a tribunal case for sex discrimination (see p283 below). Do not allow the time-limits to pass while dealing with a grievance.

■ The woman needs to decide whether she is able to remain in employment pending the tribunal case. Ideally she should request permission to work part-time until the case is completed. If this is refused, point out that she is only able to continue to work in the short-term by making awkward and temporary arrangements. Note that if the woman is in fact able to work on a full-time basis without difficulty, a tribunal may say there is no indirect discrimination.

If the member wishes to take a sex discrimination case, she must be careful about time-limits. This is a particular danger if she asks – and is refused - before she goes on leave whether she can afterwards return part-time. There is a risk that the three-month time-limit to challenge any refusal will expire during her maternity leave, when she does not feel like starting any tribunal cases. Having said that, there is strong legal authority (the Court of Appeal in the case of *Cast v Croydon College* [1998] IRLR 318) that in many situations the time-limit will continue to run until she takes up the matter again and is refused again on her return. However, it is advisable to play safe and not rely on this case applying.

Paternity leave

The right to paternity leave is set out in sections 80A-E of the Employment Rights Act 1996 and the Paternity and Adoption Leave Regulations 2002 (SI 2002/2788). The Regulations are available on the HMSO website at http://www.legislation.hmso.gov.uk. DTI guidance is available on its website at
http://www.dti.gov.uk/er/individual/patrights-pl517.htm.
The following is only a brief summary and the exact rules need to be consulted. Remember also that members may have greater rights to paternity leave under their own contract of employment.
An employee who is the father of the child or married to the mother or the mother's partner, including a same-sex partner, is entitled to statutory paternity leave if s/he will have responsibility for the child's upbringing. The employee must have 26 weeks continuous service ending with the week immediately preceding the expected week of childbirth (EWC).

The statutory leave
   – A single block of either two weeks or one week (but not two separate one week blocks).
   – Leave must be taken within 56 days of the child's birth or, if born prematurely, the expected week of birth.

The required notifications
■ In or before the 15th week before the EWC, the member must give notice of his/her intention to take paternity leave, specifying:
   – the length of leave s/he wishes to take
   – its start date
   – the EWC
■ The member can vary the date by giving 28 days notification.
■ If it is not reasonably practicable to give these notifications on time, the member must do so as soon as reasonably practicable afterwards.

Rights during leave and on return
   – The member is entitled to return to the job in which s/he was previously employed.
   – During leave, s/he is entitled to the benefit of all terms and conditions apart from pay.

Statutory paternity pay
Workers with sufficient earnings and length of service will qualify for statutory paternity pay. This is 90% of his/her weekly earnings, but subject to a weekly maximum of £106 from April 2005 (updated annually).

Adoption leave

Sections 75A and 75B of the Employment Rights Act 1996 give certain employees a right to adoption leave. This applies in relation to children placed for adoption or notified as matched with a person on or after 6th April 2003. The right is set out in detail in the Paternity and Adoption Leave Regulations 2002 (SI 2002/2788). DTI guidance is available on its website at http://www.dti.gov.uk/er/individual/adoption-pl518.pdf. The following is only a brief summary of the rules and the exact wording of the Regulations needs to be followed in any case.

To be entitled to leave, the member must be an employee who has been continuously employed for 26 weeks at the time s/he is notified of having been matched with the child. This is different from maternity leave, where no minimum service is required for the first 26 weeks of leave.

Either parent may take adoption leave, but not both. However, the other parent may be able to take paternity leave.

The statutory leave

- Ordinary adoption leave starts when the child is placed with the member or on a date up to 2 weeks earlier, which the member has notified to the employer.
- The member is entitled to 26 weeks ordinary adoption leave and a further 26 weeks additional adoption leave.
- If s/he wishes to return earlier, s/he must give her employers 28 days notice.
- S/he is entitled to 8 weeks after the disruption of any placement or if the child dies, but this cannot exceed the statutory leave period.

The required notifications

- No later than 7 days after being notified of having been matched with a child, the member must give notice of his/her intention to take adoption leave, specifying:
  - the date the child is expected to be placed with him/her
  - the date s/he wishes the leave to begin
- The member can vary the date by giving 28 days notification.
- If it is not reasonably practicable to give these notifications on time, the member must do so as soon as reasonably practicable afterwards.
- If the employer so requests, the member must produce documents from the adoption agency confirming certain dates and details.
- Within 28 days of receiving the member's notification of his/her leave date, the employers must notify her of the date his/her leave will end.
- It is assumed the member will return at the end of the 52 weeks leave. If s/he wishes to return earlier, s/he must give at least 28 days' notice.

Rights during leave and on return

  – The member's rights during ordinary adoption leave and on return are very similar to those applicable during and after ordinary maternity leave (see above).

  – The member's rights during additional adoption leave and on return are very similar to those applicable during and after additional maternity leave (see above).

Statutory adoption pay

Workers with sufficient earnings and length of service will qualify for statutory adoption pay. This is 90% of his/her weekly earnings during the ordinary adoption leave period, but subject to a weekly maximum.

Parental leave

The Maternity and Parental Leave etc. Regulations 1999 (SI 1999/3312) also grant minimum rights to parental leave. These Regulations were passed to implement the Parental Leave Directive. DTI guidance is available on its website at
http://www.dti.gov.uk/er/parental-leave.htm

Employees who have been continuously employed for one year and who have or expect to have responsibility for a child are entitled to parental leave.

The entitlement is to a total of 13 weeks unpaid leave for each parent in respect of every child who is under five, or if adopted, for the first five years of adoption up to 18 years old maximum, or up to 18 years old for a child entitled to a disability living allowance. A week's leave for a full-time employee is equal to 5 days and for a part-time employee is pro-rata.

The purpose of the leave is to "care for" the child. This means to look after the child or make arrangements for the child's welfare. It need not be connected with the child's health and could cover, for example, settling a child at a new playgroup.

It is unlawful to dismiss the member or subject him/her to a detriment because s/he has claimed parental leave.

The government has stated explicitly that it wants employers to make collective or workforce agreements which are contractually enforceable by workers on the details of how this leave will operate. The agreement must meet the minimum requirements set out above. However, if there is no collective agreement, the rules of the "default scheme" set out in Schedule 2 of the Regulations will apply. Under the default scheme, the minimum period of leave is one week and it cannot be taken in single days.

If you have not already done so, UNISON should immediately negotiate with the employers on the details of a scheme, as the default scheme can be improved in many ways. Some UNISON service groups have already negotiated or are in the process of negotiating national agreements on parental leave. You should check with your regional officer/organiser regarding the position in your service group. You can also negotiate local agreements improving further on any national agreement.

Any negotiation should fit in with and build on any entitlements to paternity or compassionate leave already existing in your collective agreements. In particular, be careful not to lose any periods which are already paid.

There is a separate statutory entitlement to dependant leave, which covers certain emergency situations and is not subject to an overall 13 week ceiling (see p277). It is important in practice that employers are not allowed to force members to use up their 13 weeks parental leave for emergency situations which are really covered by the more flexible dependant leave.

The default scheme

These are the key elements of the Default Scheme:

■ Maximum four weeks per child in any year.

■ Leave can be taken only in one-week blocks (except in respect of disabled children).

■ The member must produce on request any evidence reasonably required to establish responsibility for the child or the child's birth or adoption date or disability.

■ The member must give the employers the dates of the required leave and give 21 days' notice of the start. Where applicable, 21 days' notice need be given only of the expected week of childbirth or adoption.

■ The employers can postpone leave for up to six months where the operation of the business would be unduly disrupted, by giving written notice specifying new dates within seven days of the member's own notice. However leave may not be postponed where it is to be taken immediately the child is born or adopted.

Negotiating a better scheme

As mentioned above, UNISON has already negotiated better agreements at national level. For a summary of UNISON agreements providing improvements on basis rights to parental leave, see "Good Practice for Parental Leave and Time off for Dependants" (1.2.04), available under Resources / Documents Database on the website (search "Dependants") or on www.unison.org.uk/acrobat/B257.pdf. UNISON has also issued a Bargaining Support Guide "Negotiating parental leave", revised in February 2004, (available on its website under "Resources" or on www.unison.org.uk/acrobat/14028.pdf). The Guide contains many suggestions for negotiating an improved scheme, including:

■ Paid leave.

■ Leave entitlement in respect of children up to school-leaving age and regardless of date of birth.

■ Available to all workers, not purely employees and regardless of length of service.

■ Available to any primary carer with day-to-day responsibility for looking after a child, eg grandparents or same sex partners.

■ No limit to the annual amount, up to the 13-week maximum.

■ More than 13 weeks maximum in total.

■ Leave may be taken in single days or half days or by regular reduced days' or hours' working.

■ Clarification and limitation of the grounds on which employers can postpone leave, making it only in exceptional circumstances and introducing a balancing consideration of the urgency of the member's need. As the default scheme stands, postponement can destroy the effectiveness of the right. After all, if the member were unexpectedly ill, the employers would have to cope, and on less than 21 days' notice.

Dependant leave

The member's employers may already give rights to compassionate leave under the member's contract. Such rights are often discretionary and frequently refused by local managers as being inconvenient at the particular time requested. The Employment Rights Act 1996 at section 57A establishes a minimum right to unpaid dependant leave which the employers cannot refuse. It is also unlawful to dismiss the member or subject him/her to a detriment because s/he has claimed dependant leave.

Employees (regardless of length of service) are entitled to reasonable time-off to take action necessary for any of the following purposes:

→ To provide assistance on an occasion when a dependant is injured or assaulted, falls ill or gives birth.

→ To make care arrangements for a dependant who is ill or injured.

→ In consequence of the death of a dependant. This means making funeral arrangements, attending the funeral, registering the death, applying for probate etc, but not compassionate leave to deal with the emotional consequences of the bereavement.

→ Because of the unexpected disruption or termination of arrangements for the care of a dependant.

→ To deal with an incident involving the employee's child which occurs unexpectedly while the child is at an educational establishment.

There is no definition of "reasonable" time off. To have this right, the member must tell the employer how long s/he expects to be absent and the reason, as soon as reasonably practicable. The purpose is to give the member time to make care arrangements. S/he cannot have time off to provide the care personally beyond the immediate crisis. A "dependant" means a spouse, child, parent or person (other than a tenant, lodger or employee) who lives in the employee's household. In relation to the right to time-off to provide care for illness or injury, it also includes anyone who reasonably relies on the employee for assistance in those circumstances, eg a neighbour or elderly friend or relative who does not live with the member, but who has no one else available to care for him/her in emergencies.

The member can complain to a tribunal within three months of any refusal of such time off. The tribunal can award compensation which it considers just and equitable including for resulting loss.

The law on dependant leave is restricted in several respects and you should try to negotiate better rights. For this you should obtain the UNISON Bargaining Support Guide: "Negotiating time off for dependants". For a summary of UNISON agreements providing improvements on basis rights to dependant leave, see "Good Practice for Parental Leave and Time off for Dependants" (1.2.04), available under Resources / Documents Database on the website (search "Dependants") or on www.unison.org.uk/acrobat/B257.pdf

Flexible working

For childcare or other reasons, members may wish to change their hours of work or work partly from home. There is no legal right to do this, although refusal may in some cases amount to indirect sex discrimination (see page 283).

The government wants to encourage employers and employees to negotiate flexible arrangements. It has therefore set out a formal procedure for some workers to request flexible working and to have that request formally considered by the employers, although the employers can still say no.

Of course there is nothing to stop workers who are not covered by this statutory procedure from requesting flexible working anyway. Indeed, the member's employers may have a flexible working policy already in operation

The statutory right is contained in the Employment Rights Act 1996 and Flexible Working Regulations. The DTI has produced a useful guide "Flexible working: The right to request and the duty to consider" although it has no formal legal status. This is available on its website at www.dti.gov.uk.

The statutory right

■ The member can request a change in his/her terms and conditions of employment for the purpose of caring for a child under 6 or if disabled, under 18.

■ To be eligible for this right, the member must be

– An employee with at least 26 weeks' continuous service.

– Either the parent (including adopted or foster parents) or guardian of the child, or their partner or spouse, with responsibility for the child's upbringing.

— Agency workers are not covered.

■ Caring for a child can include collecting the child from school or simply spending more time with him or her.

■ The member can only ask for changes to hours or workplace under this procedure, eg ?   Part-time working or job-share

— Different shift-patterns

— Homeworking

— Compressed hours (working the same number of hours over a shorter period),

— Reduced hours (eg starting an hour later each day).

Remember that working fewer hours will usually mean less pay.

■ The member can only make one application under this procedure in 12 months, so s/he should choose her time carefully.

Any change will be permanent and the member will have no right to revert back to the original terms and conditions, unless agreed otherwise.

■ The employers may only refuse the request on one of the specified grounds, ie

— Additional costs.

— Detrimental effect on ability to meet customer demand.

— Inability to recruit additional staff or re-organise work amongst existing staff.

— Detrimental impact on quality or performance.

— Insufficient work during the periods the member proposes to work.

— Planned structural changes.

■ If either the member or the employers are unsure about the arrangement, a trial period with a specific end date could be agreed. This should be put in writing.

■ The best chance of persuading the employers to agree the member's request, whether or not made under this procedure, is to anticipate and deal with any workplace problems which may result from the change. Ideally the member would explain how the change may benefit the employers.

■ The DTI guide also provides useful case-studies to help persuade employers to agree flexible working.

The procedure

■ The member must make a written application, eg by letter or e-mail. There is a useful standard form on the DTI website although it need not be used.

■ The application must contain the following information:

– Its date.

– The date of any previous applications or confirmation there have been none.

– A statement that the application is being made under the statutory right to request a flexible working pattern.

– Confirmation that the member has responsibility for the upbringing of the child and his/her relationship to the child.

– The flexible working pattern applied for and the date it should come into effect.

– An explanation of what effect, if any, the proposed change will have on the employers and suggestions as to how the effect may be dealt with. The member is not expected to know exactly what the effect on the employers may be, but this is just to show s/he has considered the likely impact of the proposed change.

■ Within 28 days, the employer must either

– Write to the member agreeing the request and specifying a start date; or

– Hold a meeting to discuss it.

■ The employers must provide a written decision within 14 days of the meeting, indicating the ground of any refusal and sufficient explanation of the facts on which it is based.

■ The member can make a written appeal setting out grounds within 14 days. There is a standard form on the DTI website but it need not be used.

■ An appeal meeting must be held within 14 days and a written decision within 14 days after that.

■ The time and place of the original and appeal meetings must be convenient to each side, and time-scales can be extended by written agreement.

■ The member has the right to be accompanied by a worker employed by the same employers including a UNISON rep. This companion or rep may address the meeting and confer with the member, but cannot answer questions on the member's behalf.

■ If the employers fail to hold the meetings or notify the decision, or if a decision to reject the application is based on incorrect facts or is outside the listed grounds, the member can bring a tribunal case claiming compensation up to 8 weeks' pay.

■ S/he can also claim 2 weeks pay if the employers refuse to allow her to be accompanied.

■ The member cannot make a claim under this procedure simply because the employers refuse to agree his/her request, if they have followed the correct procedures.

■ However, the member may have other legal claims, eg

– If the employers refuse the member's request but grant a similar request to a worker of a different racial group, this may be direct race discrimination.

– If the employers unjustifiably refuse a woman's request to leave early to collect her child from school, this may be indirect sex discrimination.

– It may be unlawful discrimination to refuse the request of a member who needs to change hours or work from home due to his/her disability.

■ The member must not be subjected to a detriment or dismissal because s/he has requested flexible working under this procedure or brought a tribunal case about it.

The government is considering extending the right to request flexible working hours to carers of adults and parents of older children. Regardless of whether this change is introduced, your branch can negotiate such rights for members. Care for adults and older children tends to fall predominantly on women and refusal of flexible working to accommodate such care may be another example of indirect sex discrimination.

Part-time working

The law governing part-time working is covered by the Part-time Workers Regulations ("the Regulations") and in a slightly different way, by sex discrimination and equal pay law. Some of the key differences between the two legal areas are these:

– The Regulations give equal protection to male as well as female part-timers. Sex discrimination law generally only assists female or married workers in this respect.

– Both the Regulations and sex discrimination law require equal treatment of part-timers as compared with full-timers unless the employers can objectively justify failing to do so.

– Under the Regulations, it is necessary for the member to compare him/herself with a full-time worker doing broadly similar work or if s/he previously worked full-time, with how s/he was treated as a full-timer. Under the SDA it is not necessary to make this comparison.

– Sex discrimination law can make it unlawful unjustifiably to refuse a worker's request to change to part-time working. The Regulations do not cover this aspect, although the Best Practice Guidelines issued under the Regulations encourage flexibility by employers.

– A worker can receive higher compensation under the SDA than under the Regulations. S/he can also use the helpful questionnaire procedure available only under discrimination law (p300).

The part-time workers regulations

The Part-Time Workers (Prevention of Less Favourable Treatment) Regulations were brought in to implement the EU Part-time Work Directive.

There are currently approximately six million part-time employees in Great Britain. 40% of UNISON members work part-time and the public sector is the largest employer of part-time workers. In introducing the Regulations, the government said it believes the economy and society will gain as a whole if people are able to achieve a better balance between work and family responsibilities.

Under the Regulations, a part-timer must not be treated less favourably than a comparable full-timer on grounds that s/he is a part-timer. If the member changes from full-time to part-time working, s/he must not be treated less favourably than beforehand. As with the SDA, there is an exception if the employers can objectively justify less favourable treatment.

The member can request a written statement detailing reasons for any treatment s/he considers less favourable. S/he must not be victimised for requesting such a statement or for claiming any rights under these Regulations.

Some examples of the effect of the Regulations are that, unless the employers can objectively justify otherwise:

■ Current or past part-time status should not constitute a barrier to promotion.

■ Part-time workers should receive the same hourly rate as comparable full-time workers.

■ Part-timers should not be less favourably treated than full-timers in calculating the rate of sick pay, how long it is paid, or the length of service required to qualify for payment.

■ Employers should not discriminate against part-timers over access to pension schemes.

■ Part-timers should not be excluded from training.

■ Part-timers should not be targeted for redundancy selection.

The government has issued Guidelines for Compliance with the Regulations and for Best Practice. These are available on the DTI's website at http://dti.gov.uk/er/point-information.htm, click on "The law and best practice – a detailed guide for employers and part-timers". The Regulations themselves are on http://www.dti.gov.uk/er/ptime.htm

UNISON has sought to eliminate discrimination against part-time workers from national agreements. Branches should review their own agreements. You can use the Regulations and the Guidelines on Best Practice to negotiate to eliminate discrimination against part-time workers and to open up opportunities.

The Best Practice Guidelines recommend:

– At all levels of an organisation including skilled and managerial positions, employers should seek to maximise the range of posts designated as suitable for part-time working or job-share.

– Larger organisations should keep a database of those interested in job-share.

– Employers should actively consider whether it would be appropriate to introduce flexible forms of working, eg term-time working, lunch-time working, flexi-time, home-working, a parental leave scheme and reduced hours working.

– Larger organisations should consider whether to provide childcare facilities onsite or offer a contribution towards childcare costs.

Sex discrimination law

Sex discrimination law covers the position when a member enquires about his/her rights as a part-timer or to change to part-time working.

■ There is no absolute right to work part-time under statute, although you should check the member's contract to see if s/he has a contractual right.

■ Refusing to allow a member to work part-time or discriminating against part-timers in their terms and conditions may be indirect sex discrimination, unless the employers can justify their behaviour.

■ Even if the member's contract requires him/her to work full-time or a job is advertised on a full-time basis, sex discrimination law can override this.

■ Indirect sex discrimination claims linked to part-time working may apply to women or married workers, but are very unlikely to protect unmarried male workers. This is because women and married workers are statistically more likely to be unable to work full-time (due to child-care obligations).

■ To prove indirect sex discrimination, the member must show:
– It is a disadvantage for her/him to work full-time.
–   In the particular workplace, or in the workforce generally, women (or married workers) are at a particular disadvantage when asked to work full-time.
Note that: definition of indirect sex discrimination is in fact very complex and cases are difficult. For more detail, see p196.

■ There is no indirect sex discrimination if the employers can justify insisting on the member working full-time or giving better terms and conditions to full-timers.
– Pin down the employers on their reasons for wanting full-time work.
– Do the reasons amount to a real and legitimate need on the part of the employers?
– If so, are there other non-discriminatory ways of meeting the same aim or need?
Note that: often the real issue on whether or not the employers' behaviour is lawful comes down to whether they have a good justification.

■ Refusing to allow a woman to work part-time or modify her hours may occasionally be direct sex discrimination if, eg a man is allowed to work part-time or modify his hours for a personal reason.
■ The Part-time Workers Regulations (above) deal with part-timers' rights (male and female) to terms and conditions which are pro rata to those of full-timers.

■ Possible discrimination (unless justified) against part-timers may occur in the following ways:

– Selection of part-timers first for redundancy.

– Refusing to allow women to change to part-time working after maternity leave.

– Advertising posts for full-time workers only.

– More favourable terms and conditions for full-timers, eg higher hourly rates; faster progress through incremental scales; enhanced holiday and sick-pay entitlements. For more examples, see the EOC Code on Equal Pay.

■ As well as full-time working, similar issues of indirect sex discrimination due to childcare can arise on the following requirements:

– Working a certain number of hours every day.

– Fixed hours which clash with collecting children from school or child-minders.

– Mobility.

– Rotating and 24 hour shifts

For a full list of indirectly discriminatory requirements under the Sex Discrimination Act or Equal Pay Act, see p202.

Work and family life: myths

● *Myth:*
If the member's contract of employment says she is a full-time worker, she cannot claim the right to work part-time under sex discrimination law.

Truth:
The Sex Discrimination Act overrides contract law. If the member is unable to work full-time due to childcare and the employers cannot justify insisting on her doing so, it will be unlawful. (See p283.)

● *Myth:*
If the member applies for a job or promotion which is advertised as a full-time post, she cannot apply to take it on a part-time basis and claim indirect sex discrimination if she is refused.

Truth:
It may be indirect sex discrimination for the employers unjustifiably to insist on the member working full-time in the post. (See p283.) They cannot get around this by simply advertising the post as full-time only.

● *Myth:*

The member is entitled to work part-time on her return from maternity leave if she wants to.

Truth:

Unless she has such an entitlement under her contract, the member has no automatic right to work part-time. However, an unjustified refusal to allow her to work part-time may be indirect sex discrimination.

● *Myth:*

Employers must allow the member to work flexible hours if s/he wants to.

Truth:

The law gives certain workers a right to have their request for flexible hours seriously considered, but it gives no right to have the request granted. If the employers refuse, members can use sex or disability discrimination law, if it applies.

Work and family life: key points

- The member has a variety of rights when she is pregnant and has recently given birth. You should ensure she is aware of them.
- The member must not be discriminated against or dismissed due to pregnancy or pregnancy-related illness.
- In certain circumstances, the member is entitled to an alteration of her duties, reduction in hours or a fully paid health and safety suspension.
- There are two types of statutory maternity leave according to length of service, OML (ordinary maternity leave) and AML (additional maternity leave). The member may have more beneficial rights under her contract.
- The member is likely to be entitled to Statutory Maternity Pay or Maternity Allowance.
- Members who meet the qualifying requirements may be entitled to statutory paternity leave or adoption leave.
- There are statutory rights to unpaid parental and dependant leave. The member may also have rights to paid compassionate leave under her contract.
- Members who meet the qualifying requirements can use a statutory procedure to request flexible working. This simply gives them the right to have their request formally considered and responded to.
- There is no absolute right to work part-time, but it may be indirect sex discrimination if employers cannot justify refusing a woman's request.
- The government has issued Best Practice Guidelines encouraging employers to grant flexible working arrangements.
- Part-timers (of any sex) should not be unjustifiably treated less favourably than full-timers. See the Part-Time Workers Regulations, the Sex Discrimination Act and the Equal Pay Act.
- Workers must not be subjected to a detriment or dismissal because they have taken up maternity, paternity, adoption, parental or dependant leave or sought equal treatment as a part-timer or used the statutory procedure to request flexible working.
- The "Getting Equal" Campaign Pack (Bibliography, p314) contains a leaflet on "Getting equal pay for part-timers".

Chapter 14:

Going to tribunal

Contents

The tribunal system

Most employment cases are heard in an employment tribunal ("ET"), formerly known as an industrial tribunal. Appeals against ET decisions are made to the Employment Appeal Tribunal ("EAT"). After that, appeals go to the Court of Appeal and then the House of Lords. Where European Law is concerned, the case can be referred to the European Court of Justice by any lower court or tribunal.

There is no automatic right of appeal. The EAT restricts appeals to where the ET has made an error of law or reached a perverse decision on the facts. In most cases, the member has only one chance and his/her chances of success will be influenced by the personalities and attitudes of the particular tribunal panel which will decide his/her case.

Tribunal panels are made up of three people: a legal Chair who must be a solicitor or barrister of seven years' standing, and two lay or "wing" members. The lay members used to be nominated through the TUC and the CBI/Personnel side, but now the tribunal system is also recruiting directly from the public. All three panel members are supposed to take a neutral position and most Judgments are in fact unanimous. On the whole, the legal Chair is very influential, although not always in touch with workplace realities.

The government and unions have made attempts in recent years to ensure the make up of panels is more representative of disadvantaged groups, especially black and minority ethnic workers. However there will only be real change if all tribunal nominees, whatever their background, are fully trained to analyse the legal and practical issues which arise and to put forward their views.

Statistics on numbers and success rates of different kinds of case are released annually and reproduced in publications such as IRLB and IDS Brief (see Bibliography p314). Tribunal hearings are public and if you have not seen any, it is worth going to your local tribunal before 10 a.m. and asking at reception about which case may be interesting to sit in on. It is best to watch a few cases. Be careful not to generalise from one or two experiences. The atmosphere in the room and the difficulties facing the witnesses can vary enormously according to the particular case and the particular tribunal panel, especially the Chair.

Employment tribunals are far more formal than internal appeals hearings or other tribunals, eg social security or medical appeal tribunals. Witnesses must take an oath or affirm and answer formal questions and cross-examination. You cannot casually represent a member in ETs, even though that was the original intention when the system was set up. On the other hand, ETs are not as formal as other courts. After taking the oath, everyone sits down, no one wears wigs and hearsay evidence can be allowed. As if to symbolise this semi-formality, tribunal panels sit on a raised platform which is only 9 inches high.

Currently legal aid is not available for tribunals except in limited circumstances in Scotland. Anyone is allowed to represent the member and in theory the member can represent him/herself but realistically this is very difficult. Usually each side pays its own legal costs, whoever wins or loses. However, if the member or UNISON runs a hopeless or misconceived case or does not meet deadlines during the preparation of the case, the tribunal can make the member pay part or all of the employers' legal costs. Costs can be awarded up to £10,000 or more. Costs will not be awarded if a reasonable case is run correctly, but there are real dangers with inexperienced representatives.

This is one reason why advice and representation of the member must be taken very seriously. The representative must have a good grasp of the relevant law, be on top of the relevant facts and evidential issues, be able to assess the strengths and weaknesses of the claim and calculate its financial value, understand how all the preparatory procedural steps operate, have time to meet all the deadlines and know how to represent at the final hearing. Too often emphasis is put on the importance of the final hearing, when it is the earlier steps which affect the result. For this reason UNISON takes the training of its regional officers/organisers very seriously.

It is not the scope of this book to cover tribunal procedure. For a very full guide to each step of ET procedure with practical precedents and a guide to evidence, see Employment Law: An Advisers' Handbook by Tamara Lewis (Bibliography, p314).

Compensation and remedies

Unfair dismissal remedies

Members need to have a rough idea about what they will get if they win a tribunal case for unfair dismissal. This will affect their decisions such as:

→ Whether to bring a case at all.

→ Whether to accept any settlement package offered by the employers.

→ Whether to resign and claim constructive (unfair) dismissal.

Loss of earnings

1 Up to the date of the tribunal (past loss)

A tribunal usually awards loss of earnings, net of tax, for some or all of the time the member was unemployed. However, the tribunal may think the member should have obtained a new job more quickly. Therefore the tribunal may not award loss of earnings for the whole time the member is unemployed.

The tribunal will also expect the member to be flexible about the type of job and level of pay which s/he will accept in the future, especially the longer s/he is out of work. The member should therefore be advised to look for a new job and to keep a record of where s/he has looked

If the member received job seekers' allowance during the period of the award for past loss of earnings, this sum will be deducted from the tribunal's award and paid by the employers back to the Benefits Agency.

2 Future loss of earnings

A tribunal can award future loss of earnings too if the member has not obtained a new job by the time of the tribunal hearing. It will award loss for as long as it thinks it should take the tribunal to find a new job. It can also award the differential if the member has found a new job, but on lower pay.

Other financial awards

The tribunal can also award compensation for loss of pension rights, certain job-hunting expenses and a few smaller items.

There is an overall maximum on the compensatory award for routine unfair dismissal cases, £56,800 from 1st February 2005. There is no upper ceiling on a few of the automatic unfair dismissals and on discrimination cases

There is also a Basic Award calculated according to age, length of service and weekly pay. This is subject to a weekly maximum, £280 from 1st February 2005.

Unlike in discrimination cases (see below), tribunals do not have the power to award compensation for hurt feelings or damaged health in unfair dismissal cases.

Reductions

Compensation can be reduced for many reasons, eg

■ By the amount of any redundancy payment and, usually, any ex gratia payment made by the employers.

■ Due to the member's misconduct prior to dismissal or contributory fault.

■ Where the unfairness was solely due to procedural factors, to reflect the chance that a fair dismissal would have taken place anyway, even if fair procedures had been followed.

■ Under the new statutory disputes resolution procedures (see page

57), there will be deductions in compensation if the member failed to go through the compulsory disciplinary or grievance procedures before bringing a tribunal case.

What the tribunal cannot do

→ The tribunal can order the employers to take the member back, but it cannot insist. At most, it can order the employers to pay extra compensation (26-52 weeks pay) if they refuse. This is called an "additional award".

→ Note that a tribunal cannot order the employers to take the member back if it is not reasonably practicable to do so.

→ The tribunal is unlikely to make an order for reinstatement if it considers the member has contributed to his/her dismissal.

→ A tribunal cannot order the employers to provide a reference, let alone a good reference. This is one reason why a negotiated settlement of a case is often a good idea.

→ A tribunal cannot order the employers to apologise (although this can be recommended in discrimination cases)

Discrimination remedies

Compensation for race, religion, sex, sexual orientation or disability discrimination in the employment tribunal is not subject to any statutory ceiling. Compensation is awarded in three categories:

■ Actual financial loss, eg loss of earnings following a dismissal, loss of potential earnings on a failed promotion, loss of acting-up allowance etc.

■ Injury to feelings. This sometimes divides into two awards, one for injury to feelings and one for aggravated damages, where the employers have behaved particularly badly. It can also include compensation for injury to health. The total award for injury to feelings including aggravated damages is constantly rising and hard to predict. Awards rarely fall below £1000 and in serious cases with damage to health can reach £25,000 or more. There have been a few huge awards, but these really are exceptional. In most cases, though, tribunals can be disappointing and the member should not assume s/he will be awarded a large amount or a sum which properly reflects his/her true injury.

■ Interest.

The tribunal can also make recommendations that the employers take action which would benefit the worker concerned, eg that certain documents are removed from a personnel file, that the finding of discrimination is noted on the personnel file, that an apology is circulated etc. The tribunal cannot insist on a worker being reinstated or getting the next promotion vacancy.

If any settlement is negotiated prior to the hearing, then there is of course no limitation on what may be negotiated.

Time-limits

Unfair dismissal time-limits

Points to note:

■ A case starts when the tribunal office receives the worker's tribunal claim. This must arrive at the tribunal office on or before the relevant time-limit.

■ The normal unfair dismissal time-limit is within three months of the effective date of termination. Three months means three calendar months less one day.

For example, if the effective date of termination was 3rd April 2005, the deadline is 2nd July 2005. If the effective date of termination was 30th November 2004, the deadline is the last day of February 2005.

■ The effective date of termination is when the contract of employment ends. The three-month time-limit must not be counted from the outcome of any appeal following termination.

■ The effective date of termination can be uncertain where a member does not work his/her notice. Sometimes the member's contract terminates with immediate effect, but s/he is paid in lieu of notice. At other times, the member is not allowed to work his/her notice, but his/her contract does not end until the expiry of the notice period.

Note that the position is often ambiguous. If there is any doubt at all, the member should count the three months from the earliest possible date. Unless s/he was off sick or on holiday, for example, it is usually safest to count the three months from the last day the member worked.

■ The time-limit is extremely strict. The tribunal has power to allow in a late application if it was not reasonably practicable to get the claim in on time. In practice, tribunals rarely accept any excuse for a late claim.

— It is rarely an acceptable excuse that the application was delayed or lost in the post.

– It is unlikely to be an excuse that the member was ignorant about the law or the UNISON representative made a mistake about the time-limit.

– It is not acceptable to delay until the appeal is completed.

– Always telephone and check the tribunal has received the claim before the deadline expires.

■ If the statutory disputes resolution procedures apply (which is often unclear), the time-limit will be extended by three months if, at the time of expiry of the normal time-limit, the member had reasonable grounds for believing that a dismissal or disciplinary procedure was still being followed.

For example, if the effective date of termination was 3rd April 2005, the normal time-limit would be 2nd July 2005. If as at 2nd July 2005, the disciplinary procedure was still ongoing (eg the appeal was outstanding), the time-limit would be extended to 2nd October 2005. However, if the procedure still is not finished by 2nd October 2005, there are no further extensions and the member must start his/her tribunal case.

■ **Be careful.** A member may have several claims at once and other claims may have shorter time-limits. For example, if the member has also suffered discrimination, the three months may run from an incident occurring before the dismissal. See below for time-limits under the discrimination legislation.

■ Members should be advised about the correct time-limits as soon as they seek advice if they have a potential legal claim, even if they are very doubtful whether they will go ahead.

Discrimination time-limits

Starting a case

This is only a brief guide to discrimination time-limits under the Race Relations Act, SDA, Disability Discrimination Act, sexual orientation, religion and belief regulations. If a case appears out of time seek legal advice immediately as there may be a way progressing a legal case if action is taken quickly.

A large number of discrimination cases every year are thrown out by tribunals because the time-limits have been missed. To make sure you do not miss a time-limit, it is essential to produce a list of dates of key incidents at the first meeting and to draw up a diary plan of what has to happen by when.

In general, members should be educated in advance so that they understand the existence of strict time-limits and the importance of bringing discrimination issues to UNISON's attention immediately.

Note the following points:

■ The time-limit for starting a case is within three months of the act of discrimination, ie the tribunal claim must arrive at the employment tribunal on or before three calendar months less one day from the act of discrimination.

For example: if the act of discrimination was on 3rd April 2005, then the tribunal claim must arrive at the tribunal on or before 2nd July 2005.

■ Time runs from each act of discrimination, not just the last act. Therefore all significant acts of discrimination should be kept in time. For example:

– A woman is assaulted on 5th March 2005 and again on 6th April 2005. She is dismissed on 7th May 2005. The time-limit for the first assault is 4th June 2005. It would be particularly important to keep the first assault in time if it was more serious or easier to prove than the second assault.

– The member suffers sexual harassment on a daily basis up to 3rd November 2004 and then goes off sick for two weeks before resigning or being dismissed. To keep even the latest act of harassment in time, s/he must claim on or before 2nd February 2005 at the latest.

■ Time runs from the act of discrimination not from the outcome of any grievance or appeal. It is easy to miss time-limits because there is often a gap in time between an act of discrimination and the outcome of a grievance or appeal.

For example, the member is discriminated against by way of a failed promotion on 5th May 2005, but her grievance is not heard and rejected until 5th August 2005. The time-limit for the failed promotion is 4th August 2005.

On this example, the rejection of the grievance may or may not constitute another act of discrimination, which will be in time until 4th November 2005. However, the missing of the 4th November 2005 time-limit will mean that the tribunal is not required to make a finding on the promotion itself.

Therefore it may be necessary to lodge a tribunal claim while the grievance is still being pursued in order to protect the option of taking the case to employment tribunal. Unfortunately this can affect the employers' response to the grievance, making them more cautious. If the grievance is rejected and this appears to be a discriminatory act a further tribunal claim would have to be completed.

■ Time may be extended by three months where the statutory disputes resolution procedures apply, as explained below. However, even if there is an extension of time, the same problem arises if the grievance procedure has not been completed by the time the extended time-limit expires.

■ Although a member may refer to earlier incidents as evidence, only acts within the time-limit form the grounds of the claim. Therefore even if discrimination has been going on for some while so that earlier incidents are inevitably out of time, the more serious and provable recent incidents should be kept in time.

■ The tribunal does have power to permit a late claim to be made if it is just and equitable to do so, but it is very risky to rely on a tribunal allowing this.

■ There is case-law which may help bring a claim in time once a time-limit seems to have been missed, eg possibly where there has been a sequence of linked discriminatory incidents and only the latest is in time. This often applies in sexual harassment cases in particular. It is therefore important to seek specialist advice immediately and not to assume that a claim is necessarily out of time.

■ If further discrimination or victimisation occurs after a claim has been made, a further tribunal claim will need to be lodged within a further three-month time-limit.

Effect of the statutory disputes resolution procedures on discrimination time-limits

Where the statutory disputes resolution procedures apply, tribunal time-limits are sometimes extended. However, you need to be very careful because it is often uncertain whether the procedures do in fact apply. If you mistakenly think the procedures apply and allow the normal time-limit to pass, the member's claim will be out of time. The rules about when the procedures apply are set out at pages 57-72. Where possible and if in any doubt at all, keep to the normal three month time-limits.

If the member's discrimination claim purely concerns dismissal, the statutory dismissal and disciplinary procedure ("DDP") applies. The normal three month time-limit is extended only if a dismissal procedure (whether contractual or statutory) is ongoing at the time the normal time-limit expires. (The rule is the same as for unfair dismissal – see above.)

If the member's claim concerns other acts of discrimination and s/he has to follow the statutory minimum grievance procedure ("GP"), the rules are more complicated. For more detail on when the statutory GP applies, see pages 57-72.

■ Where the statutory grievance procedure applies, the member is barred from starting a tribunal case unless s/he has already sent a step 1 grievance letter to his/her employer.

Provided the member sends his/her step 1 grievance letter to the employer within the normal time-limit (three months from the act of discrimination), the time-limit for lodging a tribunal claim is extended by three months (making six months altogether). It is irrelevant whether the grievance has been heard or is ongoing. (**Note that** this is different from the rule applying to dismissal).

For example:

→ The member is given a discriminatory warning on 10th January 2005.

→ The normal deadline for lodging a tribunal discrimination case about the warning is 9th April 2005.

→ Provided the member sends his/her step 1 grievance letter to the employer by 9th April 2005, his/her deadline for lodging a tribunal case is extended to 9th July 2005.

■ The member must wait 28 days after sending the step 1 grievance letter before lodging his/her tribunal claim. In the above example:

→ The member sends his/her step 1 letter to the employer on Wednesday 2nd March 2005.

→ S/he cannot lodge his/her tribunal claim before Thursday 31st March 2005. (The wording of the legislation is a little tortuous, but it appears to mean the member must wait till after the 28th day.)

→ S/he can lodge his/her tribunal claim any time between 31st March 2005 and 9th July 2005 inclusive.

■ If the member sends his/her tribunal claim to the tribunal without having first sent a step 1 letter to the employer, the tribunal will send the claim back. However, as long as the claim was sent within the normal time-limit (the original three months), there will be an automatic extension of time for a further three months – up to a six months total.

The member must then send a step 1 letter to the employer, wait 28 days, and then relodge his/her tribunal claim within the six month period.

Note that all this is only allowed if the member sends his/her step 1 letter to the employer within one month of the expiry of the original time-limit, ie within four months of the act of discrimination. If s/he fails to do this, s/he is out of time for sending the step 1 letter and as a consequence, debarred from bringing a tribunal claim altogether. It is thought that the tribunal has no discretion to extend this one month rule.

For example:

→ The member is given a discriminatory warning on 10th January 2005.

→ The normal deadline for lodging a tribunal discrimination case about the warning is 9th April 2005.

→ The member lodges his/her tribunal claim at the tribunal on 15th February 2005. The tribunal sends the claim back on 20th February 2005, because the member has not yet sent his/her employer a step 1 letter.

→ The member can now send a step 1 letter at any time up to 9th May 2005.

→ Provided s/he does that, s/he can relodge the tribunal claim at any time up to 9th July 2005.

→ If the member fails to send a step 1 letter by 9th May 2005, s/he will be out of time and the tribunal probably has no discretion to extend time.

■ **The safest strategy:** The danger with the above rules is that the member may not be sure whether or not the statutory disputes resolution procedures apply at all. The safest strategy, which keeps within the time-limits either way, is to send a step 1 grievance letter within two months of the act of discrimination, wait 28 days, and ensure the tribunal claim is lodged within three months of the act of discrimination (ie the normal time-limit).

■ **Beware mixed claims:** Remember also that the claim may be mixed, eg partially related to discriminatory action short of dismissal and partially related to dismissal. As the rules for time-limit extensions differ, it is possible there will be a six month time-limit on the action short of dismissal, but only a three month time-limit on the dismissal. In such a situation, the member has to work to the shorter time-limit to avoid the need for putting in two separate tribunal claims.

Serving the questionnaire

The questionnaire is extremely important in gathering evidence for a discrimination case. It enables the member to ask employers very detailed questions regarding their actions, and for relevant information and statistics concerning comparable workers and in the workplace generally. You should ensure the member knows of the existence of the procedure and the relevant time-limits, and it should be decided who will be responsible for writing it. See Bibliography (p315) for Guides to the procedure with sample questionnaires. There are strict time-limits. If a time-limit is missed, the worker must ask the tribunal's permission to send it late. The tribunal may refuse. It is therefore vital not to miss the time-limit.

The questionnaire must be received by the employers on or before the time-limit. This is when the questionnaire is "served" on the employers.

The questionnaire may be served at any time before a tribunal case has been started. However, a tribunal case must be started within three months of the act of discrimination or any extension of time under the statutory disputes resolution procedures (see above).

Once a tribunal case has been started, if no questionnaire has yet been served, it must be served within 21 days. For example, if the tribunal claim arrived at the tribunal on Tuesday 2nd February 2005, the questionnaire must be received by the employers on or before Monday 22nd February 2005.

This is so even if the tribunal claim was lodged well within the time-limit for starting a case. Equally, it is so even if the tribunal claim was lodged on the last possible day for starting a case.

Action checklist for stewards where a legal case is possible

Cases must not be commenced without the involvement and decision of your regional officer/organiser. However you can:

■ Obtain all relevant documents from member and take a full statement.

■ Make the necessary arrangements for progressing any appeal by the member.

■ Advise the member of possible cases and the relevant time-limits. Ensure the member notes the time-limit and make your own diary note.

■ Consult your regional officer/organiser so that s/he can advise the member of his/her chances of success on any possible legal case, the pros and cons of going ahead, and the likely compensation or remedies.

→ The advantages of bringing a case are obvious if the member has reasonable chances of success. However s/he does need to be aware that success is not guaranteed and that remedies and compensation can be limited. UNISON will only pursue tribunals where there are reasonable prospects of success.

→ If the member has been dismissed, the disadvantages of going ahead with a weak case are:

— Costs of many thousand pounds may be awarded in the tribunal for running a case without reasonable prospects of success.

— It will be stressful.

— It would be a waste of time and energy.

— It will upset the employers and could cause problems with references.

→ If the member is bringing a discrimination case while still in employment, s/he needs to consider whether s/he is likely to be victimised as a result and whether s/he can cope with that.

■ Advise the member on what level of support UNISON can offer. If this cannot be decided yet, advise the member when s/he will be informed of this and by whom.

■ Discuss with the member who will put in the tribunal claim to the employment tribunal (plus, if it is a discrimination case, the questionnaire). Discuss who is responsible for ensuring the next step is taken and explain both that the regional officer/organiser is responsible for deciding if the case will be run and that UNISON can only run it if it appears to have reasonable prospects of success. Ensure the member does not write the tribunal claim and questionnaire him/herself as these are important documents. If these documents are badly written, it is likely to adversely affect the outcome of the case.

■ Discuss with the branch if required by policy.

■ **Very importantly, consider non-legal options. Where the member is still in employment, these may include negotiation or taking out a grievance or collective action.**

Appendices

Contents

List of main employment rights

Employment law is constantly changing and developing. The following list does not contain all available rights, but those most commonly encountered. The listed rights are "statutory rights", ie rights given by parliament. Different eligibility requirements apply to different rights. In addition, the member may have rights under his/her own contract.
Note that the headings in the following list are not a precise description of the actual right.
"ERA" refers to the Employment Rights Act 1996. TULR(C)A refers to the Trade Union and Labour Relations (Consolidation) Act 1992. For the full title of the other statutes and regulations, see the list at p316.

DISMISSAL
→ Statutory minimum notice or pay in lieu (unless gross misconduct). (ERA s86)
→ Unfair Dismissal. (ERA Part X)
→ Automatic Unfair Dismissal, eg for:
– asserting a statutory right (ERA s104)
– taking up health and safety issues (ERA s100)
– pregnancy-related reasons (ERA s99)
– trade union reasons (TULR(C)A s152)
– not completing the statutory disputes resolution procedures (ERA s98A)
– other reasons. (See p101.)
→ Written reasons for dismissal. (ERA s92)
→ Statutory Redundancy Pay. (ERA Part XI)
→ Right to paid time off to look for new work during redundancy notice period. (ERA s52)
→ Dismissal due to race, religion, belief, sex, sexual orientation, being married, gender reassignment, or disability discrimination. (See DISCRIMINATION below)

DISCRIMINATION AND FAMILY
→ Race discrimination. (Race Relations Act)
→ Discrimination related to religion or belief. (Employment Equality (Religion or Belief) Regulations)
→ Disability discrimination. (Disability Discrimination Act)
→ Sex Discrimination including discrimination related to gender reassignment or being married. (Sex Discrimination Act and Equal Pay Act)

→ Discrimination related to sexual orientation. (Employment Equality (Sexual Orientation) Regulations)

→ Statutory maternity, adoption, paternity leave and parental leave. (The Maternity and Parental Leave (Amendment) Regulations; The Paternity and Adoption Leave Regulations)

→ Dependant leave. (ERA s57A)

→ Paid time off for ante-natal care. (ERA s55)

→ Right to modified duties or paid health and safety suspension while pregnant.

→ Right to written reasons for dismissal if dismissed while pregnant. (ERA s92(4))

→ Equal treatment of part-timers. (Part-time Workers Regulations)

→ Right to request flexible working. (Flexible Working Regulations)

OTHER RIGHTS AT WORK

→ Minimum wage. (National Minimum Wage Act and Regulations)

→ Rest breaks, holidays, hours. (Working Time Regulations)

→ Right to receive itemised pay statements with pay (ie pay slips). (ERA s8)

→ Right to receive the main terms and conditions of employment in writing. (ERA s1-4)

→ Unauthorised deductions from pay. (ERA Part II)

→ Action short of dismissal for membership of a trade union or trade union activities. (TULR(C)A s146-151)

→ Right not to suffer a detriment for taking up health and safety issues. (ERA s44)

→ Preservation of terms and conditions and continuity of service on a transfer. (TUPE Regs)

→ Access to data and information. (Data Protection Act; Freedom of Information Act; Freedom of Information Act (Scotland).)

COLLECTIVE

→ Consultation with trade union or appropriate representatives over proposed redundancies. (TULR(C)A)

→ Consultation with trade union or appropriate representatives over a transfer of an undertaking. (TUPE Regs)

→ Information and consultation. (The Information and Consultation of Employees Regulations)

Glossary

BREACH OF CONTRACT
If the worker or the employers break a term in the contract of employment, they are acting "in breach of contract".

CLAIM TO A TRIBUNAL, TRIBUNAL CLAIM
A worker starts a case by lodging a Claim (sometimes known as a Tribunal Claim) at the appropriate employment tribunal, ie the worker writes out the basic particulars of his/her claim, and makes sure it arrives at the tribunal within the relevant time-limits. See page 294. From October 2005, the claim must be completed on standard form ET1.

CODE OF PRACTICE
There are various Codes of Practice relevant to employment law, particularly discrimination law (see list on page 318). Generally speaking, these provide guidance on good practice within the law and should be taken into account by tribunals where relevant. However, they are not usually legally enforceable in themselves.

CEHR, COMMISSION FOR EQUALITY AND HUMAN RIGHTS
Plans are underway to set up a new Commission for Equality and Human Rights, whose remit will cover all areas of discrimination law (race, sex, religion and belief, sexual orientation, disability and age) as well as human rights. It will replace the current CRE, EOC and DRC.

COMMISSION FOR RACIAL EQUALITY
The CRE is the organisation set up under the RRA with overall responsibility to work towards the elimination of race discrimination and to keep the workings of the RRA under review. As well as its policy and educational functions, it has unique powers to conduct formal investigations and to take up cases regarding pressure or instructions to discriminate. The CRE also runs individual tribunal cases of race discrimination in employment.

CONSTRUCTIVE DISMISSAL
This is where a worker resigns, but the law regards him/her as having been dismissed. It happens only where the worker's resignation is because the

employers have broken his/her contract in a very serious way. Constructive dismissal is hard to prove. There are many misunderstandings about what it means. See page 118.

CONTRACT, CONTRACT OF EMPLOYMENT, CONTRACTUAL RIGHTS
Every employee works under a contract of employment, which may be written or verbal or partly written. The contract is made up of a number of terms and conditions representing the agreement between worker and employers on matters such as hours, pay and workplace. The worker's rights under his/her own contract are called her "contractual rights". S/he will also have other rights given to him/her by parliament ("statutory rights") or by previous case-law.
In theory, a worker's contract can only be changed or "varied" by agreement. In practice, problems arise when the employers try to unilaterally vary (ie change without agreement) the contract. See page 118.

CONTRACT WORKER
This phrase is often used to describe workers who are employed on fixed term contracts as opposed to permanent workers. However, the phrase has a different and technical meaning under the RRA, SDA, DDA, sexual orientation regulations and religion and belief regulations. It refers to a worker who is employed by one organisation ("the employer" but sent to work for another organisation ("the principal") under a contract between the employer and the principal. Such workers can bring discrimination cases against the principal if the principal discriminates against them.

CRE
See Commission for Racial Equality.

DDP
See Dismissal and disciplinary procedures.

DIRECT DISCRIMINATION
Under discrimination law, direct discrimination is where a worker is treated differently or less favourably due to his/her disability, sex, being married or gender reassignment, or due to his/her own or someone else's sexual orientation, race, religion or belief. See page 165 (race).

DIRECTIVE

Directives are issued by the EU on certain areas of employment law. Usually member states are given a few years to implement the Directives into national law. Where member states do not do this correctly, workers can sometimes go direct to the European Court of Justice, though not necessarily.

DISABILITY RIGHTS COMMISSION

This has similar powers to the CRE and the EOC except in the field of disability law.

DISCRIMINATION LAW

This is understood by employment lawyers to mean cases under the Race Relations Act , Sex Discrimination Act , Equal Pay Act, Disability Discrimination Act , Employment Equality (Religion or Belief) Regulations or Employment Equality (Sexual Orientation) Regulations. By December 2006, age discrimination will also be covered.

DISMISSAL AND DISCIPLINARY PROCEDURES

Under the statutory disputes resolution procedures (below), a statutory minimum dismissal and disciplinary procedure ("DDP") must be followed where the employer contemplates dismissing an employee or taking relevant disciplinary action. See p57.

DISPUTES RESOLUTION PROCEDURES

Under the Employment Act 2002 and the Employment Act 2002 (Dispute Resolution) Regulations 2004, statutory minimum disciplinary and grievance procedures must be followed in most workplace situations before bringing tribunal claims. See pages 57-72.

DL56

The standard form on which a questionnaire under the Disability Discrimination Act is usually written. See page 300.

DRC

See Disability Rights Commission.

EAT

See Tribunal.

ECJ

See European Court of Justice.

ELIGIBILITY, ELIGIBILITY REQUIREMENTS

Statutory employment rights given to workers by parliament each have their own eligibility requirements, eg that a worker cannot make a claim until s/he has acquired a certain length of service. It is important to know whether the member is eligible for each of the possible rights s/he may claim.

EMPLOYEE

Certain employment rights are only available to employees. Not all workers are employees and in border-line cases, it is hard to know whether or not a worker is really an employee (whatever s/he is labelled by the employer). See page 96.

EMPLOYMENT APPEAL TRIBUNAL

See Tribunal.

EMPLOYMENT TRIBUNAL

See Tribunal.

EOC

See Equal Opportunities Commission.

EQUAL OPPORTUNITIES COMMISSION

The EOC, set up under the SDA, has similar powers to the CRE except with regard to sex discrimination and to the workings of the Sex Discrimination Act and Equal Pay Act.

EQUAL PAY

Sex discrimination in pay is dealt with by the Equal Pay Act, whereas race discrimination pay is covered by the Race Relations Act. References to "equal pay" therefore usually refer to equalising pay between men and women. Unfortunately this can obscure race issues and it sometimes gets forgotten that black women are often at the very bottom of the pay-scale.

ET

See Tribunal.

EUROPEAN COURT OF JUSTICE

The ECJ is the most senior court deciding cases under European law. European law applies to discrimination, TUPE, collective consultation and certain other areas. National tribunals and courts at any level can refer a case to the ECJ to provide legal guidance.

FIXED TERM CONTRACT

This is a contract where the worker's last day of work is stated or can be worked out. It is irrelevant that the contract allows for earlier termination by ordinary notice.

GRIEVANCE, GRIEVE

Under statutory disputes resolution procedures (above), an employee must follow a statutory minimum grievance procedure before bringing a tribunal claim concerning most workplace issues. See p59. This has spawned a new meaning for the verb, "to grieve", ie "to bring a grievance under the procedure".

GROSS MISCONDUCT

Where a worker is guilty of gross misconduct, the employers do not need to give notice if they dismiss the worker. However, whereas some misconduct is obviously gross misconduct, eg theft, other misconduct is not so obviously gross and will depend on all the circumstances, eg swearing. It is not gross misconduct just because the employers say it is. Note that for unfair dismissal purposes, employers usually still need to follow fair procedures.

INDIRECT DISCRIMINATION

Under the RRA, SDA, religion and belief regulations and sexual orientation regulations, indirect discrimination is where the employers treat the worker in a way which has an adverse impact on the worker's racial group, married workers, or those of the same religion, sex or sexual orientation. See pages 169 (race) and 196 (sex).

ET1

The standard form on which a tribunal claim is usually written.

LODGING A CLAIM OR APPEAL

A worker starts a tribunal case by "lodging" his/her claim at the tribunal.

His/her claim is "lodged" when the document arrives at the tribunal office. A worker's appeal to the Employment Appeal Tribunal against an employment tribunal Judgment is "lodged" when the Notice of Appeal arrives at the EAT. The relevant documents can be sent or hand-delivered (and in some cases, faxed), as long as they arrive within the relevant time-limits.

QUESTIONNAIRE

A special procedure available under discrimination and equal pay law, which is extremely important in collecting evidence. Note that strict time-limits apply. See page 300.

RELEVANT DISCIPLINARY ACTION

This is a particular phrase used under the statutory disputes resolution procedures. If you hear it in that context, it means any disciplinary action except warnings or paid suspension. So, for example, it would cover unpaid suspension or a disciplinary demotion. Under the statutory procedures, a DDP must be followed in respect of dismissal or "relevant disciplinary action".

RR65

The standard form on which a questionnaire under the Race Relations Act is usually written. See page 300.

SD74

The standard form on which a questionnaire under the Sex Discrimination Act is usually written. See page 300.

SERVING A DOCUMENT OR QUESTIONNAIRE

A questionnaire is "served" on the employer when it arrives at their address. The relevant documents can be sent or hand-delivered (and in some cases, faxed), as long as they arrive within the relevant time-limits.

STATUTE, IMPOSED BY STATUTE, STATUTORY RIGHTS

Many workers' rights are given by parliament. These are called statutory rights. Legislation in the employment field is a very political area and constantly changes. Most rights and duties are agreed by the worker and the employers ("contractual rights"), but parliament has set a few minimum statutory entitlements which cannot be agreed away, eg minimum notice, maternity leave, and equal pay between men and women.

STATUTORY DISPUTES RESOLUTION PROCEDURES
See Disputes Resolution Procedures (above).

TERMS AND CONDITIONS
A worker's contract of employment is made up of a series terms and
conditions regarding hours, pay, workplace, notice rights, sick pay
entitlement etc. See Contract above.

TIME-LIMITS
All employment claims have time-limits or deadlines within which they must
be started. It is essential to know what the time-limits are on any potential
claims the member has. For time-limits on unfair dismissal, discrimination
and questionnaires, see pages 294-300.

TRIBUNAL, EMPLOYMENT TRIBUNAL (ET), EMPLOYMENT APPEAL TRIBUNAL (EAT)
Most employment claims are dealt with by an employment tribunal. Appeals
against an ET Decision go to the EAT. There is no automatic right of appeal
and the ET must have made a mistake of law or reached a decision which is
perverse on the facts.

TUPE
This is the name by which the Transfer of Undertakings Regulations are
commonly known. The Regulations protect workers when the service in
which they work is sold or contracted out. See Chapter 7.

UNFAIR DISMISSAL
There is a statutory right not to be unfairly dismissed. However a member
can only claim if s/he meets the eligibility requirements. See page 96.
Unfair dismissal must not be confused with wrongful dismissal.

UNILATERAL VARIATION
In theory, employers can only change contractual terms and conditions if
the worker agrees. If the employers go ahead, eg by giving notice that they
are going to change the contract anyway, without the worker's agreement,
they are trying to vary the contract unilaterally. This change will not be
effective provided the worker does not implicitly agree to the change by
inaction. See page 20.

VARIATION

See Unilateral Variation

VICTIMISATION

Under discrimination law (above), a worker is victimised if the employer punishes him/her or treats him/her less favourably because s/he has made a complaint of discrimination. See page 164 (race).

WORKER

Certain employment rights are given to "employees" and certain rights to "workers" in the wider sense. The relevant statute will define what it means by "worker" but this is usually similar to the definition used for the Working Time Regulations (see page 30.) In this book, the word "worker" is used in a loose sense to describe all workers, but it is specified where it must be an employee.

WRONGFUL DISMISSAL

There is a contractual right not to be wrongfully dismissed. This means a worker must not be dismissed in a way which the contract does not allow. Usually this simply means s/he must be given his/her correct contractual notice. Sometimes more serious procedures have been ignored. Unlike unfair dismissal, wrongful dismissal is not about whether the dismissal was fair. See page 92.

Bibliography

UNISON website: http://www.unison.org.uk

UNISON GUIDES

Many advisory briefings and negotiating guides can be downloaded from the
UNISON website or are otherwise available from Mabledon Place or
UNISONDirect (telephone 0800 5979750). The following guides may be of
particular interest:

→ Negotiating Parental Leave (revised Feb 2004). (Stock no: 1402)
→ Harassment: A UNISON guide to policy and representation. (Stock No:
1359)
→ Getting Equal Campaign Pack. (Stock no: 1836)
→ Transgendered people's rights at work. (Stock no: 1938)
vA Guide to Branches on the Race Relations (Amendment) Act. (Stock No:
2122)
→ Identifying Legal Cases in the Workplace. Ed 2. (LAOS Activists
Catalogue, No: Act 172)
→ Best Value Code of Practice on Workforce Matters in Local Authority
Service Contracts in England and Police Authority Service Contracts in
England and Wales (July 2003). Available at
www.unison.org.uk/acrobat/13612.pdf.
→ Whistleblowing – Speaking out without fear
→ A Guide to Statutory Recognition
→ UNISON Guide to the Human Rights Act
→ Health and Safety advisory leaflets

BOOKS

→ **Employment Law: An Advisers Handbook.** By Tamara Lewis.
Published Legal Action Group. Tel: 0207 833 2931.
Practical and understandable guide by author of this book, to law, evidence
and tribunal procedure from the worker's viewpoint. Large discrimination
section. Updated with new editions every 2 years. Next edition due October
2005.
→ **Butterworths Employment Law Handbook.** Edited by Peter Wallington.
All relevant Statutes, Regulations and Codes fully reproduced. No
commentary. The Book is regularly reissued with latest Statutes.
→ **Harvey on Industrial Relations and Employment Law.** Published
Butterworths. 6 volume loose-leaf, regularly updated. The most authoritative

academic text on employment law. Reviews case-law and reproduces key Statutes.

→ **Maternity Rights 2.** By Camilla Palmer and Joanna Wade. Published Legal Action Group and Maternity Alliance.

A detailed guide to a very complex area. Edition 3 is due in late 2005.

→ **Legal rights to child-friendly working hours.** Published Maternity Alliance.

NON UNISON BOOKLETS AND GUIDES

→ **RRA Questionnaires: How to Use the Questionnaire Procedure in Cases of Race Discrimination in Employment.** By Tamara Lewis. Published Central London Law Centre. Guide to procedure and sample Questionnaires for many situations. Hard copy of ed 2 available from CLLC (tel administrator: 0207 839 2998). Ed 3 available from 2005 on CRE website.

→ **SDA Questionnaires: How to Use the Questionnaire Procedure in Cases of Sex Discrimination in Employment.** By Tamara Lewis. Published Central London Law Centre. Guide to procedure and sample Questionnaires for many situations. Ed 2 due October 2005 and available from CLLC (tel administrator 0207 839 2998).

→ **DDA Questionnaires: How to Use the Questionnaire Procedure in Cases of Disability Discrimination in Employment.** By Tamara Lewis. Published Central London Law Centre. Guide to procedure and sample Questionnaires for many situations. Hard copy available from CLLC (tel administrator: 0207 839 2998). Ed 2 available from 2005 on DRC website.

→ **Discrimination Questionnaires: How to use the Questionnaire Procedure in Cases of Discrimination in Employment.** By Tamara Lewis. Published Central London Law Centre. Guide to procedure and sample Questionnaires under sexual orientation and religion and belief regulations, equal pay, sex, race and disability discrimination. Available from CLLC (tel administrator: 0207 839 2998).

→ **Proving disability and reasonable adjustments: A worker's guide to evidence under the DDA.** By Tamara Lewis. Published Central London Law Centre. Available October 2005 from CLLC (tel administrator: 0207 839 2998).

LAW REPORTS

→ **Industrial Relations Law Reports** ("IRLR")

Fully reproduced law reports. Essential if using cases in an employment tribunal, but you need to know what you are looking for.

→ **IDS Brief.** Published twice/month by Incomes Data Services Ltd. Tel: 020 7250 3434. Readable summaries of latest cases. Subscribers also receive occasional specialist handbooks.

→ **Industrial Relations Law Bulletin.** Published twice/month Industrial Relations Services. Tel: 020 7354 5858. Similar to IDS Brief: readable summaries of latest cases and excellent feature articles on various aspects of employment law.

→ **Legal Action magazine.** Published Legal Action Group. Tel: 020 7833 2931. Employment Law update in May and November issues written by Central London Law Centre's Employment Unit. Useful summary of key statutes and cases in the previous 6 months, selected from the worker's point of view and put into an understandable context.

→ **Equal Opportunities Review.** Published every month by Industrial Relations Services. Tel: 0207 354 5858. Excellent publication. Case summaries and commentaries on all key discrimination, maternity and equal pay cases; news, features and reports on initiatives in the equal opportunities field.

STATUTES AND CODES OF PRACTICE

The following are set out in Butterworths and Harveys (above) but can also be obtained separately. This is not a full list of all employment Statutes and Codes.

STATUTES AND REGULATIONS
Employment Rights Act 1996.
Employment Act 2002
Employment Act 2002 (Dispute Resolution) Regulations 2004 (SI 2004/752)
Race Relations Act 1976.
Race Relations (Amendment) Act 2000

Employment Equality (Religion or Belief) Regulations 2003 (SI 2003/1660)

Sex Discrimination Act 1975 (as amended).

Employment Equality (Sexual Orientation) Regulations 2003 (SI 2003/1661)

Equal Pay Act 1970 (as amended).

Disability Discrimination Act 1995.

Protection from Harassment Act 1997.

Human Rights Act 1998.

Trade Union and Labour Relations (Consolidation) Act 1992

Transfer of Undertakings (Protection of Employment) Regulations 1981 (SI 1981/1794).

Collective Redundancies and Transfer of Undertakings (Protection of Employment)(Amendment) Regulations 1999 (SI 1999/1925).

Working Time Regulations 1999 (SI 1999/3372).

National Minimum Wage Regulations 1999 (SI 1999/584).

Management of Health and Safety at Work Regulations 1999 (SI 1999/3242).

The Maternity and Parental Leave (Amendment) Regulations 2002 (SI 2002/2789).

The Paternity and Adoption Leave Regulations 2002 (SI 2002/2788).

Part-time Workers (Prevention of Less Favourable Treatment) Regulations 2000 (SI 2000/1551)

Flexible Working (Eligibility, Complaints and Remedies) Regulations 2002 (SI 2002/3236)

Flexible Working (Procedural Requirements) Regulations 2002 (SI 2002/3207)

Disability discrimination (Meaning of Disability) Regulations 1996 (SI 1996/1456)

EUROPEAN DIRECTIVES

Equal Pay (75/117/EEC)

Equal Treatment (76/207/EEC)

Equal Treatment Amendment Directive (2002/73/EC)

Business Transfers (Acquired Rights) (77/187/EEC and 98/50/EC)

Collective redundancies (98/59/EC)

Working Time (93/104/EEC)

Parental Leave (96/34/EC)

Part-time work (97/81/EC)

Equal Treatment (Race and Ethnic Origins) (2000/43/EC).

General Framework (2000/78/EC).

CODES

ACAS Code of Guidance on Disciplinary and Grievance Procedures.
CRE: Code of Practice for the elimination of racial discrimination and the promotion of equality of opportunity in employment. (1983).
EOC: Code of Practice for the elimination of discrimination on the grounds of sex and marriage and the promotion of equality of opportunity in employment. (1985).
EOC Code of Practice on Equal Pay.
Commission Recommendation 91/131/EEC and Code of Practice on the protection of the dignity of women and men at work.
DRC: Code of Practice for Employment and Occupation. (2004)
Guidance on matters to be taken into account in determining questions relating to the definition of disability.
Code of Practice on Age Diversity in Employment.

USEFUL WEB-SITES (alphabetical listing)

→ **ACAS** www.acas.org.uk
→ **Bully on Line**
www.successunlimited.co.uk
→ **Campaign for Freedom of Information**
www.cfoi.org.uk
→ **Commission for Racial Equality**
Includes guidance booklets and research reports. www.cre.gov.uk
→ **Department of Trade and Industry**
Very informative web-site. Publishes Regulations and Government Guidance in many areas of employment law. www.dti.gov.uk
→ **Disability Rights Commission**
Includes useful links to other specialist sites.
www.drc-gb.org/drc/default.asp
→ **Employment Appeal Tribunal judgments**
wood.ccta.gov.uk/eat/eatjudgments.nsf
→ **Equal Opportunities Commission**
Good source for research briefings on male/female work patterns.
www.eoc.org.uk
→ **Great Place to Work**
Case-studies of organisations that have achieved results by involving and developing people. www.greatplacetowork.gov.uk

→ **Maternity Alliance** www.maternityalliance/org.uk

→ **Health and Safety Executive** www.hse.gov.uk

→ **HMSO**

Publishes full text of all UK statutes since 1988. www.hmso.gov.uk

→ **Incomes Data Services**

Pay, employment, personnel and pension issues. www.incomesdata.co.uk

→ **Industrial Society** www.indsoc.co.uk

→ **Institute of Employment Rights** www.ier.org.uk

→ **International Labour Organisation** www.ilo.org

→ **Labour Research Department** www.lrd.org.uk

→ **Low Pay Unit** www.lowpayunit.org.uk/eras.index.ht

→ **National Assembly for Wales:** Industry and Training
www.wales.gov.uk/polinfo/industry

→ **Northern Ireland: Department of Higher and Further Education:**
Training and Employment www.northernireland.gov.uk/hfe.htm

→ **Public Concern at Work** www.pcaw.co.uk

→ **Scottish Executive:** Enterprise and Lifelong Learning
www.scotland.gov.uk/who

→ **Thomsons Labour and European Law Review** Review of rulings under UK
and European law affecting trade unions and their members.
www.thomsons.law.co/ltext/libindex.htm

→ **TIGER – Tailored Interactive Guidance on Employment Rights**
www.tiger.gov.uk

→ **TUC** www.tuc.org.uk

→ **UNISON** www.unison.org/uk

→ **Work Life Balance** – key facts and case studies from the DfEE
Key facts and case-studies from the DfEE. www.dfee.gov.uk/work-lifebalance

INDEX